Innovations in E-Government

Innovations in E-Government

The Thoughts of Governors and Mayors

Edited by
Erwin A. Blackstone,
Michael L. Bognanno,
and Simon Hakim

ROWMAN & LITTLEFIELD PUBLISHERS, INC.
Lanham • Boulder • New York • Toronto • Oxford

ROWMAN & LITTLEFIELD PUBLISHERS, INC.

Published in the United States of America
by Rowman & Littlefield Publishers, Inc.
A wholly owned subsidiary of The Rowman & Littlefield Publishing Group, Inc.
4501 Forbes Boulevard, Suite 200, Lanham, Maryland 20706
www.rowmanlittlefield.com

PO Box 317, Oxford
OX2 9RU, UK

British Library Cataloguing in Publication Information Available

Library of Congress Cataloging-in-Publication Data

Innovations in E-government : the thoughts of governors and mayors / edited by Erwin A. Blackstone, Michael L. Bognanno, and Simon Hakim.
p. cm.
Includes bibliographical references and index.

ISBN: 978-0-7425-4912-8

1. Internet in public administration—United States. 2. Internet in public administration—Canada. I. Blackstone, Erwin A., 1942– II. Bognanno, Michael, 1962– III. Hakim, Simon, 1944–
JK468.A8I56 2005
352.3'8213'02854678—dc22 2005009263

Printed in the United States of America

∞™ The paper used in this publication meets the minimum requirements of American National Standard for Information Sciences—Permanence of Paper for Printed Library Materials, ANSI/NISO Z39.48-1992.

Contents

Note to the Reader

The chapters contributed to this book were written in the period from 2002 to 2005. Because of this, some chapters refer to points in the future that have already passed. As well, some of the mayors and governors who contributed chapters are no longer in office. Please keep this in mind when encountering date references and authors writing in the present tense or from the perspective of currently serving in office.

Part I

INTRODUCTION

1

Electronic Government: Review, Evaluation, and Anticipated Impact

Erwin A. Blackstone, Michael L. Bognanno, and Simon Hakim

The benefits of e-government have become manifest in numerous ways since the late 1990s. With the high rate of Internet usage today and the extent of interaction between the public and business over the Internet, the expectation of a similar level of convenience in dealing with the government has developed. This expectation is being met with information technology (IT) expenditures in the tens of billions of dollars annually at the federal, state, and local levels. This chapter categorizes e-government activities and considers the potential savings of delivering public services through e-government, as well as the potential implications of further advances in e-government on the organizational structure of government. We believe that new technologies will enable a smaller, leaner, and more responsive government, and we make some projections based partly on the experiences of the private sector.

The annual percentage rate of increase in Internet usage is necessarily falling since the Internet already reaches most of the adult population in the United States. However, despite the small annual percentage increase, the aggregate number of people coming online each year is large. Data from a Harris Interactive telephone survey in 2002 found that an estimated 137 million adults were online in the United States, or 66 percent of the adult population (Taylor 2002). The rate of increase slowed markedly after 2000, when penetration had already reached 63 percent of the adult population. Still, the rise of just 2 percent above the level of usage in 2001 equated to millions of additional Americans online. The early growth in Internet usage was remarkable. In 1996, only 33 million, or 9 percent, of U.S. adults were online; this jumped to 59 million (30 percent) in 1997, 70 million (35 percent) in 1998, 113 million (56 percent) in 1999, and 121 million (63 percent) in 2000.

Not only is 66 percent of the U.S. adult population online, but according to comScore Media Metrix Canada,[1] 42 percent of online citizens in the United States visited a government website in May of 2003. This amounts to more than 50 million Americans visiting a government website in a single month. These citizens increasingly expect interactions with government to be available online and to be able to operate seamlessly across the relevant government agencies. While the initial fixed costs of setting up online systems are high, costs savings should eventually result because the marginal cost of online service is very low. It is estimated that providing service to citizens by telephone costs $6 to $10 per contact, while similar Internet service costs as little as 4 cents per contact.

Despite tremendous advances in e-government, Accenture (2001) estimates that countries at a mature stage of e-government have still realized less than 20 percent of the technology's full potential. For this reason, and to meet the expectations of the public, it is important that the commitment to e-government not be lessened despite public-sector budgetary difficulties. This is the case at the federal level that has funded continuous growth in IT spending, particularly in 2003. Fiscal year 2003 federal IT spending was projected to be more than $58 billion (Office of Management and Budget 2003). The federal government IT spending estimate for 2002 it was $44.9 billion; for 2001, it was $44.5 billion; and for 2000, it was $41.3 billion (R. Brown 2001). Growth in IT spending is not happening at the moment at the cash-strapped state and local levels. Even though state and local IT spending in 2003 was an estimated $41 billion, it was 6.5 percent below the 2002 level. Nevertheless, state and local spending is projected to increase strongly in the middle of the decade (K. Brown 2003).

There are various ways to categorize the numerous aspects of e-government. We simply divide e-government into three general categories: improving internal government operations, improving the government-to-business interactions, and improving the delivery of services to citizens. Following a discussion of each of these categories, we give examples from the chapters contributed by mayors and governors that follow in this book. To conclude this chapter, we provide projections for the future of e-government.

INTERNAL GOVERNMENT OPERATIONS

Governments can use the Internet to improve internal operations both by improving communication and collaboration among government agencies and by raising the accountability of government employees through the use of new technologies such as geographical information systems (GIS). The Internet also reduces the costs of contracting with others to produce goods and services; thus, it can reduce the size and scope of internal government agency production. In particular, the Internet reduces required travel and facilitates document exchange and communication (Goldsmith and Eggers 2004, 17). We consider uses of GIS and the increased potential for outsourcing below.

Geographical Information Systems

GIS is computer software that links desired geographical databases and creates easily understood digital maps tailored to specific purposes. It enables obtaining visual or statistical associations among variables. Technologies like GIS improve emergency response and enhance service production and the accountability of public-sector managers. State and local governments make wide use of GIS for descriptive and decision-making purposes.

In the past, the construction of maps and complicated tables was often costly and required considerable time. GIS provides timely and cost-efficient information that expresses data in more useful and more easily understood formats. For example, most communities have digital maps showing water, sewer, telephone, electricity, and gas lines. When the fire department responds to an emergency, it can, while on route to the site, obtain prespecified information as to the nature of the building and surrounding structures. This allows them to evaluate risks better and to take steps like shutting off gas and electric lines. Access to water and the optimal route to the site can also be determined. GIS enables the relevant information to be processed quickly to aid even in time-critical missions.

GIS is crucial preparation for, effective response to, and recovery from either a terrorist attack or a natural disaster. GIS can play a critical role in the first response to a disaster. The number of possible targets in America's cities is almost unlimited, making prevention exceptionally difficult. Additionally, the type of attack could take different forms—conventional, chemical, biological, or nuclear. Thus, a system to aid in a rapid and effective first response to any type of situation is extremely useful. GIS can provide overlays of maps that include the roadways and railways; oil, gas, and water pipelines; surrounding structures and population concentrations; neighboring volatile materials; schools, hospitals, and nursing homes; and so forth. Clearly, the prompt availability of such information allows various concerns to be considered, along with optimal strategies.

Police use GIS to achieve more effective spatial deployment of patrol officers and greater accountability of their commanders. Spatial data on all crimes, once recorded, can be posted immediately in a map format. Precinct commanders in the New York City Police Department (NYPD), which pioneered this approach, daily obtain a GIS-generated map of crime incidents to detect trends and deploy their patrol resources most effectively. The top commanders of the NYPD meet periodically with all of the precinct commanders to assess their performance. Beyond police use, the allocation of any mobile resource can be examined. For instance, GIS permits managers to monitor the location and operation of trash trucks to optimize the efficiency of their use.

Technologies like the Global Positioning System (GPS) and GIS improve the measurement of government production, leading to the increased accountability of bottom-line workers. For example, in some cities, drivers can report the location of potholes in the road by dialing a number or calling 311.[2] GPS enables the public works department to locate the pothole and send the repair team to fix it. GIS enables the efficient deployment of workers throughout the jurisdiction and allows for their output to be measured. The time required to fix potholes can be mapped across various sectors of the city and the location of trucks monitored. Managers can be called to account for their performance. This provides an increased ability to hold workers accountable, reward productivity, and provide stronger incentives to workers.

Outsourcing

We classify "outsourcing" within internal government operations because it constitutes a fundamental change in the activities performed by government. Drawing lessons from the private sector, we observe that outsourcing has been expanding to take advantage of efficiencies and to focus on core business activities. Corporations often choose to focus on their core business and outsource other activities to specialist firms. Numerous examples of firms that are outsourcing exist. DuPont outsources legal, security, travel, IT, and other noncore functions to other entities. Nike outsources production while retaining design and other core business areas.

A trend toward outsourcing in the public sector is becoming evident. Federal government employment is decreasing and is likely to continue to decrease, while state and local employment has grown. Between 1999 and 2002, federal government employment decreased by 50,000, while contract-generated jobs increased by 700,000 (Goldsmith and Eggers 2004, 11). Between 2002 and 2004, federal employment decreased by an additional 38,000 to 2.73 million. State and local governments have also increased their contracts with the private sector. Between 1996 and 2001, state government contracts grew by 65 percent to a total of $400 billion (Goldsmith and Eggers 2004, 11). Nevertheless, state employment over that time period grew by about 300,000, and combined state and local employment grew by 1.6 million. Between 2001 and 2004, state and local employment grew by an additional 500,000 to almost 19 million (U.S. Department of Labor 2005).[3]

New public-sector outsourcing opportunities have been brought about through the technologies enabling e-government. The tasks to which technology can be applied, and the technologies themselves, are quite similar across units of government. This enables a small number of firms in a specific area, through economies of scale, to act as service providers at costs below those that would encumber a unit of government performing the service itself. Technology allows many tasks to become "commoditized," thus provided very cheaply. Outsourcing also allows services to be delivered by companies with substantial purchasing power and the most efficient specific technology. Experience has shown that the price paid for outsourced services is often below the cost of internal production. Although outsourcing is taking place in the public sector, the opportunity for greater usage exists and is expected to take place in the future.

GOVERNMENT TO BUSINESS

A major area of change in the relationship between government and business is expected to be in the area of electronic procurement. E-procurement has a number of advantages over the traditional method of awarding contracts. Cost savings should result because information concerning a contract is disseminated more widely, exposing it to more bidders. This has the advantage of increasing competition, making collusion between bidders more difficult, and increasing transparency. Additionally, units of government can cooperate in joint e-procurement, increasing the scale of their orders and saving money by avoiding having to set up duplicate e-procurement systems. The early trends in e-procurement and the sources of cost savings are discussed below.

Electronic Procurement

Jupiter Media Metrix estimates that online purchases by government will grow to $286 billion by 2005, fully 17 percent of the total government purchases. This amount is more than 50 times greater than e-procurement in 1999, which stood at $5.5 billion. It is, according to Jupiter, state and local governments that lead the way in e-procurement, despite their falling well below the overall level of federal government expenditures on goods and services provided by business. Fueling this projected growth in e-procurement is the size of potential cost savings. Online procurement is estimated to save government as much as 18 to 45 percent, or $50 billion, in 2001 of their direct and indirect purchasing costs (Wyld 2001, 142). To put these figure in the context of spending overall, in 2000 the federal and state governments purchased $1 trillion worth of goods and services. In terms of number of purchases, the federal government made about 28 million purchases in 1998, of which 98 percent were valued at no more than $25,000 (Moon 2003, 181).

Governments are often the victims of overpayment for goods and services. The media is particularly fond of showing the high prices for some Pentagon purchases. Unjustifiably high prices often result from a lack of competition, either because the market for a specific product has few suppliers or because the geographic market is limited. However, another reason for overpayment is that the government is sometimes the victim of price-fixing conspiracies.

In the past, a local government's request for bidding went to only a few suppliers in its immediate area. Often, governments published their procurement requests in local newspapers. This limited the number of bidders. The use of the Internet in e-procurement can more widely disseminate the information about available government contracts and thereby increase the number of bidders. This has two primary benefits with regard to the price of a contract. First, with more bidders, competition for contracts will be stronger, and contracts will more likely be exposed to low-cost providers. These factors should reduce the price of contracts. Second, increasing the number of bidders will decrease the likelihood of successful collusion among bidders. It is more difficult and risky for bidders to attempt to collude when their numbers are larger. In fact, increased numbers of bidders in sealed-bid auctions have been shown to decrease prices in the case of highway construction (Gupta 2002, 14).

Opportunities for joint purchasing also hold the potential for cost savings in public-sector purchasing. Joint purchasing in the private sector has been pursued to a limited extent to reduce procurement costs. Five large automobile companies formed Covisint Inc. to create a platform providing procurement information to suppliers, hence making such information ubiquitous and increasing competition. Although Covisint Inc. ultimately ran into difficulties, state and local governments could form a joint-purchasing platform to generate savings from greater bargaining leverage. Efforts in the private sector have not flourished, in part because the savings are relatively small and because the creation of monopsony power could raise antitrust issues; joint purchasing in the public sector does not raise the same antitrust issues. Small jurisdictions could combine their purchasing activities and enjoy greater purchasing power. We could witness greater interjurisdictional cooperation where large local governments provide services involving significant scale economies to their neighboring smaller localities. Such opportunities were not even considered before the Internet reduced transaction costs substantially.

GOVERNMENT TO CITIZENRY

Changes in the way that government interacts with the citizenry are present in many forms. The most basic change is in information delivery. The maintenance of websites providing various types of information is now standard. Increasingly, complete interactions with government take place online. In a step beyond the posting of information, numerous types of applications, permits, payments, inquiries, and licenses have been made available for online submission. The Internet and e-mail have fostered communication between citizens and government. These serve to enhance democracy by closing the information and communication divide. The last change in the way government and citizens interact that we consider is in Internet voting. This holds the potential to increase democracy as it may increase voter participation.

Information Delivery

A virtual bulletin board provides a way of making information easily accessible to the public at minimal cost. Municipalities use their virtual bulletin boards to present information about their leaders, the structure of the government, and their activities. Some specific examples of information posted include such timely information as beach conditions, inspections of nursing homes and healthcare facilities, and health advisories. The Pennsylvania Healthcare Cost Containment Council provides extensive information on the mortality experience and other aspects of hospital performance. New York City posts restaurant-inspection reports. This type of information allows consumers to make better choices and provides strong incentives for establishments to achieve high marks on the inspections. To some extent, providing this information to the public creates market incentives that augment the incentives created by government sanctions and could eventually serve as an alternative to government sanctions.

Online Government Services

Government services provided on the Internet include renewing driving licenses, paying fines, filing taxes, and obtaining building permits and fishing licenses. All states offer downloads of professional licensing forms, but only two, in 2002, allowed completion of the entire process online (Gant and Gant 2003, 63). Eighty-four percent of the states make their tax forms available online, and most make online submission possible. Citizens increasingly demand that governments provide both 24/7 service and seamless services that cross over various relevant agencies and governments.

Online transactions provide significant savings for governments. Arizona saves 76 percent for online vehicle registrations compared to paper registrations received in the mail. An e-payment costs 2 cents, compared to 43 cents for issuing a check (Eggers 2004, 28). On the other hand, online automobile registration in Alaska in 2000 was calculated to cost 27 cents more per transaction than mail-in registration because a development cost of 85 cents was included (Cohen and Eimicke 2001, 23). Whether development cost is appropriately added is debatable. Savings should result as more people use the online automobile-registration system at a very low marginal cost, while no additional funds for development need be incurred.

Democracy Enhancement

With the expansion of e-mail, citizens are able to transmit their preferences to their representatives and to other government officials more easily and in a timelier manner. In 2003, 91 percent of government officials had e-mail addresses on the jurisdiction website, an increase from 68 percent in 2000. In 2003, 12 percent of governments enabled citizens to obtain e-mail updates about their jurisdiction's activities, an increase from 5 percent in 2000. In a 2003 study of the human-services departments of all 50 states, 68 percent responded to an e-mail question about their hours of operation. In fact, 62 percent responded within 24 hours, showing the benefit citizens derive from e-mail (West 2003, 15).

In the other direction, citizens are able to learn easily about their public officials' voting and activities. Transcripts and real-time video transmission of meetings and hearings are available. All of that increases accountability and transparency, thus enhancing democracy.

The Internet has enhanced citizen involvement in the political process. Political candidates can get their messages across cheaply and promptly. The campaigns of former Minnesota governor Jesse Ventura and U.S. Senator John McCain of Arizona relied substantially on the Internet to present the candidates' policy positions, attract volunteers, and obtain campaign contributions. Both President George W. Bush and Sen. John Kerry used their respective websites to express their views and counter their rival's positions. The Internet permits popular candidates with no party support to challenge the leading candidates by raising campaign funds inexpensively and quickly. After his 2000 New Hampshire victory, Sen. John McCain raised $20,000 through his website in the first hour and $2 million within one week. Gov. Howard Dean, in 2003, raised a record $15.9 million via his website in a single three-month period (Eggers 2004, 161–69).

The Internet, e-government, and communications in general serve to increase democracy in the world. Citizens in deprived and undemocratic nations learn about how governments operate in nations with personal and economic freedom, causing pressure to replace undemocratic regimes. The use of the Internet is significantly lower in less-developed nations than in the democratic and developed nations and is limited to better-educated and wealthier citizens. However, that slice of the population is usually instrumental in bringing about political change. Indeed, this is an important long-term contribution of e-government.

Internet Voting

Voting over the Internet will further enhance citizens' participation in electing their representatives. Internet voting is simply the use of any computer with Internet access to cast a vote. Such voting does not require the use of computers only at polling places. To achieve security, a process similar to that for electronic payments can be used. The objective is to increase voter participation through eliminating the need to travel to and spend time in a queue. That this is important is highlighted by the decline in voter participation. Voter participation in presidential elections has declined from almost 58 percent during the 1972–1996 period to slightly more than 50 percent in 2000 (Done 2003, 251). Polling places, libraries, and other public places can be used to provide access to voters who lack their own electronic access. However, the need for such outlets will diminish with time as entire cities become wireless enabled and as prices decline for the equipment needed to connect to the Internet.

Internet voting could involve simply obtaining the forms, then mailing in the ballots, which would be similar to the process currently used for absentee ballots. This system allows handicapped, infirm, and rural constituents, as well as those absent from their jurisdictions, to vote more easily. It also permits signature authentication and avoids problems like people hacking into or jamming the Internet voting site (Elliott 2004). The more complete form of Internet voting avoids the use of the mail and involves submission of the electronically authenticated ballots.

Complete Internet voting would employ a similar method to the credit card system used for electronic payments. This voting, which would preclude the use of mail and associated processing, has some inherent problems, including the possibility of hackers altering individual voting, jamming of the system, and possible coercion through the lack of secrecy provided by the traditional polling place. In 2005, efforts were underway to develop standards for Internet voting to ameliorate the secrecy and reliability problems (Levy 2005).

E-voting was implemented in its full form for the March 2000 Democratic primary in Arizona. Any computer that complied with security and privacy requirements could be used. The system used a secure communication link and electronic signatures. Individual votes required personal identification numbers, as well as ballot control and inscription. Access to the computer tabulating system was strictly controlled. Forty-one percent of all votes were cast on the Internet, and three times as many votes were cast in 2000 as in the 1996 primary (Done 2003, 43). Even though the 2000 presidential primary may have held more interest than the 1996 primary, the increase in turnout was impressive.

EXAMPLES OF E-GOVERNMENT INNOVATIONS AMONG CITIES AND STATES

The extent to which e-government is serving the functions of government varies across states and cities. In this book, we provide a snapshot of e-government development and initiatives across cities and states as of 2002 to 2005. When we began soliciting chapters for this book, we started by finding cities and states recognized for specific innovative projects in various publications, such as *Government Technology*, *Mobile Government*, *Governing*, *Public CIO*, and *American City and County*, as well as those highly ranked in general by the Center for Digital Government's Digital Cities Survey and Digital State Survey. The chapters included reflect recognition of excellence in general or in relation to a specific project.

Government's improvement in service delivery to the public receives the most attention. This is partly the result of the state and local government emphasis of this book, thus reflective of the fact that e-government is most important to citizens at the local level, where more than 80 percent of transactions occur.

Internal Government Operations

Internal government operations are the focus of the chapter by Mark Forman, the top federal e-government administrator in the first term of the Bush administration. The initiatives begun under Forman were intended to bring down the walls preventing the sharing of information between government agencies, allow government bodies more convenient information regarding grants, reduce redundancies, unify the thousands of individual websites, and increase cybersecurity. The efforts outlined at the federal level are complemented by the accounts of the use of GIS in managing city departments submitted by Baltimore mayor Martin O'Malley and former New York mayor Rudolph Giuliani. The city of San Francisco's centralization of GIS information to bring efficiency to the interdepartmental sharing of data is discussed in the chapter by Mayor Willie Brown. Indianapolis mayor Steve Goldsmith discusses the use of information technology in reforming city management.

Another example of using technology to increase accountability in government is provided in the chapter on regulatory reform by Gov. Bill Owens and Executive Director of the Department of Regulatory Agencies Rick

O'Donnell. Colorado's Regulatory Notice system requires all proposed regulations to be subject to public disclosure. Any interested party may subscribe to the system and receive e-mails of proposed regulations that fall within their areas of interest. The public feedback to proposed regulations, via e-mail response to the regulation, can impact whether a cost-benefit analysis of the regulation is conducted. Information on hearings and agency contacts is also provided. Regulators in Colorado no longer act within a bubble, insulated from public feedback. They receive rapid feedback from business and the public, allowing the citizenry to play an influential role in regulatory decision making.

In reaching a higher-level of e-government, Mayor Kay Barnes and Gail Roper discuss the importance of an IT strategic plan and the steps taken to produce one for Kansas City. Newark mayor, Sharpe James, provides an account of the transformation of that city's once overburdened municipal court and the enhancement of public safety through the use of new technology. The chapter by Mayor Neil Giuliano of Tempe, Arizona, presents a solution to communication problems between various public-safety agencies at numerous special events throughout the year, such as the Fiesta Bowl.

Government to Business

Government-to-business interactions have been facilitated with some of the same tools used with the citizenry, such as Web portals. However, the content is tailored to the business community, providing information on topics such as compliance, zoning, applications, and permits. An example is provided by Mayor Anthony Williams of Washington, D.C. The District has built a comprehensive online business resource center that, in addition to information resources and online transactions, even provides consulting guidance in areas from applying for a loan to creating a business plan.

Another aspect of government-to-business interaction takes place in purchasing. Virginia is one of the states that leads the way in e-procurement, government purchases from vendors over the Internet, and that state's efforts are documented in the chapter submitted by Gov. Mark Warner. Another state embarking on a Web-based procurement system is Florida. The chapter by Gov. Jeb Bush discusses Florida's vision for streamlined interactions with vendors.

Government to Citizenry

Examples of the use of e-government to better serve the citizenry abound. All but two states offer online licensing and permission forms. Seventy-six percent of the states make their forms available online and make online submission possible. The online payment of fees and tickets has become commonplace.

The delivery of information to the public has been undertaken in a wide variety of areas from program eligibility and public services to reports on restaurant inspections and traffic conditions.

The chapter by Gov. Edward Rendell discusses the evolution of online services in Pennsylvania. The chapter by Gov. Mike Huckabee details the steps taken in Arkansas to replace the once frustrating process of vehicle registration with an online alternative. The chapter by Gov. Mike Foster and Joan McGee documents the development of the Louisiana Services Directory, which provides a comprehensive, single-entry portal to information on state services. The chapters submitted by Gov. M. Michael Rounds and Otto Doll of South Dakota and Gov. Sonny Perdue of Georgia also speak of the development of their respective state Web portals and online services. Charlotte's mayor, Patrick McCrory, discusses the evolution of the city's award-winning combined city and Mecklenberg County website, as well as efforts to reduce the digital divide and provide online services. Mayor Bill Smith provides insight into the process of carrying out e-business innovation for the citizens of Edmonton, a city in which the average citizen visits the city's website more than three times a year. Mayor Lee Brown discusses the launch of Houston's award-winning eGovernment Center and the use of services provided online. Mayor Vera Katz presents the evolution of Portland's e-government system. They now provide a host of online services, from the mapping by address of characteristics from property assessments and crime statistics to environmental hazards and zoning to resources for housing and carpooling.

Mayor Pam Iorio discusses Tampa, Florida's award winning Neighborhood Information page, which provides information on topics from land use and population to public safety and recreation and also allows citizens to compare neighborhoods instantly to citywide averages.

Providing more innovative services and using e-government to improve public safety is the focus of the chapter by Honolulu's award-winning mayor, Jeremy Harris. Technology is also being used to enhance democracy as is detailed in the chapter by Gov. Tony Knowles and Lt. Gov. Fran Ulmer of Alaska. Calgary's mayor, David Bronconnier, presents the development of fiber-optic infrastructure to aid in the development of intelligent transportations and provide bandwidth for city services. Mayor Bob Corker and David Eichenthal of Chattanooga, Tennessee, discuss the implementation of a 311 call number in that city for the reporting of nonemergency conditions and requests for service and information; they discuss as well the opportunity the system provides for better city management. Corpus Christi, Texas's mayor, Loyd Neal, and Susan Cable, the director of e-government services, write about that city's use and development of e-government. Corpus Christi ranked among the top ten U.S. digital cities in both 2003 and 2004 in a survey conducted by the Center for Digital Government.

THE FUTURE OF E-GOVERNMENT

In some sense, the future of e-government is more of the same. In particular, more widespread and varied use of GIS, more outsourcing (especially of tasks commoditized through technology), and greater use of e-procurement are expected. In information delivery, websites will often become more expansive, more relevant, and easier to navigate. Interactions of business and citizens with government will, to a greater extent, be fully available online. We also expect some expansion of Internet voting. Beyond the expansion of forms of e-government that are already in evidence, we expect changes in the organizational structure of government to take place as well. Of course, for these changes to occur, it is important that strong leadership be provided. We discuss some of the challenges facing e-government below.

Success in e-government implementation depends upon two key factors. First, having a committed political leader to champion e-government initiatives is critical. In the chapters selected for this book, the role of a champion as an important criterion for success is evident. A study by the U.S. General Accounting Office (1997) revealed that the most important factor determining the extent of privatization in state and local government is the existence of a strong political champion that advances the change. The same would apply for any major governmental initiative, including the adoption of electronic government. One insight from this book is the recognition of the strong impact made by leaders in government.

The second factor critical to the success of e-government is establishing an organizational structure to implement initiatives, become a resource for other agencies of the jurisdiction, develop comparability standards, and evaluate other jurisdictions' efforts. Such an agency already exists in the jurisdictions in the form of the chief information officer and associated staff. One challenge faced by this organizational structure is overcoming workers' fears. Ameliorating workers' concern about loss of employment through increased use of technology and including workers in the decision-making process are important.

Modern business-information systems and better communications enabled by the Internet have changed the corporate structure. A study of 300 large U.S. firms found that between 1984 and 1999, more individuals reported directly to their chief executive officers, and the number of intermediate supervisory levels and positions decreased (Malone 2004, 32). If government adopts these technologies with the vigor of competing businesses, changes to the structure of government will also result.

E-government is expected to make middle management of lesser value and to flatten the pyramid of management in government. Improved communications, measurability of output, and greater worker accountability will reduce the necessary levels of worker supervision and middle management. In turn, decisions by top management will become more transparent, and its accountability will also rise. With the decline in the number of middle-level managers, the responsibilities of frontline workers will rise; more decision-making responsibilities will shift from middle management to these workers. Thus, as a result of improved technology, government could become leaner and workers more empowered, efficient, and accountable.

When considering the long-term effects of e-government on the structure and activities of government, increased transparency becomes a most beneficial aspect. When activities are reported, meetings are broadcast, and information is easily accessed, citizens become more informed. This will make government more accountable, and good governance in one locality will increase pressure on others to adopt the same innovations.

E-government is a technological innovation and moves from an inefficient and mainly unaccountable bureaucracy to a new entrepreneurial and accountable culture. It enables workers at lower levels of the hierarchy to take part in and be accountable for decision making. E-government is being used to improve the management of cities and to achieve a more efficient use of resources. In the long run, opportunities exist for e-government to bring about a reorganization of government, one that will reduce excessively bureaucratic processes and organizational structures. It is these changes that may ultimately bring the biggest cost savings to taxpayers.

ENDNOTES

1. Press release: strategis.ic.gc.ca/epic/internet/inspp-pps.nsf/vwapj/gtec-081003-e.pdf/$FILE/gtec-081003-e.pdf. Last visited 1/11/2005.

2. Such a service has already been provided in Akron, Ohio, and Birmingham, Alabama. The Customer Service Request (CSR) System enables assignment of the work, follows it up to completion, and reports back to the resident who first complained. The 311 system enables residents to complain about any problem without directing it to a specific municipal agency only during work hours (Dombrowski 2005).

3. Series IDs for the tables are as follows: Federal Employment CEU9091000001, State Employment CEU9092000001, and Local Employment CEU9093000001.

BIBLIOGRAPHY

Accenture. 2001. "Rhetoric vs. Reality: Closing the Gap," at www.accenture.com/xdoc/en/industries/government/2001FullReport.pdf (accessed February 15, 2005).

Brock, James. 2005. "Automobiles," in *The Structure of American Industry*, ed. Walter Adams and James Brock, 11th ed., 96–118. Upper Saddle River, NJ: Pearson Prentice Hall.

Brown, Ken Spencer. 2003. "Cities and States Look to Tech for Savings," *Investors Business Daily*, April 10.

Brown, Richard. 2001. "Making Government Pay: Times Make BTG Look Attractive, but Beware," *E-Business News*, August 27.

Cohen, Stephen, and William Eimicke. 2001. "The Use of the Internet in Government Service Delivery," in *E-Government 2001*, ed. Mark A. Abramson and Grady E. Means, 9–43. Lanham, MD: Rowman & Littlefield.

Dombrowski, Cathy. 2005. "One Call Away," *American City and County* (January): 46–51.

Done, Robert S. 2003. "Internet Voting: Bringing Elections to the Desktop," in *E-Government 2003*, ed. Mark A. Abramson and Therese L. Morin, 237–65. Lanham, MD: Rowman & Littlefield.

Eggers, William D. 2004. *Government 2.0: Using Technology to Improve Education, Cut Red Tape, Reduce Gridlock, and Enhance Democracy*. Lanham, MD: Rowman & Littlefield.

Elliott, David M. 2004. "Examining Internet Voting in Washington." Discussion paper from the Assistant Director of Elections, the state of Washington, at www.electioncenter.org/voting/InetVotingWhitePaper.html (accessed January 14, 2005).

Gansler, Jacques S., and William Lucyshyn. 2004. *Competitive Sourcing: What Happens to Federal Employees?* Washington, D.C.: IBM Center for the Business of Government (October).

Gant, Diana Burley, and Jon P. Gant. 2003. "Enhancing E-Service Delivery in State Government," in *E-Government 2003*, ed. Mark A. Abramson and Therese L. Morin, 53–80. Lanham, MD: Rowman & Littlefield.

Giuliani, Rudolph W. 2002. "From In-Line to Online: The E-Government Revolution in New York City," in *The New Public Management: Lessons from Innovating Governors and Mayors*, ed. Paul Andrisani, Simon Hakim, and E. S. Savas, 99–106. Boston, MA: Kluwer.

Goldsmith, Stephen, and William D. Eggers. 2004. *Governing by Network*. Washington, D.C.: Brookings Institute.

Gupta, Srabana. 2002. "Competition and Collusion in a Government Procurement Auction Market," *Atlantic Economic Journal* (March): 13–25.

Levy, Steven. 2005. "A Step Forward in the Voting Wars," *Newsweek* (February 7): 12.

Malone, Thomas W. 2004. *The Future of Work*. Boston, MA: Harvard Business School Press.

Moon, M. Jae. 2003. "State Government E-Procurement in the Information Age: Issues, Practices, and Trends," in *E-Government 2003*, ed. Mark A. Abramson and Therese L. Morin, 177–231. Lanham, MD: Rowman & Littlefield.

Office of Management and Budget (OMB). 2003. "Bush Administration Moves to Get Volume Discount on Software," Press release 2003-16, June 5.

Pryor, Fredric L. 2001. "New Trends in U.S. Industrial Concentration," *Industrial Organization* 18 (3) (May): 301–26.

Stowerse, Genie N. L. 2001. "Commerce Comes to Government on the Desktop: E-Commerce Application in the Public Sector," in *E-Government 2001*, ed. Mark A. Abramson and Grady E. Means, 44–84. Lanham, MD: Rowman & Littlefield.

Taylor, Humphrey. 2002. "Internet Penetration at 66 Percent of Adults (137 Million) Nationwide," Harris Poll #18, April 17, at www.harrisinteractive.com/harris_poll/index (accessed February 4, 2005).

U.S. General Accounting Office. 1997. *Privatization: Lessons Learnt by State and Local Governments*, GAO/GGD-97-48, Washington, D.C., March.

U.S. Department of Labor (DOL), Bureau of Labor Statistics. 2005. "Number of Government Employees 1995–2004," at www.bls.gov/ces/home.htm (accessed February 15, 2005).

West, Darrell M. 2003. "State and Federal E-Government in the United States, 2003." Discussion paper, Center for Public Policy, Brown University, Providence, Rhode Island, September, at www.insidepolitics.org (accessed January 10, 2005).

Wyld, David C. 2001. "The Auction Model: How the Public Sector Can Leverage the Power of E-Commerce through Dynamic Pricing," in *E-Government 2001*, ed. Mark A. Abramson and Grady E. Means, 85–161. Lanham, MD: Rowman & Littlefield.

Part II

INCREASING THE EFFICIENCY OF INTERNAL GOVERNMENT OPERATIONS

2

Information Technology and Homeland Security: The Federal Perspective

Mark Forman, Administrator, U.S. Office of E-Government and Information Technology

The federal government is on the cusp of transforming the way government works. Our current technology and management knowledge allow this change, and the need for homeland security demands it. This chapter focuses on federal initiatives for managing information technology (IT), particularly initiatives that enable federal, state, and local governments to work together effectively.

The President's Management Agenda, which is the administration's overall management reform approach, encompasses five components. The first component is the strategic management of human capital, which will become increasingly important as 50 percent of the federal workforce becomes eligible for retirement in the next five years. The second component is financial management, which addresses the federal government's chronic problems with erroneous payments, financial-management systems, and other areas of accountability. The third component, which the federal government is just starting, is competitive sourcing. This consists of public–private competition for commercial functions. The fourth component is performance integration, which ties budgeting and spending to results. The fifth component is expanding e-government, the component for which I am responsible. E-government focuses on modernizing the federal government.

E-GOVERNMENT

The purpose of e-government, as of the entire management agenda, is to make government more citizen centered and less agency centered. The $58 billion we spend on IT must make a difference in government's service to citizens. A key result I anticipate is making government—typically thought of as slow and bureaucratic—work faster. It's as simple as shrinking decision-making time from weeks to hours.

E-government means more than just putting up websites; it means using digital technologies to transform the way we do business, making our services better and more efficient. E-government initiatives are unique because they always impact other components of the management agenda; for example, using technology to improve business processes will help federal workers be more productive. Overall, e-government is both making the federal government simpler and unifying government organizations, thus improving efficiency, effectiveness, and service quality.

With the advent of the Internet, the way people work has changed. However, the federal government does not yet fully understand that. The federal government is still largely paper based. Yet, in the private sector, people have adapted to a real-time environment where decisions are made rapidly because information is shared and business processes are conducted online.

Interaction with government has changed from a physical to an electronic process; every week, half of the people in America are online dealing with a government website. So, we need to focus not just on having more IT but on working together—government with government, agency with agency—to reach citizens the way they expect to reach us.

Services to Citizens

A well-managed e-government approach has to look at what our citizens—our customers—want. They want services and information that are easier to access. Hence, we focus on simplification. They also want better coordination of information across federal, state, and local levels, which e-government can provide and is required for homeland security. To give citizens better services, the administration has adopted a four-part e-government strategy. First, to reduce redundancy across federal agencies, we have created "one-stop shops" such as FirstGov.gov, our official Web portal. Whether you're in state and local government, a business, or a citizen, you can access the portal's easy-to-use, consolidated services.

Second, we have highlighted government-to-government cooperation. We have leveraged technology to reformulate the way governments work together, from grant management to disaster planning. For example, we are working to make grant processes simpler, and are focused on getting better results.

Third, because most federal transactions are with the business community, we are simplifying and putting these transactions online (over 8,000 are online right now), making them easier to carry out. The Paperwork Elimination Act requires that by October 2003, all of our transactions must be electronic.

We are, however, running the risk of merely shifting the bureaucratic burden online. So, instead, we are leveraging e-business approaches to reduce the burden on business as we put transactions online.

Fourth, we are integrating our administrative processes so that there is no unnecessary paper passing, even electronically. This means that the federal government is applying technology to simplify and integrate such functions as purchasing, payroll, recruitment, and security clearances.

To implement this strategy, we consolidated 400 redundant agency projects into 24 cross-agency projects, thus simplifying and unifying federal services around the customer. We organized these projects into four portfolios in line with the four-part e-government strategy. I will highlight the government-to-government projects since we are focusing efforts on restructuring the way governments work together. But there are other important projects, such as e-authentication to provide trustworthy transactions as government goes online. From these efforts, we have learned that restructuring government services is complicated—because the government is! A key issue is that several agencies perform the same work. I know state and local governments are dealing with the same sorts of issues. Grappling with these complexities is necessary to modernizing government processes.

Modernizing Federal Government Processes

We know that IT solutions alone will not make government run more effectively. We also need to address problems with underlying organizational issues, which is a key focus in modernizing the federal government. An important component has been reducing redundant buying to achieve economies of scale and interoperability. Also, because of the cost overruns in many programs, we have looked at changes in program management. Since the federal government has so much invested in IT, we have had to set some priorities, figuring out the relationship between organizational change, process redesign, and the use of IT. We call these "modernization blueprints."

Another key element of modernization has been reducing "islands of automation." In June 2001, we found that the government already had 22,000 websites. Thus, it was almost as difficult to work with the government online as in person! The fact is that the federal government depends on local and state governments to deliver services. So, we have focused on simplifying and unifying these independent IT investments not only to improve citizen services but to meet the demands of homeland security that our people be able to use their computers to work together effectively. For example, if terrorist threats have to be handled by government agencies that share information, then there have to be organized processes and interoperable IT available to allow that exchange. Also related to homeland security, of course, is cybersecurity. Making communications across organizations secure has been a challenge, but we are continuing to make progress by using a structured approach to alleviating cybersecurity issues.

We have made significant progress in our modernization efforts, with 23 of the 24 cross-agency projects making key deployments. Any resistance to change hasn't come from the average federal employee but from those intimidated by changes in the bureaucratic culture. Nevertheless, we have worked as a team and achieved important results. For instance, FirstGov has evolved from an inefficient search engine to an efficient "three clicks to service" model. The numbers tell the story: in 2001, 6.7 million Americans tried to get service at FirstGov; this year we're servicing six million a month. We are also seeing significant results in business-to-government transactions. Almost 50 percent of all businesses conducted online transactions with us in January 2003. Furthermore, the partnerships across agencies that make efforts like FirstGov successful have also motivated greater teamwork within the agencies.

We are also making measurable progress in cybersecurity. We have gone from about 30 percent of systems secured to 50 or 60 percent, with a goal of 80 percent in 2003. Interestingly, we're finding that when IT projects have not built security in from the beginning, we have had to do costly patching. But, when we can build security in from the start, it actually costs less. We are trying to make progress in IT workforce reforms, too. Over 80 percent of the federal IT workforce comes from the vendor community. I want the federal employees who work in IT to focus on project management because that's what drives the reengineering that makes us more effective.

Our future work will remain dedicated to improving policy results. We want to reduce the cycle time, or the response time, of government, which is very important in providing homeland security. And more broadly, the E-Government Act commits us to using IT to foster ongoing dialog with state, local, and tribal governments and to finding innovative ways to collaborate.

GOVERNMENT-TO-GOVERNMENT PROJECTS

Finally, I want to focus on five initiatives linking government to government, some of which are relevant to homeland security. These were identified two years ago through focus groups, which consisted of state and local government officials.

- *Grants.gov.* This project, already operational, creates one portal for all federal-grant customers, making it easier for potential recipients at other government levels to learn about and apply for grants. This eliminates waste, such as the need for governments to hire "bounty hunters" to find grants. Hitherto, grants have been managed so that we don't know which grants best meet recipients' needs; this project addresses that problem. Grants.gov is currently in its pilot phase, offering its "find grants" capability. By October 2003, we hope to launch the "apply" capability for the bulk of grant moneys. This will allow governments to complete joint applications or to use a single, integrated application, eliminating wasteful paper-based processes.

- *E-vital.* This project, just rolling out beyond the initial states, will establish common electronic processes for federal and state agencies to process, verify, and share birth- and death-record information. Accurate and consistent vital statistics are important for homeland security and for avoiding waste through erroneous payments to deceased recipients.
- *Disaster management.* This initiative is crucial to homeland security. It allows us to provide federal, state, and local emergency managers with online access to disaster-management information and to planning and response tools. After September 11, 2001, state and local first responders told us that figuring out whom they were suppose to work with in the federal government was taking so much time that it hurt their ability to save lives and protect property. We have established a consolidated website, www.disasterhelp.gov, which gives all jurisdictions a toolkit for interoperability. The site pulls together geographic and disaster-response tools, such as secure instant messaging, which makes it simpler for federal, state, and local first responders to work together. Now we are testing the interoperability system through disaster-preparedness exercises. We have also been working to simplify and unify the processes that first responders undergo when working with the federal government.
- *Geospatial One-Stop.* Here we have consolidated information to give federal, state, and local agencies a single point of access to geographic data. Studies showed that 50 percent of governments' geospatial information was redundant, so we developed standards for the interoperability of that data. We also constructed a portal, www.geodata.gov, that provides governments and citizens access to basic frameworks and tools for sharing data on geospatial categories, such as transportation and climate. Thus, data will no longer have to be collected and purchased separately. This unification is important for disaster planning, environmental response, and infrastructure decisions related to homeland security.
- *Project Safecom.* This initiative is intended to help federal, state, local, and tribal public-safety agencies improve response through more effective and efficient interoperable wireless communications. Again, we are addressing an issue very important to homeland security. When we started this initiative, we had over 1,000 interoperability wireless pilots

underway; we saw that it was unrealistic to reach interoperability with so many projects. Project Safecom will identify the key elements of IT architecture and applications, then work to unify wireless communications systems. The radio and voice piece is important, but local governments and law-enforcement officials tell us that the essential information they need for public safety comes from computers at the base station. For a fraction of the cost of most trunk radio systems, we can use IT to get much better data directly to first responders. But we still need to construct interoperability—decide on systems architecture, requirements, and agreements between jurisdictions. Most important, this initiative has to develop from the local level up. In all five initiatives, in fact, we are trying to change the top-down way the federal government has worked in the past.

Of the five projects, only Safecom and E-vital are nonoperational; however, they are very close to full implementation. In June 2003, the Safecom project held the kick-off meeting for its IT architecture work. State and local public-safety associations, county-manager associations, the National League of Cities, and the National Association of State CIOs are all involved in working on the architecture.

OTHER KEY E-GOVERNMENT PROJECTS

Two other major projects deserve notice, one regarding government-to-citizen interactions and the other regarding government-to-business.

- *GovBenefits*. This initiative provides a single point of online access for citizens, community organizations, or faith-based organizations to determine their eligibility for government benefits and services. As an example of the integration involved, there about 410 federal programs for social services, each of which had been providing its information separately. The GovBenefits website is intended to reduce that to one-stop shopping, whereby citizens can gather information regarding the aforementioned 410 programs from one source. Any citizen can seek and find relevant federal benefits programs through use of the GovBenefits eligibility-screening tool. Most state and local government benefits programs are tied to GovBenefits, and we have been working with states and some localities on an integrated benefits application form. Citizens, organizations, and caseworkers can use the GovBenefits tools.
- *Business Compliance One-Stop*. This initiative aims to reduce the burden on businesses by making it easier to find, understand, and comply with relevant laws and regulations. For example, businesses need fed-

eral, state, and local licenses for transportation and other aspects of their activities. We want to reduce the paperwork burden this involves, so we've been working to convince all government levels to integrate their processes. This project is also working to harmonize reporting requirements in a variety of areas.

CONCLUSION

There is a lot of exciting work involved in the pursuit of e-government. How do we motivate that change at the federal level? All of the items on the President's Management Agenda and the agencies involved are scored on their status and progress every quarter. An agency or agenda item that is not making progress gets the president's attention since he is very concerned about the quality of government management. Thus, there is accountability for results at the highest level, and that motivates change. Also, we can analyze an agency that is not progressing in e-government and understand how to improve efforts, looking at chronic problems that may be preventing modernization.

To move forward, however, we not only have to assess our own progress, but we must work with others. We must work with everyone involved to get the "breakthrough thinking" we need to innovate. This is not government business as usual. Since we are dealing with issues as important as homeland security or Internet access to services, business as usual is not an option. We are finding that once we break through to new ways of operating, like those I've discussed in this chapter, our performance improves significantly. And that requires help from interested individuals. I encourage such individuals to get involved in our initiatives, whether in business case development or helping us deploy e-government solutions. We have an open-door policy, and we especially encourage those interested to work with us on the disaster-management and wireless-communications projects.

We are already working with many groups, as previously stated—governments, businesses, and organizations like PTI, a technology nonprofit funded by numerous local governments. We look forward to this collaboration. We know that we can't create e-government magically; we need the ideas and assistance of everyone involved.

3

Using Technology to Strengthen Government Accountability and Achieve True Regulatory Reform

Bill Owens, Governor of Colorado, and Rick O'Donnell, Executive Director of the Department of Regulatory Agencies for Colorado

Using technology to empower entrepreneurs and give them a direct voice in the state regulatory process is at the core of a first-of-its-kind tool in place in Colorado—a tool that is helping us stop needless, expensive regulations. The Regulatory Notice system exposes all proposed regulations to the scrutiny of full public disclosures and gives citizens the tools to react quickly and easily. As a result, Colorado regulators have new incentives to consider the real-world effects of proposals on jobs, our economy, and our state as a whole.

This is a vital development because modern regulation constitutes one of the most significant avenues for the exercise of government authority, even as it remains the least understood sphere of government activity in the popular mind. For example, in 2002, Congress passed 269 bills, while federal regulators issued 4,167 new regulations. Lawmaking at the state level is no less active: in Colorado, the state general assembly passed 460 bills in the 2003 regular legislative session alone.

In the face of such a tremendous volume of government activity, the public's capacity for monitoring the actions of the public sector is easily overwhelmed. The resulting "accountability gap" that is created by this popular lack of understanding of, and involvement in, the regulatory process has not gone unnoticed—or unexploited—by bureaucrats and special interests.

As Fred Smith, president of the Competitive Enterprise Institute, has noted,

> Efforts to control Leviathan have evolved slowly throughout our history. As the disciplining effects of controls in the tax and spending area have improved, there has been a natural tendency by regulators to select the least disciplined instrument of regulation. For that reason, regulations have become the preferred

> tool of special interests and those who believe the public interest is best advanced by expanding political interference in the economy.[1]

Regulatory Notice is a tool of good government that involves the public in the operation of government precisely where it is needed the most—at the contact point between the "rubber" of legislative will (the exercise of which usually enjoys a good deal of public scrutiny) and the "road" of bureaucratic implementation (the practice of which generally goes unnoticed and unreported).

USING TECHNOLOGY TO TAKE REGULATORY REFORM TO THE NEXT LEVEL

In most cases, the regulatory-reform efforts of government have ignored technology and relied instead on two methods to control the regulatory world. The first method has been for the elected head of the executive branch to impose a generally deregulatory governing philosophy on the bureaucracy. Imposing a mindset that respects the fact that regulation makes life hard for individuals and businesses is never a bad thing, but like most approaches to changing organizational culture from the top—whether by managerial decree or executive order—this approach has its inherent limitations.

The most significant limitation is the simple, practical impossibility of imposing the will of a relatively transient political leader on the organizational culture of what, in government, is typically a human organization with relatively static membership. Given that our philosophical view of government tilts strongly toward the free market, smaller-government side of the spectrum, we do our best—often with admirable success—to implement our philosophy operationally. At the same time, given that the state of Colorado consists of 19 executive departments that employ more than 47,000 people to promulgate and administer bureaucratic rules on a vast array of subjects that often require highly specialized knowledge, it is easy to see that even the best cabinet may find it difficult to impose philosophical consistency on every regulatory action that an administration undertakes on a daily basis. This problem is likely to be even more challenging in many other states; Colorado, after all, has a relatively lean state government by most measures.

Since philosophical direction by the chief executive and his or her appointees has its practical limitations, even when that executive's philosophy is generally hostile to regulatory excess, the executive's check on the regulatory power of state government is next to meaningless when the elected head of state is not a friend of regulatory restraint. The transience of political power further limits the strength of an elected executive to make a lasting difference through the imposition of his or her philosophical approach.

Since many state employees here in Colorado were on the job before the Owens administration began five years ago and since nearly as many of them will likely remain with the state government after the end of the second term, you begin to understand that even an effective administration may ultimately find its regulatory discipline to be, at best, short-lived.

The second traditional method for controlling the regulatory apparatus of state government has been the employment of cost-benefit analysis to evaluate proposed regulations and determine their economic impact (for example, overall cost to the economy and costs of implementation). This method of restraining the regulatory power by requiring rational justification of its exercise decreases the chances that a bad regulation will slip through. However, in the end, it is really little more than an additional hoop that regulators must jump through since any analysis can only be as good as the rigor that is brought to its conduct. When the regulator that proposes a rule is the same entity that is charged with carrying out the cost-benefit analysis, benefits are often inflated and costs discounted.

Fred Smith recently referred to the deficiency of employing cost-benefit analysis without sufficient legitimacy safeguards when he noted that

> indeed, the push for cost-benefit or net-benefits analysis has diverted attention from more effective ways of prioritizing regulation. . . . More importantly, cost-benefit review has relatively little restraining effect. As long as the regulatory agency can argue that a rule has more benefit than cost, it is home free.[2]

Subjectivity is inherent in cost-benefit analysis, and to the extent that this is true, cost-benefit analysis alone provides only a pretense of genuine comfort against the prospect of bad regulation.

Colorado's Regulatory Notice system, in contrast, is more effective than either executive fiat or cost-benefit analysis at screening out bad regulation. This is so because it harnesses the energy of the individuals and businesses most likely to be affected by a proposed regulation and affords those parties the opportunity to present a perspective separate and apart from the perspective of the regulator. By facilitating such a dynamic, the Regulatory Notice system shines the light of accountability onto the traditionally hidden workings of the regulatory bureaucracy and thereby permits a broader application of the very same basic theory of political accountability that legitimizes elective democracy.

THE REGULATORY NOTICE SYSTEM AT WORK—ENDING THE PRACTICE OF REGULATION WITHOUT REPRESENTATION

The process of regulation in Colorado begins whenever an agency determines that a new or modified rule is required to implement a statute. We amended the Administrative Procedure Act to require that whenever state rule-making entities propose a new regulation or an amendment to regulations, they must submit a draft to the Office of Economic Competitiveness and Regulatory Reform (OECRR). This ensures that a particular, identifiable entity has the responsibility for reviewing every proposed new regulation in Colorado. To accomplish the submission process without creating another level of paperwork, we created a paperless system that allows regulators to submit their proposed regulations electronically via the Internet.

The OECRR then evaluates proposed regulations on three specific criteria, with adverse effects on: economic competitiveness, job creation, and small businesses in Colorado. Should a proposed regulation present signs of concern to the OECRR, a cost-benefit analysis will be ordered, requiring a detailed examination of the regulation's impact in these three spheres. The Regulatory Notice system has revolutionized the way OECRR carries out what might otherwise be its fairly traditional core functions.

Here is how Regulatory Notice works: A subscriber can sign up for the free service on the OECRR's website (www.dora.state.co.us/oecrr) and pick from among 40 subject areas of interest (e.g., labor and industry, natural resources, or health). Once signed up, subscribers receive automatic e-mails whenever proposed regulations are submitted in the subject areas they selected. These e-mails provide the interested citizen with several key pieces of information, including a link to the proposed regulation; time, date, and place of the hearings on the regulation; agency contacts who will address questions and concerns; and a contact at the OECRR who is responsible for gathering feedback on the proposed regulation to evaluate whether a cost-benefit analysis should be requested.

Regulatory Notice provides every Coloradan the ability to track proposed regulations effortlessly. At the same time, it ensures awareness among regulators that their submissions are subject to public review from the very beginning of the proposed regulation's life. And what has been the end result? Colorado benefits from a more thoughtful regulatory process because citizens are involved on the front end, not just once a regulation has been promulgated and already carries the force of law.

To ensure even more transparency and accountability, in those cases in which a cost-benefit analysis has been requested by the OECRR, that cost-benefit analysis becomes a part of the rule-making record. More importantly, once the cost-benefit analysis has been submitted to the OECRR, Regulatory Notice subscribers again receive an automatic e-mail, this time containing a link to the cost-benefit analysis. This step allows Coloradans to review the analysis for accuracy and to submit testimony or rebuttal analysis during the public rule-making hearing, all with the objective of arriving at the best possible end result for the "clients" of the regulatory process. By subjecting the cost-benefit analysis of a proposed regulation to "peer review" by the stakeholders who feel themselves likely to be impacted by the proposed regulation, we go a long way toward guaranteeing better regulatory outcomes for all Coloradans.

The Regulatory Notice system benefits small-business owners and entrepreneurs in particular. Unlike many large corporations with entire departments of regulatory-compliance staff, regulatory attorneys, and lobbyists, small businesses rarely have the time, energy, or staff to track regulations. Now, they can be actively involved in the regulatory process with the simple click of a mouse. This levels the playing field for big and small business.

Such citizen and business involvement exposes the regulatory guts of government to the public in a meaningful manner, thereby ending the practice that those of us critical of the current system like to call "regulation without representation."

The World Bank, in its *Doing Business in 2004: Understanding Regulation*, noted, "Although macro policies are unquestionably important, there is a growing consensus that the quality of business regulation and the institutions that enforce it are a major determinant of its prosperity."[3] The Regulatory Notice system places Colorado on the cutting edge of regulatory reform through the innovative use of basic, widely available technology to promote a better regulatory environment and to strengthen our state's prosperity.

EVALUATING THE EFFECTIVENESS OF THE REGULATORY NOTICE SYSTEM

Vindication of our intuitions about the existing regulatory process was not long in coming. Once we embarked upon the task of implementing the Regulatory Notice system, it came in the unexpectedly direct form of comments from many of our regulators themselves. At training sessions on use of the system, many of our state regulators repeatedly objected to the idea of publishing cost-benefit analyses through the Regulatory Notice system, often with comments such as, "I have no idea if and how my regulation impacts small businesses." Our response to those folks was simple: "If you are not considering the impact your regulation has on Colorado's economy, then you are an irresponsible regulator and this system was designed for you." This is a stern message but also an important one. The simple opportunity to convey this message to our regulators in a formal setting was itself a major and early benefit of adopting the Regulatory Notice system.

When we launched the system on September 22, 2003, our private-sector stakeholders responded with great enthusiasm. From the National Federation of Independent Business (the largest association of small business owners in the United States) to Americans for Tax Reform, a number of groups heaped praise on the Regulatory Notice system and publicly hailed it as a revolutionary tool for keeping Colorado's government appropriately in check.

In just over two weeks, more than 1,000 Coloradans signed up for the free e-mail alert service. Given the fact that a less proactive system in Rhode Island (under which e-mails notified subscribers only after a regulation was promulgated) failed to surpass this same number of registrants until well over one year after its launch, we feel confident that Regulatory Notice is off to a great start and will continue to grow in use as the system becomes more widely known. And, of course, as more individuals subscribe, the work of regulators can be expected to receive correspondingly greater scrutiny, which is good news for friends of regulatory accountability.

The following is a tangible example of the impact that the Regulatory Notice system is having on the process. During the system's first week of operation, one of our regulators pulled a proposed regulation after he realized that the feedback he was receiving through the OECRR was heavily critical of it. One retracted regulatory proposal shows deterrence at a late stage in the process; a less tangible indicator of deterrent effect would be the regulatory proposals deterred prior to being proposed in the first place. Evidence of such early-stage deterrence is necessarily elusive. However, we do know that the OECRR constantly receives telephone calls from regulators who are concerned that a regulation they may want to propose could be hit with a cost-benefit analysis or could inspire a deluge of adverse responses from Regulatory Notice subscribers. Extrapolating from these inquiries, we are highly confident that a deterrent effect has been created and is operating in many cases to keep bad regulations from even being proposed.

CONCLUSION

The simple fact is that the economic impact of regulation cannot be ignored. Economist Clyde Wayne Crews Jr., director of technology studies at the Cato Institute, recently estimated in the annual survey of regulatory trends called *Ten Thousand Commandments* that the annual cost of federal regulation is $860 billion.[4] Crews points out that this figure is greater than Canada's gross domestic product and the combined pretax profits of all U.S. corporations.[5] After adding the cost of state regulations, the annual cost of regulations easily enters the trillion-dollar range. Our economic health is already burdened by this reality, and so, it is obvious that additional regulatory pressures would be even less desirable. This is at least the case for those concerned with lessening the drag that government imposes on economic performance.

With the Regulatory Notice system, Colorado is well on its way to fostering a better and more responsive state government. We eagerly encourage our sister states and the federal government to adopt the Regulatory Notice system so that the United States can continue to be the premier example of transparent government in the world.

Ronald Reagan once said, "A big business is what a small business would be if only the government would get out of the way and leave it alone." His insight remains instructive today. While it is imperative for the government to protect consumer health and safety, we must be mindful that onerous regulatory burdens on business detract from job creation and hamper economic growth.

The Regulatory Notice system here in Colorado harnesses available technology in a very straightforward way to create a seamless e-government process that subjects regulators to accountability. The Regulatory Notice system can empower Coloradans, who otherwise might never have had the ability to monitor the government actions that threaten to affect the way they do business and earn a living, to become engaged in the regulatory process and to compel the government to make its case for regulating free market behavior.

By approaching the regulatory enterprise with three distinct, yet synergistic, methods aimed at ensuring good government, we in Colorado are heartened by the prospect of minimizing regulation without representation. Moreover, we hope to ensure that the power of state government continues always to be exercised with a clear understanding of just who government exists to serve in the first place—the people.

ENDNOTES

1. Fred L. Smith Jr., Testimony before the Committee on Government Reform in the U.S. House of Representatives, July 22, 2003.
2. Smith, Testimony, 7.
3. *Doing Business in 2004: Understanding Regulation*. The World Bank, 2004, at rru.worldbank.org/Documents/DBoverview.pdf.
4. Clyde Wayne Crews Jr., *Ten Thousand Commandments: An Annual Snapshot of the Federal Regulatory State* (Washington, D.C.: Cato Institute, 2003), 4, available at www.cato.org/tech/pubs/10kc_2003.pdf.
5. Canada's GDP is $701 billion, and the combined pretax profits of all U.S. corporations is $699 billion. Crews, *Ten Thousand Commandments*, 5–6.

4

CitiStat and Operational Efficiency in City Government

Martin O'Malley, Mayor of Baltimore, Maryland

Joe Kolodziejski stands before me looking as if he needs a cigarette and blindfold. The chief of Baltimore trash-collection efforts is next up at CitiStat, our new high-tech program for government efficiency that requires city supervisors, such as Kolodziejski, to appear before me and my cabinet every two weeks to defend their work.

I adopted the statistics-driven concept from New York City, where police leaders use their CompStat system to map crime daily on computers in an effort to hold officers to a greater level of accountability. But Baltimore may be the first city in the nation to use the idea to measure other urban problems and issues, such as vacant housing, trash dumps, drug treatment, and lead-paint abatement. And the process is attracting attention from other cities, as well as from former vice president Al Gore. Representatives from former vice president Gore's office visited city hall for a demonstration of what some observers say could revolutionize the delivery of government services nationwide.

"I think it can have an enormous impact," Fred Siegel, an urban affairs expert from the Progressive Policy Institute in Washington, said recently after sitting in on a session. "If this really works in Baltimore, people are going to pick it up."

The CitiStat updates take place in a sixth-floor conference room at city hall that looks like something out of *Star Trek*. In a glass-enclosed control room in the rear, technical wizards click away on computers that track and map everything from the number of citizen complaints per department to the amount of overtime worked by city crews. It is all charted, graphed, and flashed, in a multimedia blitz, onto two 6′ × 10′ movie screens that hang above the managers' heads.

Then, the questions begin. My staff and I ask about matters that in the past might have come up only once a year, during budget sessions. Managers must explain any increase in bad news. Why, for example, is more overtime required in one public works yard than another? Why aren't the sanitation trucks washed on a regular basis? Why is one out of every five of a particular group of employees absent every day without penalty?

"It's like facing the Spanish Inquisition," said one city supervisor. "And they told us that this was the 'honeymoon.'"

Critics of the process worry that putting supervisors on the spot to show improvement could result in more theater than progress. Others say that forcing departments to spend their time gathering statistics keeps them from doing their jobs. Others worry that measuring city woes through data and computer maps fails to take into account the political dynamic interwoven in daily government decisions. "If your statistics show you need a drug-treatment center in a neighborhood, who's going to go to that neighborhood and get the community's approval?" asked former city real estate officer Anthony J. Ambridge, a former East Baltimore city councilman. "It's hard for the administration to translate the statistics into reality." I, however, contend that the system is sparking landmark improvement in city government.

During CitiStat's three-month trial run, overtime in the Department of Public Works' Water and Waste Water Division dropped by about 25 percent. Unscheduled leave in the agency fell by more than one-third, translating to an average of 28 more workers on the job each day. And administration pressure to clear up a 2,000-order backlog for installing new water meters will add an estimated $150,000 in revenue from water fees this year. There is an old adage: that which gets watched gets done. We're watching every day.

When I asked the outgoing director of public works how many vehicles the city had in its municipal fleet, he replied, "I don't know. Maybe 6,000 or 6,500." Note that this was an area over which his department had management responsibility. It was then, a few weeks before I took the oath of office as mayor of a city with 15,000 employees and a $1.8 billion budget, that it became clear to me that Baltimore had a long way to go to become a city that effectively managed its resources.

Little in city government seemed to be measured in a consistent, real-time manner. Information was collected faithfully. However, it was not necessarily the right information, and it was rarely used to manage. And if information was used to make policy changes, they came as a result of yearly reviews. Implementation took months, even years. By the time the contemplated change was in place, the conditions that prompted the shift might no longer be relevant.

I thought of the idea for CitiStat while touring East Baltimore with CompStat creator former New York deputy police commissioner Jack Maple, who pioneered the effort in police departments by teaching cities across the nation to track crime daily to deploy officers more efficiently. After viewing the police system, I wondered aloud whether it could be used to measure other city services. It could, Maple said, if four principles were applied: accurate and timely data; rapid deployment of staff; establishment of efficient tactics to address problems; and follow-up and assessment.

As we watched our police department dramatically improve its performance, just like New York's had, it became clear that Comstat could change how the rest of government operates as well. Instead of checking performances every few months or scheduling an annual review meeting, the leaders of the police department met every week. Crime-fighting strategies and resource deployment were adjusted constantly, and follow-up was never allowed to slip for more than a week.

Those same principles have become our prime tool in achieving efficient, effective, and accountable government. Today, this is how we run our 16 city agencies. And we have used the tool to focus on specific problems, creating outbreak measurements such as LeadStat, which tracks kids with high levels of lead poisoning, and KidStat, which follows at-risk youth. By using the same process as police (GIS mapping, weekly strategy meetings, and relentless follow-up) strategies are being developed and employed, managers are being held accountable, and results are being measured—every week.

Kolodziejski, the trash administrator and a Vietnam War veteran, said that the sessions sometimes feel like a court-martial. "You get nervous and sometimes you feel on the spot because these are your superiors," he said. Kolodziejski said he has learned to use the sessions to explain his agency's needs to the administration. "If the administration doesn't know what I'm going through, they won't know how to help me," Kolodziejski said. "The information works both ways. They have to know what I need."

On the issue of absent workers, Kolodziejski explained at one CitiStat session that the finance department has a policy of eliminating from an agency's budget the positions of any fired worker. But, he said, his Bureau of Solid Waste would rather deal with problem employees than a shortage of employees on the 1,000-member force. As a result of that discussion, I asked city finance officials to change their policy for public works. The charts and graphs are nice, but the real benefit of this is the dynamic that occurs around the table.

The data also highlights successes. In analyzing trash collection, city officials kept noticing that one sanitation yard in East Baltimore outperformed others. I began rewarding high-performing workers with everything from Orioles baseball tickets to $150 cash bonuses. It's not a lot, but at least it shows people that we appreciate them. Building the computerized conference room cost the city about $20,000 in off-the-shelf software, with public works crews helping to construct it. The largest expense is the salaries of the five full-time employees who operate the control room, which add up to $285,000 a year.

The CitiStat room is similar to the Comstat control room in the police department. It has a control room with two computers, which are used to project GIS maps, charts, graphs and other information onto 6′ × 10′ screens. Agency managers stand at a podium for 90 minutes in front of the screens and are questioned by the panelists, led by the deputy mayor and myself. They are asked to explain increases and declines in indicators like overtime, complaints, or absent employees so that problems can be eliminated and successes duplicated in other areas of the organization.

Hired to be the director of operations for CitiStat was Matt Gallagher, a Baltimore native who served as deputy mayor in Philadelphia during that city's resurgence in the 1990s—a success story that became the subject of a book, *A Prayer for the City*. "Philadelphia did a great deal of . . . reporting every quarter," Gallagher said. "This is reporting to the *n*th power. Every two weeks, you're in here asking, 'What did you do last week? What are you doing next week?'"

Kolodziejski and others have acknowledged that supervisors gripe about gathering the statistics. Furthermore, Kolodziejski states that preparing for the meeting can take up to four days. Yet the 25-year department veteran is starting to see the benefits. "The charts and maps have told me stories about my own department that I didn't see before," he said. "It's given me a better understanding."

Here are a few concrete examples of how it's making a difference. During an initiative focused on cleaning up Baltimore's troubled Eastern District—targeting crime and grime—the Departments of Housing and Community Development and Public Works coordinated their boarding efforts for the first time. Moving in a structured manner in a targeted area, with cleaning crews going through first, followed closely by boarding crews, we cleaned and boarded 1,000 vacant houses in three weeks—almost half the total for the year before we took office.

In the Bureau of Water and Wastewater, through CitiStat, we reduced overtime by 23 percent in the first 20 weeks. This has been accomplished by requiring supervisors to demand more from their employees in terms of reducing unscheduled leave, which was cut by 37 percent during the same period. They are also required to check up on employees who are out on accident leave in order to get them back to work faster. As a result, accident leave was also cut by 29 percent. This increased supervision—tracked through CitiStat—has put, on average, 49 additional workers on the job every day, cutting overtime expenses and increasing productivity. Like Woody Allen says, 90 percent of life is just showing up.

In the past, these numbers were never regularly measured, so they were never managed to make the workforce more efficient. We are making similar overtime reductions elsewhere in the Department of Public Works and throughout city government, which will save money and improve performance. In the first year, we cut overtime across the board by $6 million. We are using CitiStat to prioritize the use of resources. For example, the Bureau of Water and Wastewater found that there were nearly 2,000 bypassed water meters in the city and surrounding counties that we serve. This oversight costs the Bureau of Water and Wastewater $150,000 in revenue per year. By setting and enforcing a September 1 deadline and following up every other week at CitiStat meetings, we eliminated this waste, bringing in additional revenues and eliminating a situation that was fundamentally unfair to customers who were bearing this cost.

Additionally, CitiStat helped us discover that, while fleet maintenance was repairing thousands of vehicles every year, we had a perpetual shortage of critical vehicles, like ambulances, police cruisers, garbage trucks, and street sweepers. Giving priority to repairing these vehicles and monitoring their availability every week has virtually eliminated this problem.

We are also finding new ways to evaluate and motivate our frontline workers to bring urgency and accountability to their jobs. One leading example of this is the CitiStat Management Improvement Index, which is a contest we've started among the trash-collection teams. We are ranking teams by lost workdays, overtime, and complaints, which were the primary problems we uncovered, and a cash bonus is paid right before Christmas to each member of the top three crews and the crew with the greatest improvement. Furthermore, we have implemented a merit-based incentive project in our Department of Housing and Community Development. By setting performance goals, tracking output, and offering a modest bonus, housing inspectors have, on average, doubled and even tripled their daily inspection output.

Today, our public works director can answer the question that baffled his predecessor. After months of counting, our CitiStat office determined that Baltimore has 4,500 vehicles in its city fleet. However, while Baltimore does not have as many cars as suspected, we determined that we still have too many, and they are being used inefficiently. Thus far, we have cut 175 vehicles from the public works and police fleets. And take-home privileges have been reduced by almost half—from 194 to 101—in these two agencies. We are now moving on to make similar cuts in other agencies, and the effort is continuing in public works and the police department. Our housing department has already cut take-home vehicles from 20 to 5. We saved $2 million by reducing and reorganizing our fleet. And we will save $500,000 annually through reduced maintenance costs, reduced fuel costs, and better management.

Increasingly, city employees are starting to view the funds city government receives from residents, businesses, the state, and federal government as investments rather than entitlements. Our 15,000-person organization is beginning to realize that those who invest in Baltimore have a right to expect a return on their investment, so we must make wise use of our investors' capital, and we must produce results. Every wasted dollar is a dollar that cannot be spent serving the public. And we estimate that we've saved the city about $44 million through new revenue streams and cutting waste.

CitiStat also puts information into the hands of many managers, rather than a few. Just like in the private sector, shared knowledge allows for government to change and adjust more quickly to better serve the public. And longtime managers, who have come up through a system in which supervisors managed by "feel" rather than facts, are learning new things about agencies where they have worked for years.

More than 2,700 illegal dumping grounds inside the city limits have been eliminated, with fewer than 200 remaining. Even potholes are filled with amazing efficiency. I guaranteed that all city potholes would be filled within 48 hours, and so far, we have reached the mark 97 percent of the time. And citizens do phone them in, at the rate of 1,500 per month. Previously, pothole repair wasn't even tracked.

If there is one thing we've been able to achieve here, it's building the expectation of improvement into the system. The people of Baltimore want more and better, and they're getting it.

Col. Alfred Foxx Jr., the city transportation director, adjusts his tie behind the podium. A large projection screen over his right shoulder shows a Microsoft Excel spreadsheet detailing all tickets handed out by officers citywide during a recent two-week period, comparing that period with other two-week periods for the previous several months.

Over Foxx's left shoulder another screen projects maps illustrating the activity. Michael Enright, my chief of staff, had opened the session precisely at 8:30 a.m. and went straight to the chart's hot spot like a bear to honey.

"Col. Foxx, I see these parking tickets went up dramatically from 322 during the last two-week period to 1,128. Is there something going on here?"

"We've had a couple of training sessions recently," Foxx replied. "We've also added new field staff, bumping up from 47 to 51 officers."

"Four new officers, more than tripling the total?"

"It could also be an increase in productivity. I've got four supervisors there, and they're staying on top of things."

Next on the agenda, the previous night the local evening news reported an exposé on the city's car pound. Tow trucks have been dumping rotting, abandoned vehicles smack up against brand new cars towed in for violations. Worse, the new cars have been broken into, and stereos have been stolen. Gallagher tells his staff in the projection room to roll the film. It's two minutes of agonizing embarrassment.

"Can't we put some razor wire up there?" I ask.

"I think we'd face significant liability," City Solicitor Thurman Zollicoffer says.

"Even if we put up a warning sign?"

"The legal advice we now have says we'd probably still face liability."

"Can you get me another legal opinion?" I ask as the room breaks into laughter.

Next is snow removal, and Foxx calls his division head to the podium to stand with him. Because all of Baltimore's Orbital snow removers are equipped with Global Positioning Systems and antennae, the entire snow-removal effort is fast-forwarded and replayed on a detailed map projected on the wall. Each individual vehicle pushes up and down the computerized maze of city streets like avaricious Pac-Men. One of the vehicles moves to the city's eastern boundary and just keeps going, straight into the next county. Enright is on it like a magnet, flashing a red laser pointer from his seated position next to me.

"Where's he going?" Enright hollers.

"I'm informed he was . . . ah . . . lost," Foxx says. "But he was contacted by radio and directed back in."

"Did he know where he was going?" Enright asks.

"He was new, just trained, and he was taken aside and reinstructed," Foxx says.

Enright is dogged.

"Did he have his blade down? Was he distributing salt?"

"From the point of radio contact, I'm told his blade was up and no salt distributed," Foxx says.

In 55 minutes, Foxx is questioned on tickets, the city's abandoned-vehicle program, the car-impound problem, and the city's ongoing paving projects. He is accountable, poised, polite, and in command.

When we arrived, it was basically, "If the mayor really wants to know, we can find out, but we'll have to pull people off their jobs, and it'll take weeks," or "We'll get to that as soon as we can, but it'll take a few months because of budget cuts," or even "That's the way we've always done it," or "We're already doing that," or "We tried that, and it didn't work." We still have some people who come in here and act like victims, but the best and most successful are those who start to do it internally as well. It challenges people to step up, be prepared, and be ready.

The charts and maps are critical. They show you where your problems are. A map doesn't care whether you're rich or poor, black or white, or whether a judge, congressman, or senator lives in a given neighborhood. It just knows where the problems are, and that's where we deploy our resources. It sounds like a really simple concept, but it's something that's rarely ever done in representative democracies.

On another day, the health department faces the firing squad that also consists of the personnel director, labor commissioner, city solicitor, finance director, and chief information officer. Sifting through health department numbers, Enright stops where aberrations stand out. The questioning begins.

"Why the dip in average restaurant inspections performed?"

The manager in charge of inspections moves to the podium as a graph pops up on the screen behind him. It shows that average inspections increased substantially after CitiStat began, reaching a plateau of 5 per day, but have fallen back to 4.5 in previous weeks. The manager responds that his staff is going full guns and that to work them harder would sacrifice the quality of their inspections.

Someone chimes in from behind the desk. "There's no room for improvement?"

"I'm satisfied with our performance," the manager says.

Enright remains skeptical. There is a backlog of hundreds of restaurants to be checked. He flips to a spreadsheet showing how many jobs individual inspectors are doing, pointing out employees whose inspection numbers are down. "No city agency is running at optimal levels," he says. "You're telling me you're at peak performance?"

Enright likes the immediate give-and-take of the session. "There is a great creative dynamic because all of the principals are in the room," he said. "We don't need 22 memos to get an issue resolved."

That dynamic has helped abate many problems such as lead poisoning. In LeadStat, cases of poisoning in children were marked on a map with red dots, and many players involved in lead abatement—health, housing, and city and state environmental officials—began meeting every other Tuesday to figure out what it would take to turn each dot to green. Through LeadStat, the agencies identified the many cross-jurisdictional barriers that had prevented Baltimore from abating a single case of lead poisoning in ten years. The group agreed to cross-train housing and health inspectors to end the overlap in enforcement efforts. In one year, 127 red dots were turned to green, and when all outstanding cases are finally abated, the city will turn to taking a more proactive stance to prevent lead poisoning from happening in the first place.

Through the work of Kolodziejski and hardworking men and women like him throughout city government, Baltimore is using technology and old-fashioned accountability to deliver cost-effective, quality services to the citizens of our city. The number of outstanding requests for dirty-lot, alley, and illegal-dump cleanup have decreased by 47 percent, with response times declining from as high as 120 days to 24 days. The penalties from fines collected through sanitation enforcement have more than doubled from $373,249 to $791,946.

The number of playgrounds renovated has increased from a total of 6 in 1999, when this administration took over, to 28, with 40 more slated for this year. Pothole complaints have decreased by 30 percent from 2,555 to 1,792. The number of abandoned cars towed increased 22 percent from 28,998 to 35,377.

We are measuring. We are managing. And increasingly, we are producing results. Through CitiStat, Baltimore is mapping the future of city government.

The city of Baltimore—through CitiStat—has taken public-sector performance measurement to a whole new level. CitiStat has become an instrumental component in managing the day-to-day operations of Baltimore's municipal government. It has become what I like to call the "dashboard" of the city.

I've tried to ease worker anxiety by trying not to embarrass the managers and by being selective about whom they invite to the sessions. I want to allow supervisors to become comfortable with speaking to the cabinet in the forum. The goal is not to shame workers but to get them to cooperate and even to suggest ways to improve city efficiency, he said. I intend to make the sessions more public, including posting data on the city's website at www.baltimorecity.com. And my staff tries to determine accuracy by holding routine spot inspections.

In addition to CitiStat, we have added CitiTrack, the city's 311 "One Call to City Hall" service. Since being implemented in 2000, 450,000 customer-service requests have been recorded and memorialized in the CitiTrack system. Each complaint receives its own number. Since the system's initiation, 91 percent of the calls have been answered by the responsible agency, leaving a detailed audit trail of what actions by which individuals were involved in each closure. Baltimore was the first city in the nation to deploy 311 as a police "nonemergency" telephone number, so it was fitting to expand the role of 311 to include all city services and to become one of the first municipalities to provide comprehensive service.

Neither CitiStat nor CitiTrack/311 should be viewed as a magic elixir capable of curing Baltimore's municipal government of all its operational inefficiencies and customer-service deficiencies. These tools do, however, provide managers, frontline employees, and the public the mechanisms necessary to measure progress toward meeting goals, assess effectiveness, and make more prudent decisions. This is not some sort of torture chamber. This is how we do business.

5

Efficiency, Effectiveness, and Accountability: Improving the Quality of Life through E-Government

Rudolph W. Giuliani, Former Mayor of New York, New York

Two-and-a-half months after I addressed Temple University's Center for Competitive Government's Conference of Mayors, our world was changed forever, but the policies and systems that have been instrumental to the renaissance of our city were an important reason our response to that change was so successful. Although the building I gave my welcoming remarks in, the World Trade Center 7, no longer stands, our commitment to bringing the principles and systems of accountability to government should remain unwavering.

I was recently asked what the worst day and the best day were in the course of the past eight years. September 11, 2001, was the darkest day in our city's long history. But I also believe that September 11 was our best day. New Yorkers responded to the attack upon our nation immediately, courageously, tirelessly, and generously. The response of our city's agencies was, likewise, tremendously effective. This is because during the past eight years, accountability has become an integral part of city government's character. CompStat was the program that first introduced systematic accountability to the police department. It then became the model for accountability throughout city government through CapStat and paved the way for New York City to become a leader in e-government. The Mayor's Office of Emergency Management (OEM) is the embodiment of the lessons we have learned from CompStat, its technological adaptations, and the principles of accountability that have proven to be so successful.

In April 1996, the OEM was created to improve the city's planning and response to emergencies. OEM is responsible for coordinating the planning effort of city, state, and federal agencies, as well as corporate and not-for-profit entities. OEM responds to multiagency events and coordinates the city's response on behalf of the mayor. The agency is responsible for running the city's Emergency Operations Center (i.e., the command center), which acts as the central point for information exchange during an emergency.

Since 1996, OEM has prepared for natural disasters and possible terrorist attacks by conducting tabletop exercises and full-scale drills for emergencies ranging from chemical and biological terrorism to aviation disasters and Year 2000 preparedness. In 1997, OEM conducted "train the trainer" classes for more than 5,000 responders to prepare for response to incidents involving weapons of mass destruction.

OEM was designed to coordinate immediate and efficient responses to natural disasters or attacks upon our city, such as the one perpetrated on September 11. Ironically, at 5:20 p.m. on September 11, the building that housed OEM and its command center collapsed due to terrorist attacks.

One of the remarkable, untold stories from the hours and days after September 11 was the speed with which OEM was able to reconstruct a new command center. The original command center was not designed to handle the magnitude of destruction from the attack of September 11. Nobody could have ever predicted such a barbaric attack upon our nation. But while the city operated out of a temporary command center at the Police Academy, OEM built a new command center in 72 hours. More than 100 government, private, and nonprofit organizations had computers, networks, and telephones set up for them. The size of the new command center, located on a pier on the Hudson River, provided room to grow and effectively address the staffing and technological requirements of such a massive undertaking.

Agencies were organized in clusters as they were in the original command center. An area for press conferences was built. A large roundtable and a walled-off room were built for daily briefings where the governor and I would hear reports from commissioners and agency directors. There was room to have the Red Cross provide food, drinks, and medical attention to everybody who was working. There was even a large space set aside with cots so that people could get some sleep. Moreover, OEM operated from a podium in the middle of the command center, just like at the original location.

OEM's staff, and the staff of every agency that participated in its drills since 1996, was so well prepared that there was nearly a seamless transition during unbelievable circumstances. One of the reasons for this was the tremendous leadership of men like Fire Commissioner Tom Von Essen, Police Commissioner Bernard Kerik, and OEM Director Richard Shierer. But the other reason the city's response was so effective is the culture of accountability that has been cultivated throughout city government, especially in the aforementioned three agencies. This mentality within city government is a result of the leadership shown by Essen, Kerik, and Shierer, as well as the very important systems that paved the way for e-government, such as CompStat. The culture of accountability, along with these systems, made it possible for the city of New York to respond to the worst attack upon our nation in an effective and efficient manner.

In 1991, David Osborne published *Reinventing Government* while cities across America were suffering from rising crime and welfare rolls and a corresponding low quality of life. New York was considered unmanageable and ungovernable. The Internet was still in its infancy and virtually unknown to most Americans. Years later, much of urban America is thriving, and a new consensus has emerged from a new philosophy of governing. Best practices have become apparent, and the use of new technology as a management tool has increased government accountability and effectiveness. In the process, residents' faith in the future of their cities has been restored.

The rise of e-government offers an unprecedented opportunity to reinvent government by fundamentally changing the structure of government itself to incorporate the lessons we've learned. Those of us who have fought to bring greater efficiency, effectiveness, and accountability to government will find that e-government allows us to engrain those management principles into the structure of government in a way that was never before possible.

E-government represents not only a shift in the technological means of delivering services, but also a shift in the culture of government itself—a movement away from inefficient bureaucracy and toward a more entrepreneurial culture of accountability. The experience of longstanding and distinguished corporations evolving into e-businesses provides a blueprint for those of us in government who are attempting to lay the foundation for e-government.

Much like the corporations that needed to adapt their business models to meet shifting consumer expectations, municipalities face not a technology problem but a management challenge. We need to incorporate new technologies into the business of government. This isn't a chore but a tremendous opportunity.

The United Parcel Service (UPS) provides an interesting blueprint for evolution. Several years ago, UPS decided that it needed to embrace the possibilities of new technology to grow. This meant reexamining the systems its company had used successfully for decades. UPS evolved into a business that offers services, solutions, and strategic partnerships with its customers, not just overnight package delivery. In doing so, it became the first package-delivery company to go online and use technology to offer those services at any hour of any day. To express the new possibilities that new technology had brought to their company, UPS launched a new ad campaign with the tagline "Moving at the Speed of Business."

This is the kind of innovation we need to bring to government; e-governments can learn from UPS's success in the marketplace. "Moving at the Speed of Business" suggests a proactive, 24-hour information network, moving rapidly with thorough professionalism and accountability.

Now, I ask you to consider the government equivalent to that slogan. Historically, government has not provided a model for efficiency or effectiveness. That is why the notion of "Moving at the Speed of Government" might seem absurd to most people. But we have already discovered that with new technology, "Moving at the Speed of Government" is already much faster than standing in line. And one of the primary goals of e-government is to move city services online so that people no longer have to wait in line

The rise of e-business has inspired the rise of e-government. Both are about providing not only better value but better service as well. Many mayors, including myself, grew up in an age before personal computers were widely used. But we can demystify e-government if we understand that it is fundamentally about improving the quality of life. The type of transition that e-government offers has happened before in the private sector, where new technology is regularly employed to offer greater convenience to consumers.

For example, 20 years ago, ATMs were nonexistent. Americans had access to their money only when banks were open, and banks' hours of operation were limited—typically from 9:00 a.m. to 3:00 p.m., Monday through Friday, and never on holidays. It was an unofficial but generally accepted practice in New York City government to give employees an extra half hour for lunch on Friday so that they could go to the bank, fill out a withdrawal or deposit slip, wait in line, and meet with a bank teller to complete their transaction. Getting money on a Saturday or Sunday was impossible because banks were closed.

In retrospect, this weekly ritual seems unnecessary and absurd. The availability of new technology created a paradigm shift in the banking industry that has made it much more customer oriented. Government is still operating within the old paradigm. But that is changing rapidly because traditional bureaucratic structures initially built in the nineteenth century are being replaced with a twenty-first-century technological infrastructure that is directly responsive to the people it serves.

One of the most significant early uses of technology in my administration was the development of a program called CompStat. The movement toward e-government started with the attempt to solve one problem: crime. At the time, we did not fully understand that this process of collecting crime statistics combined with a computer pin-mapping system was, in fact, the first step toward e-government in New York City. The lessons we learned and the systems we developed were then applied to three or four other problems, and now they are applied to virtually all of the problems that New York City faces.

In the beginning of the 1990s, New York City was notorious for its crime. With 2,245 murders in New York City in 1990, we were setting records. We had more people on welfare than we had ever had before in our history. By 1992, we had reached one million people on welfare. Our city had a population then of 7.3 million; so, one-seventh of the people in the city were on public aid, and that number was predicted to grow to 1.5 million.

We were losing jobs at a record rate as well. New York City had lost 320,000 jobs since 1990. We had a deficit of $1.6 billion that grew to $2.3 billion. And, according to a poll, in 1993, more than half of the people who lived in the city would have preferred to live somewhere else, which is very much a sign of a society that is in decline rather than a society that is growing.

We realized that the first thing we had to do was make New York City safe. We had to make it a place where people could feel secure, where they didn't have to worry about going out at night to the movies, going to a restaurant, visiting here, doing business here. First things first. If people don't feel safe, nothing else can happen.

During the mid-1970s and the early 1980s, crime statistics were studied in a very inefficient manner. Studies were released from the federal government that would say things such as New York City was number one for homicide or Washington, D.C. was number one for grand larceny, another city was number one for robbery, and some other city was number one for property crime. They'd all be on a long list, and it always occurred to me that this was kind of crazy; we were reporting on what happened roughly six months or a year ago.

There was nothing anybody could do about the crimes at that point. The murders had already taken place; the robberies had already taken place; the burglaries had already taken place. And it was interesting sociological data, it was interesting news, interesting political information, but it had no relevance to management. It had no relevance to anything that you could do about it because it all happened six months, a year ago.

What we decided to do was to capture all that information on a daily basis. Using CompStat, we figured out every day how the Federal Bureau of Investigation (FBI) was going to measure us a year later. Then, we figured out how to improve our crime-fighting strategies so that when New York City was measured, we would be able to demonstrate substantial crime reduction. So, we launched CompStat, with which we collected crime data every single day from every single precinct in the city of New York. This allowed us to respond to areas of the city that were subjected to specific types of crime waves.

Rather than just collecting the raw data, we started putting it on a map so that we could figure out that in particular areas of precincts within the city we were having a significant number of robberies, grand larcenies, or car thefts. With that type of information, we were able to allocate our police officers in the right way. We were able to put them in the right place at the right time.

After several months of collecting this data, we were able to figure out on which days of the week we were making the most narcotics arrests—it happened to be on Wednesdays. And we discovered what time of the day we were making the most narcotics arrests, which was roughly in the middle of the day, the middle of a tour. The same thing happened with shootings. Which days of the week did we have the most shootings? Thursdays and Fridays. We could then have our police officers assigned where they were needed, any time of day, in any precinct, right down to the exact street corners where crimes were increasing.

Anytime we begin to see increases in crime, we can usually—not always—figure out the reason for it: We have the police in the wrong area. We have more police officers assigned during times when there's less crime rather than more crime. Sometimes, the increase in crime that we have is an increase in auto theft, while there's a decrease in shootings. So, then we have to move in more police officers who have expertise in catching people who are stealing cars or in reporting the crimes more effectively.

Sometimes, we start to see an increase in shootings. Whenever we see an increase in shootings, we know that shortly we're going to start seeing an increase in murders. So, then we try to figure where the shootings are located, and if they are gang related. If they are gang related, we needed to bring in police officers who have expertise with gangs. If the crimes are related to domestic violence, then we put more emphasis on addressing domestic violence.

Fundamentally, CompStat takes statistics, which used to be just a political or sociological tool, and uses them as a management tool. This is like thinking of the police department as a bank with 77 branch offices. Every day, we get the performance results of every branch office. If it has good results, fine. But if there are bad results, then we want to know why and how we are going to improve it. We're going to want to look at the offices that have good results and figure out what they're doing right so that the offices with bad results can figure out how they can build from that.

The results of using the CompStat program for the police department have been impressive. Those annual 2,245 murders have fallen to fewer than 650. For the last three years in a row, we have had less than 700 murders. Our FBI index of crimes—all the ways in which they measure crime—over the last four years has us down to the lowest level in the history of the city. New York City used to be thought of as the crime capital of America. Now, we're ranked 192 on the FBI's list of cities with populations of a 100,000 or more. Murder is down almost 67 percent, shootings are down 69 percent, grand larceny is down 46 percent, auto theft is down 73 percent, robbery is down 67 percent, burglary is down 69 percent, rape is down 39 percent, and assault is down 44 percent.

From this success, we decided to adapt the CompStat program a number of years ago and start applying it to other areas of government.

We first applied it, after the police department, to our corrections department. We organized a program in the corrections department called the Total

Efficiency Accountability Management System (TEAMS). It measures every incidence of violence, slashings, and stabbings. We tried to take a look at when our corrections officers were assigned, what areas they were assigned in, and whether they were having an effect in reducing the amount of violence that went on in the jail.

We also took a look at management and budget issues in this program, such as the relationship between the amount of actual overtime and its effectiveness in reducing violence. As a result, over six years, through TEAMS, we've cut violence by 93 percent in our city jails.

We've also used it to great effect in our Human Resources Administration (HRA), which is where we deal with our welfare program. We'd had 1.1 million people on welfare. Today, we've reduced the number of people on welfare by 695,000. That's larger than the population of most cities in the United States. We've helped more than 375,000 of those 695,000 people find jobs. We've either found the job for them or helped them find the job, and we did it with a program called JobStat.

We've taken our welfare offices, of which we have 32, and we've changed the name from "welfare office" to "job center." The purpose of a welfare office in New York City, now, is not to put you on welfare. It's not to help you become dependent. It's not to help you drop out of society or to encourage you to do that, which is what we used to do. The purpose of a welfare office is to help you be self-sufficient, to help you help yourself, to help you help your family—by helping you find a job. That's why we call it a job center.

We even have our job centers compete with each other to find jobs for people. We reward the job centers that find the most jobs for people, not the offices that put the most people on welfare. We reward the welfare workers who have turned themselves into employment agents as opposed to dependency enablers.

We've created a totally different mindset, and the difference is that you take a city that had 1.1 million people on welfare, and now you have 695,000 fewer people dependent on the government of the city. And you have 375,000 who have jobs.

I hold town hall meetings once a month—I'm going to do my ninetieth tomorrow night—and people will say to me, "I can't find a job." I've not yet failed in finding a job for someone who wants to work.

So, basically, JobStat is not only a statistical program; it's also changed the philosophy of the city. It's changed the thinking of the city from encouraging dependency to encouraging people to work, to help themselves, to take care of themselves. And, today, the city cares about them in a deeper way than it used to.

Another program in which we found this CompStat approach enormously helpful, which is somewhat different from the other two, is the HealthStat program. This began about a year and a half ago.

There's a debate throughout America about universal health insurance, about how we can make certain that people are covered and have health insurance. The reality in New York City is that we have a tremendous number of people—about 300,000 children, maybe as many as 600,000 or 700,000 adults in addition—who are eligible for health insurance but don't apply for it. They don't know how to fill out the forms, or they don't realize that they can fill out the forms, or they don't know how to accomplish it, or they just don't want to.

So, we've done exactly the same thing we did to reduce crime. We've created pin maps. We're trying to figure out where in particular the children are who aren't covered by health insurance. We've taken all of the agencies of city government, and every week, they meet, and we go out and try to sign up all of the children that we can for health insurance. Then, we measure it, we pin-map it, and we try to figure out how successful we are. We've signed up about 195,000 children so far who would't have been covered but for the outreach program.

So, this method and approach to management, which grew out of CompStat, has become enormously valuable. The principles have been adopted throughout every city agency through a program called CapStat.

CompStat was an important first step toward e-government because it spread the principles of efficiency, effectiveness, and accountability citywide. The purpose of e-government is to create transparent government—a government that people can watch, understand, and hold accountable. But before becoming transparent, it is important to be organized correctly. If you're disorganized and transparent, it's a disaster. You first have to organize yourself, and then you can accomplish what government really has to accomplish, which is to become transparent. Transparent government allows people to look online at all of the things we've discussed and see how good a job we're really doing and where they can find information.

On NYC.gov, for example, you can look at my addresses, my messages, and every press conference I hold. I do a radio show that's also on there.

People can also access the city agencies, like the police department. The crime statistics that I mentioned before are on our website. Anybody in New York City can now get the crime statistics for their police precinct.

The New York Police Department really led the way in illustrating the potential for e-government and what e-government will ultimately do for all areas of government. The principles of efficiency, effectiveness, and accountability are now part of the character of city government. Adapting CompStat has helped us reduce bureaucracy, save time and money, improve the delivery of services, and create a transparent government with managerial responsibility built into it.

E-government is going to make it virtually impossible for people to roll back the organizational reforms we've made. The presence of performance indicators—objective measures of success—on the Internet will let every resident see how well a particular administration is doing its job by comparing current results to those for previous years. The condition of the city will be apparent to all, and much of the information that mayors get across their desks every day will be available at home to the average citizen.

As we move away from the brick-and-mortar bureaucracy of traditional city government, e-government offers us an opportunity to add a degree of common sense to the sometimes confusing process of getting information from city agencies.

Longtime employees of city government often become so familiar with the structure of the city government that they speak in an alphabet soup of acronyms. They forget that many New Yorkers don't know what DOH (Department of Health) or ACS (Administration for Children's Services) is; the public just wants to know where they can get a copy of their birth certificate or receive information about adoption.

The new NYC.gov is organized in such a way that visitors don't need to understand the intricacies of city government to get the information they want or need.

We call it an "I Want To . . .," which allows visitors to access a full range of city information based on their individual needs, regardless of the city agency that provides the services they're looking for.

NYC.gov is already being used by thousands of New Yorkers each day and had 34 million visitors in the last calendar year alone. Listed below are just some of the functions that visitors can access to make their lives easier.

- *View traffic cameras:* There are 60 traffic cameras placed throughout the five boroughs to help New Yorkers with their commute to and from work. By logging on to NYC.gov, visitors can see the state of traffic along different routes in real time. As a result, they can avoid traffic jams and cut their commute considerably.
- *Pay parking tickets:* One of the most used functions on NYC.gov allows New Yorkers to pay parking tickets conveniently and securely by credit card. Should they choose to contest the parking ticket, they can submit a plea to the violation and present a defense for review by an administrative law judge, rather than taking a day off from work and waiting for hours at a central adjudications bureau to have their case heard. This is a much more efficient and fair way of addressing contested parking tickets, rather than making a person take a day off of work.
- *Check restaurant inspections:* The result of restaurant inspections has been unexpectedly popular. When the Department of Health first placed its restaurant-inspection results online in May 1999, the site received an average of 45,000 visits per hour in its first day. That's significantly more

inquiries than the department received about restaurant-inspection results during the entire previous year.

- *Reserve a baseball field:* Not many New Yorkers have the time to come down to the parks department to fill out the necessary forms to reserve fields for a little league game. Now, New Yorkers can log on to the parks department website, fill out an application, and make their plans accordingly.

STEPS TO E-GOVERNMENT

These are all examples of the potential of e-government, but there are several evolutionary steps toward a fully integrated e-government.

In the first stage of e-government, municipalities merely publish existing information on their websites. Limited, but specific, information is available to the public, but there's no interactive component. It's a largely passive and early form of e-government.

In the second stage of e-government, it's possible for visitors to interact with the agencies they are accessing, but in a limited manner. They're able to submit information, but no transactions are possible.

The third stage of e-government allows for interactive information gathering—that is, for full business transactions such as the payment of parking tickets.

New York City is now in the process of fully evolving to the fourth stage of e-government, which allows full-service delivery from multiple agencies through the creation of virtual agencies. E-government will be completely customizable according to the needs and interests of the individual.

Once a municipality has its own website fully in order, it's time to look beyond its own borders. It will become increasingly important for residents to be able to access information not only from their city but from their corresponding state's or neighboring counties' websites. In the fifth stage of e-government, information and government websites are integrated to provide for maximum convenience.

Business owners will find that e-government has transcended bureaucratic structures and processes by creating a much more streamlined and efficient way to interact with the government. For example, in the past, an individual wanting to start a small business, such as a restaurant, had to navigate a bureaucratic maze to get the necessary forms he or she needed filled out from various city and state agencies. This could be a very confusing process, with various forms needing to be approved by multiple agencies. Some businesses understandably resorted to hiring third-party expeditors to help them cut through all of the red tape.

E-government will make the process of filling out forms in triplicate a thing of the past. A small restaurateur just starting out can apply for all the necessary permits from different agencies at once, online, rather than filling out endless forms and waiting for weeks for a reply. With one application, a credit card, and an electronic signature, all corresponding city, state, and federal forms will be filled out automatically. Appropriate personnel will review the applications simultaneously on their computers, instead of sequentially on paper.

As a result, a process that used to take weeks will only take days or even hours, and companies will be able to check on the status of their application online at their own convenience. We view this as an issue of competitiveness in the new economy: as businesses are increasingly mobile, they will bring their jobs to cities that make it easier to do business.

An estimated 50 percent of all New Yorkers have access to the Internet, but we're determined not to leave any New Yorkers out of the new world of opportunity that e-government provides. That's why we've taken proactive steps to help bridge the digital divide.

The city is deploying information kiosks—interactive, multimedia information booths—in prominent neighborhood locations such as libraries, train stations, and shopping malls throughout the five boroughs. Through these kiosks, every e-government function that's available online will be accessible to people without a computer at home. There will be at least one kiosk in every one of the 59 community districts.

Beyond kiosks, our long-term goal is to do everything we can to encourage the development of a computer-literate citizenry that can take full advantage of the promise of e-government and the new economy. That's why buildings in the New York City Housing Authority also offer computer access and classes to young residents, while 15 recreation centers spread throughout the parks in our city do the same.

Through an initiative called Project Smart Schools, we have given every middle school classroom in the public school system access to computers:

- *High-speed Internet in schools:* Through a partnership with AOL Time Warner and Cablevision, all New York City public schools will have high-speed Internet access in the future.
- *Web phones:* Furthermore, the city is actively encouraging the placement of pay telephones that offer access to the Web throughout New York City. This will make Internet access available on nearly every street corner.

This generation of mayors has overseen a tremendous transformation in urban America. In New York City, we've been able to reduce crime, reform welfare, encourage economic growth, and improve the quality of life. This reflects a profound social and cultural transformation: we've changed the way people think about their city. New York is no longer considered an ungovernable, unmanageable city doomed to perpetual decline.

Now, e-government gives us the opportunity to change the way people think about government. We're going to go from a government structure that makes people wait in line to one that offers virtually all those services and all of that information online.

Those of us serving in government today have a historic opportunity to create an entirely new twenty-first-century infrastructure that will return government directly to the people it serves.

We have an obligation to make the most of it.

6

Information Technology as a Tool for Government Reform

Steve Goldsmith, Mayor of Indianapolis, Indiana

Information technology (IT) now proudly takes a place at the table as a full partner in all significant government-reform efforts. But it hasn't always been so.

When I first attempted to bring online access to government information in the mid-1980s, cities and counties provided most technology services through cumbersome mainframe computer systems using incomprehensible legacy systems. These systems were controlled by an internal, centralized government monopoly that dictated what information was available and controlled both the terms and pricing of access. When I was an elected county official—a district attorney—office-reform efforts tended either to ignore technology or sought ways to subvert outdated rules imposed by the centralized IT department, which functioned more as the technology-regulatory police than it did as a service agency.

In the next phase of IT-enhanced government reform, occasionally mainframe systems operating enhanced software actually produced something of value to public managers. These systems could sort large amounts of information and produce reports that, with enough effort, yielded leads about the performance of public employees. No matter that techies produced the reports in two-foot piles of paper print outs or that requests needed to be made weeks or months in advance to allow time for inflexible programming changes. At least there was some effort to connect the reports to reform. But as a district attorney attempting to evaluate programs, courts, and deputies, I found that each report produced insights that led to more questions, which led to more requests for a different data element or look, which led to more delays and push back from the overextended IT staff.

Then, government IT reached a new level and even got its own name, E-Gov, and many of us rushed to deploy its wonderful tools. Citizens could find information and accomplish transactions online. E-Gov itself was the reform, a very exciting prospect as CIOs (Chief Information Officers) began to take a seat at the table. In this phase, technology (E-Gov) was not so much an enabler of reform as it was the reform itself.

Now, an entirely new approach is evolving; the E-Gov model is now obsolete as technology and electronic access are no longer an alternate, "reform" path into government but rather are part of the technology keys that unlock the kingdom of far-reaching reform. Even more importantly, government itself has changed. Increasingly, today, government responses involve networks of public, private, and not-for-profit partners. The traditional, hierarchical model of government simply does not meet the demands of this complex, rapidly changing age. Rigid bureaucratic systems that operate with command-and-control procedures are particularly poorly suited to confront complexities that span organizational silos. Homeland security provides an obvious example. By themselves, neither the Federal Bureau of Investigation nor the Central Intelligence Agency can stop terrorists. Nor could they solve the problems even if they were perfect partners. An effective answer requires the participation of many different government and private partners brought together to solve a common problem through sophisticated IT tools.

As William Eggers and I set out in our book, *Governing by Network: The New Face of the Public Sector*,[1] public officials no longer center their time exclusively on managing people and programs but on organizing resources—often belonging to others—to produce public value, a trend better described as "governing by network."

For example, most job-training programs operate by intersecting with welfare reform and involve federal funding, administered by local workforce boards through networks of private and nonprofit providers. Wisconsin's welfare-delivery model engages multiple levels of government, multiple state agencies, a handful of nonprofit and for-profit administrators, and dozens of community-based subcontractors. Thus, today, IT networks provide both the critical infrastructure of, and metaphor for, government reform. Unlocking information unleashes the power of networks to fulfill public services and discharge government duties.

DEFINING NETWORK GOVERNANCE

A networked government is one where a government official, concentrating on producing public value rather than managing inputs, assimilates all of the resources at his disposal into a package that's most useful for the customer.

It allows public officials to extend effective services to their constituents via a variety of channels, whether they are public, private, not for profit, or faith based. Within this networked-government model, information moves horizontally (i.e., from agency to agency) and vertically (i.e., from constituent to agency) effortlessly. Key components of a networked government include widely deployed information technologies and e-government services. These components permit managers to move ideas and information through the once-sturdy barriers imposed by layers of bureaucracy.

During my tenure as mayor of Indianapolis, this principle of widely deployed information technology as an information mover came to fruition when the American Federation of State, County, and Municipal Employees (AFSCME) union leaders in the solid-waste department requested that computer terminals be placed next to the time clocks. This investment enabled union leaders to monitor service complaints personally and communicate ideas to me directly, without the barriers imposed by bureaucratic layers of management.

TOOLS FOR A NEW NETWORK GOVERNANCE MODEL

A combination of technology tools presents network governance with many advantages over the older public processes. The traditional government structure, by necessity, produces red tape. After all, a significant number of employees spend each day shuffling papers, completing forms, examining completed forms for rule compliance, and requesting revisions for inaccurately completed forms. In this model, government transfers the responsibility for navigating the municipal red tape to the citizen. This is rationalized by the argument that government employees are too overwhelmed with forms to adequately guide citizens through the maze.

Clearly, new processes and technologies allow citizens to accomplish work on their own terms. But IT tools facilitate other reforms as well. They enable a single view of the client. Even progressive government officials operate inside relatively narrow program silos, delivering their necessary services according to their own rules. And the situation looks even worse to the citizen who, looking up, sees a multiplicity of agencies.

By establishing a virtual filing system that automatically sends citizen-submitted data to the correct location, technology—middleware and personalization software—allows officials now to see the client more completely. Coordinating support services for a poor mother in need of a job requires that the manager understand how she's dealing with social welfare, transportation, job training, child-care agencies, and more. Until recent technological advancements—including middleware, wireless, and date warehousing, and, of course, the ubiquity of the Internet itself—care coordination relied on difficult phone calls and meetings.

These workplace changes free government to accomplish more of its mission with the resources available due to the increased accuracy and efficiency provided by e-government services. The Indianapolis building-permit office furnishes an example. Delays in securing building-permit applications have haunted many cities, and Indianapolis was no exception. It took my entire eight-year tenure as mayor to successfully modernize the process of securing a permit. However, instead of developing a clear vision from the outset, we took a series of sometimes well-intentioned, but not always successful, steps.

The first step in reforming the department involved outsourcing the drainage-permit review because it was the slowest part of the process. When a year of outsourcing only marginally reduced total permit-acquisition time, I inquired about the insufficient progress. The vendor replied that there were many ways to streamline the permit-acquisition process but that the city had only asked him to speed the drainage-review process, not streamline the overall permitting system. That conversation was the catalyst for a five-year effort to digitize every land-related record that the city possessed, such as zoning regulations and variances, covenants, and previous permits, and to move from a sequential permit-processing system (i.e., employees frantically scouring their offices in search of in-process files) to a team-oriented, concurrent, digitized permit-processing system.

In the initial system, plans passed sequentially from specialist to specialist. Each reviewed areas related to his or her specialty and frequently inserted changes that affected another reviewer. Sequential processing created an efficiency model comparable to a cat chasing his tail. Concurrent processing was impossible prior to the advent of digital files and shared databases. But as the use of the databases and files became widespread and Inter- and intranet capability became a reality, the efficiency of the permit-processing system increased markedly. Not only could members of a processing team access and manipulate a digital file and apply different specialties simultaneously, but applicants could also file permit applications, respond to questions, or make modifications online, avoiding form-weary bureaucrats and the ordeal of traveling and waiting.

IT can redouble its focus on helping citizens solve problems, identifying those not following the land-use rules and providing more information in a transparent way to neighborhood groups about their community. Indeed, when officials are freed up from day-to-day ministerial duties, they can allot more time to upholding core public values, such as safeguarding the privacy of confidential information and facilitating fair and equitable access to public services and public information.[2]

Government reform, of course, requires that managers measure performance. Here again, technology provides the keys to the kingdom. In a complex, multiactor organization, measuring and tracking performance is a major challenge for public innovators. Distributed IT, networking, and digital record keeping now allows service providers to see each other's information immediately, while the contract monitors can follow individual cases and aggregate data for online reporting.

INFORMATION AS A PRODUCT

Networked government, powered by new technologies, can indeed be transformative. Government now can use information in totally new ways to produce value. It can use the information to predict areas of investigation; it can integrate disparate experiences into a sophisticated knowledge-management system that shares information, or it can make information itself the product. Placing information about child-care providers or restaurant code violations online helps citizens make better decisions about where to leave their children or where to dine.

Technologies help reduce waste, fraud, and abuse as well by directing investigators to areas that the data suggest are high in errors or exceptions to the rule in such areas as eligibility determination or Medicaid payments. Similarly, simple IT rules reduce input errors. The move to a concurrent and digitized permit-processing system further increased efficiency because system designers built error-reduction rules into the e-government system. For example, automatic systems made it impossible even to file permit applications for locations not appropriately zoned. E-government transforms information from an intangible used by the government in its duty to deliver a product into a product in its own right.

Reform means more engaged and active citizens. New technology allows a public official to provide personalized information to a neighborhood association about crime, development, and housing. It can produce more demand for school reform by organizing clear, disaggregated data about school performance. Government can procure and audit with more transparency, thus inducing trust. It can provide feedback mechanisms that are instant and easy to monitor, allowing citizens more input.

Local officials stand at the front line of innovation, often by necessity. E-government and related technology advances provide progressive managers with tools to dramatically increase constituent services. When well executed, the quality of the work can go up, the cost can go down, and the public servant can enjoy a more satisfactory and fulfilling career.

ENDNOTES

1. Stephen Goldsmith and William D. Eggers, *Governing by Network: The New Face of the Public Sector* (Washington, D.C.: Brookings Institute, 2004).
2. Goldsmith and Eggers, *Public CIO* 2004; forthcoming.

7

A Strategic Plan Is Not Optional

Kay Barnes, Mayor of Kansas City, Missouri, and Gail Roper, Chief Information Officer, Kansas City, Missouri

Relatively few local government information technology (IT) organizations have a strategic plan. I have concluded this because wherever our chief information officer travels, people from cities, big and small, look at her in amazement when she describes our plan. Some of them react as if Kansas City had discovered a new business concept or some revolutionary way of operating.

Nothing could be further from the truth. A strategic plan is just sound business sense. To me, it is amazing that more IT departments do not have one. However, in a sense, I do understand why since creating an effective and visionary IT strategic plan is a lot of work. I know because I have seen what our IT department had to go through to create one. It is even more work to carry out this plan. Sticking to your plan, month after month, in the face of naysayers and opposition, is the truly hard part.

As a result, many IT organizations struggling with day-to-day projects, budgets, brush fires, and the demands of elected officials like me just do not undertake one. I believe that is a mistake. In today's business environment, an IT strategic plan is not a luxury or an option. A strategic plan is every bit as important to the mission of our IT department as our other IT resources, such as staff, hardware, software, and technical expertise.

WHAT A STRATEGIC PLAN IS—AND IS NOT

There is no magic involved in an IT strategic plan. A good one, like other types of plans, is primarily a road map. It is not a technical document about bits and bytes or a compendium of short-term tactical plans. Rather, a good strategic plan defines where you are trying to go and tells you what steps you need to take to get there. It tells how you can use IT effectively as a business tool and how you can use technology to help your organization transform itself.

Kansas City calls its document a *competitive* IT strategic plan in recognition of the fact that local government IT organizations are very much in competition with private-sector IT services to provide technology solutions. The diverse internal and external communities that a local government IT department serves are no longer compliant "users" who can be dictated to and for whom the internal IT organization is the only option. They are our customers—the savvy, demanding people who see private companies and other local governments harnessing technology to do great and wonderful things, especially on the Internet—and they want the same opportunities. If they cannot get what they need from IT, they will get it elsewhere. This push toward electronic government can only accelerate. Thus, our internal IT organization had better be able to serve its customers efficiently, expertly, and cost-effectively, or we may find the IT function outsourced, and rightly so.

An IT strategic plan helps answer questions like these:

- In migrating from an IT organization that primarily does programming to one that primarily does consulting and project management, what does the organizational structure need to look like?
- If we want to implement emerging technologies, what building blocks, such as a stable network infrastructure, do we need?
- What industry standards will we need to follow, and what industry trends do we need to take into account?
- Where must we be, organizationally and technologically, before we can successfully implement an intranet?

E-GOVERNMENT IS BUILT IN

A thread running throughout Kansas City's plan is e-government. The plan calls for developing the basic technology foundation and basic business processes to make Kansas City a fully functional e-government entity. The primary objective of e-government is to provide the widest possible range of city services via the Web or other technologies. The idea is to automate those services, make them more efficient, and make them available to citizens on demand.

The plan specifically outlines several components of e-government for the city to develop, including the following.

An E-Portal

A portal is a gateway to a host of related services and resources, and this is one way for Kansas City to improve its interactions with constituents, suppliers, potential businesses, and existing companies. The portal represents, at its heart, the externalization of the city's business. If built properly, it will empower stakeholders to access information on demand that is

- *Relevant:* The appropriate information is provided to the appropriate individuals and groups.
- *Valuable:* Enough information is conveyed to meet the user's need.
- *Consistent:* The information is communicated so as to promote the city and the city's message and marketing plan.
- *Timely:* The information is delivered as soon as it is requested.

Branding

Branding simply consists of making people aware of the city in a positive way. It is a way to promote Kansas City from a global perspective. Due to the Internet, the opportunities and challenges for the city are no longer confined by geographic boundaries. The city is competing in a 24-hour business world, nationally and sometimes even internationally. We are competing with other cities for conferences, conventions, tourists, sporting events, company relocations, and people looking for housing and schools.

E-Procurement

Electronic procurement provides significant and almost immediate improvements and financial advantages over the old methods of bidding and buying. Our strategic plan makes e-procurement a top priority.

It's a Business Plan, Too

Kansas City's IT strategic plan goes beyond being solely a road map or a vision. It contains components that help us understand why we are here, and it gives us purpose. It tells us what the benefits to the organization will be as the plan is implemented. And, perhaps most importantly, it is a business plan as well as a strategic plan. The plan takes into account important but often ignored concepts such as return on investment and the total cost of ownership of our computer hardware, software, and other assets. It matches technological innovation with business value, otherwise known as "added value."

Keeping one eye on business value prevents us from deploying technology just because we're dazzled by it. The IT department should do more than create a computer system for customers; it has the obligation to help people do things better and more economically. Business value means helping our organization and our customers to realize those cost savings and better services.

Business value can be derived from something as simple as a downloadable form that saves staff members and citizens time. We have city-earnings tax forms on our website that get downloaded thousands of times during tax season. Think of the staff time, postage, and aggravation this saves firms.

Or, business value can be derived from something as elaborate as a new multi-million-dollar system that integrates all of the city's accounting, purchasing, bidding, human-resources, and asset-management processes. This is known as enterprise resource planning, or ERP, and Kansas City currently is installing such a system. It is modular, so we can add new components as we need them, and each component exchanges data with the others. This interrelationship will allow us to derive insights from the data that we never saw before to work smarter and to make better decisions.

But business value means more than economic value. It also refers to the feelings of IT's constituency about the department. Historically, there have been trust issues between IT and its customers; the IT department was not always trusted to provide what the customer wanted in a timely and cost-effective manner. A good strategic plan, by helping IT become competitive and customer centric, builds trust. We begin to share information. We become partners with our customers. We develop goals and timetables together. As we put more and more of the city's business and information online, our external customers—the citizens—begin to see the doors of city hall swing open. You cannot put a dollar figure on that kind of value.

Government IT's business value goes well beyond its impact on the internal organization and individual citizens. Many elected officials, managers, and even IT directors do not realize that local government IT can be a powerful economic-development tool affecting the entire community. Innovative, progressive cities gain a reputation as good places to live. Why would I want to live in a city that has no technology advantages, where I cannot pay my telephone and electric bills online? Why would I want to live in a city where I cannot pay my water bill, my taxes, and my traffic tickets online?

The city's reputation and technological amenities are as important to businesses as they are to individuals. Companies want to do business in the most efficient way possible. They conduct business with local government, just as their employees do. They want those transactions to be smooth and hassle free. They may want such things as access to geographical information systems maps. They will certainly need other local government data—for instance, real estate records or information about taxes or zoning and development opportunities—and they will expect to find it online. Most companies would prefer to take care of the following online: securing city permits and licenses, finding out about bids and requests for proposals, and communicating with city officials. An IT strategic plan helps build toward providing those online services to businesses. Companies can also recruit good employees more easily in a city with a reputation for technological excellence.

The concept of the wireless hotspot is a small example of an economic-development contribution from IT. Hotspots are physical locations where, if you are within range and have a device such as a laptop computer with a wireless network card, you can log onto the Internet, often for free. Hotspots are fast becoming a tourist amenity and a convenience for the locals. Our IT department is currently working with my office to install hotspots at various downtown sites, including in some retail space in a new city-owned parking garage. These hotspots and others we hope to deploy elsewhere in town will not only appeal to tourists and businesses but will be useful to city staff members who need to connect to the city hall network. That's business value.

HOW WE BEGAN

In formulating its IT strategic plan, Kansas City enlisted the help of the META Group, a consulting company. The IT staff began in the summer of 2000 by interviewing the internal department directors and their designees. This group of interviewees, called the Information Technology Steering Committee, was composed of 27 city employees representing 14 departments and divisions.

At that point, IT was trying hard to standardize and solidify our enterprisewide network and to get some things in place that would improve efficiency (i.e., to get a foundation in place). But it was still the old IT, and that is certainly how the departments viewed it in those interviews. Our chief information officer, Gail Roper, called it "having to confront our demons." A lot of departments wanted to discuss not where they wanted IT to go but where IT had been and what it had or had not done. Gail and her staff sat for weeks on end and listened to her customers, who in many cases were not at all happy with what the IT department had provided them in the past, before Gail's tenure. This process had to happen, but it was hard, knowing where IT wanted to be in two years and knowing that few people yet understood the vision.

The IT staff talked with the other departments about where the IT organization was and what the departments' goals were (i.e., what they needed technology to do for them). The IT department then developed a gap analysis, which measured the space between where it thought the IT department was and where the departments thought IT was. IT had to eliminate the gap to meet the departments' goals. This helped us to understand areas in which we needed to improve productivity, efficiency, and effectiveness.

In identifying key issues, steering committee members used their own experiences with the city's IT systems and processes. META and another consulting group led the team to develop recommendations. In October 2000, the committee boiled down the information gathered during the assessment phase of the work and identified seven core areas for improving IT's competitiveness and service efficiency:

- Staff development
- Purchasing IT equipment
- Communication and coordination
- Organization of IT service delivery
- Budgeting and funding of IT projects
- Network and applications issues
- Statutory and legislative mandates

We also needed to learn from our external customers, the citizens of Kansas City, so the IT staff talked to citizen groups. One of these groups was the Citizen Review Committee, which I appointed and which consisted of small-business owners. The IT staff met with the committee over a period of about five months. This group actually appeared before the city council later in support of one of IT's initiatives.

WHAT WE CAME UP WITH

What emerged from all this groundwork with our customers and META was a three-year IT strategic plan. IT would have preferred a five-year plan, but in today's dynamic technology environment, it is hard to project accurately much farther than three years ahead.

Year one called for IT to define its sourcing strategy, meaning the department had to decide which vendors to work with and standardize on, what functions to outsource, and what criteria to use to determine those things. The department also defined best practices and sought to develop performance measures so we could determine whether the IT staff was doing a good job.

Year two required IT to have defined return-on-investment and cost-of-ownership models. The department was to develop methods of analyzing project proposals and to have a better handle on the applications we already were running, such as knowing how old they were, how best to replace them, and how much maintenance they required. And, the department was to have a firm idea of its customer requirements.

In year three, IT wanted to be enablers of business transformation, that is, to be able to go to its customers and offer solutions, functionality, and experience and to anticipate those departments' needs rather than react to them. We wanted to offer solutions that would transform the way departments do business and the way citizens did business with us.

Our strategic plan defined a series of benchmarks for IT best practices and "best actions." These benchmarks were designed to lead to competitive improvements that would help position city departments to provide better service to our constituents.

Three of the best practices were

- Implementing service level agreements (SLAs)
- Instituting a governance structure for IT initiatives
- Introducing an executive oversight steering committee (EOSC)

An SLA, in our case, is an agreement between IT and another department as to what each will provide in doing business with the other. IT and the health department created Kansas City's first-ever SLA early in 2003, the third year of our strategic plan. Since then, several more SLAs have been completed or are in the works. SLAs are wonderful tools for spelling out expectations, avoiding disagreements, and measuring progress.

A governance structure refers to the whole mechanism for providing oversight of the IT function within the organization. It means providing a hierarchy of committees or entities that can address technology issues at many levels. For example, a committee called the Information Technology Advisory Board, which represents all city departments, advises IT on a wide range of technology issues, and the Internet Policy Oversight Group guides the direction of the city website and intranet. A third tier, technical liaisons within each department, handles that department's simple computer problems and provides a way for feedback to move between IT and other city employees.

The EOSC, actually another level of the governance structure, is made up of City Manager's Office representatives and department directors or their designees. It is a high-level group that oversees all major IT initiatives. The EOSC gives decision makers a way to communicate better on IT issues, to collaborate on enterprisewide projects, and to deal with funding issues.

We are finding, in the IT industry, that these governance structures are a good way to gain buy-in. They also provide a forum in which IT can educate the organization from a business perspective on what IT does. Thus, IT no longer does its work in a dark corner and can begin to acquire some much-needed credibility with other departments. In fact, many private-sector companies have set up their own governance models to support IT initiatives.

IT has also gained credibility by creating an enterprise project-management office (EPMO), which, as its name implies, is a centralized office where major projects can be tracked. This office was created to rectify inconsistencies in city departments' approach to planning, estimating, and tracking project resources and timelines, which made it tough for IT to provide high-quality service to those departments. The EPMO applies an enterprise approach to project and portfolio management based on industry best practices for project management. For the first time, the whole organization has the opportunity to standardize project-management practices and know the status of its major projects at any time. The projects themselves can be made to follow city standards.

To me, the real gauge of our success in gaining trust is the number of major projects that other departments have turned over to the EPMO, which valued $61 million at last count. Those departments would formerly have managed these projects because they did not trust the IT department.

In conjunction with EPMO, the IT department trained dozens of IT staff members in formal project planning and required them to get certification. This allows those who manage or plan projects to speak the same language, take a common approach, spot problems earlier, and use solid progress measurements. When other city departments found out what IT was doing, they started requesting the same training.

UNDERSTANDING THE BUSINESS SIDE

I believe it is just as important to understand the business side of IT as the technology side. Our IT department has a group of business analysts who do business planning. You just did not see that in old IT. Fully a third of our IT department staff is nontechnical but understands the business aspects of what we do and knows how to communicate with our customers.

An example of how the department applied its business expertise is the city's telephone system, which IT administers. IT recommended in 1999 that the city own its own phone system. That decision was made after an extensive analysis of what the existing system was costing us. The city had never before done an analysis regarding which phones were being used and where they were. We found phone lines costing $59 a month that had not been used in five years. The cost-benefit analysis led us to buy our own private system with 16 PBXs spread across the organization. We awarded a contract on a seven-year lease-purchase so that after seven years, the city owned the equipment.

Owning the system allows us to capitalize on some functionality that we would have paid extra for if a telephone company owned the system. For example, we own our voicemail system, so virtually every city employee with a phone has voicemail, and it does not cost us $3.95 a month per person. That was certainly a factor in the cost-benefit analysis. We also looked at such things as long-range maintenance costs, parts, and the cost of labor to maintain the system. We also viewed standardization as economically essential. As part of the strategic plan, we worked hard with the other city departments to develop standards in several key areas dealing with the purchase of hardware and software.

Now, Kansas City has a Microsoft site license for the entire organization. A department can no longer go to Best Buy for a copy of Microsoft Office or decide to buy a competing product. After much give-and-take among the departments, we inaugurated a PC life cycle program under which nearly all personal computers are leased on a three-year cycle. A computer at the end of its cycle must go back to the life cycle vendor. Our PC support staff no longer has to contend with outdated PCs running on outdated operating systems. As part of the life cycle, we worked out with the departments a standard for high-, medium-, and low-end personal computers. An employee must present a business case to receive one of the fancier machines. And, wonder of wonders, PCs are now delivered within a week or two, instead of months, of being ordered.

By the midpoint of the three-year period, the plan called for the IT department to reach "operational excellence," which we define as efficiency and effectiveness. It means being able to match supply with demand. At one time, the IT department more or less sat and waited for customers to come to it. As we approach a model of excellence, IT develops a catalog of services to offer its customers. The department can go to the customers and say, "Look what this new technology can do for you. Look what this new initiative will do for our organization." We gain tools that give the organization new ways of doing business. IT becomes partners with upper management. It can come to those managers and elected officials and say, "You have the business knowledge. We understand the technical side. Let's get together and provide a technical solution for this issue that will transform the organization." To an elected official, that is not only refreshing—it is exciting.

As it approaches excellence, IT also becomes more creative in financing these technology initiatives. Partnering with private industry becomes more common, as do such approaches as bank financing and public-safety bonds.

WHAT HAPPENS NOW

Like all strategic planning, this is an ongoing process, not an end result. A strategic plan is a working tool intended to allow for change over time. It serves as a guideline for actions that can be revised as new technologies emerge and the organization's needs change.

We are near the end of the three-year plan. At the finish, we will assess the IT department and the infrastructure and systems that have been built, the processes we have put into place, the issues, and the current challenges. We will look at the economy, economic-development incentives, and the initiatives the city has in progress, and IT will develop a strategy for the next three years.

That may mean developing a whole new IT strategic plan, or it may mean modifying the current plan. With the first plan, we have taken IT from being effective and efficient to being a transformation agent for the city. The new, refocused plan will support the transformation of our business processes based on the foundation we have created.

We hope to have an infrastructure in place that is flexible and can grow. We have centralized various systems so that we are not spending money for needless duplication. IT is in partnership with the other city departments. It is a catalyst for business and for business-process reengineering.

The last three years have been, for IT and the rest of the organization, a discovery process, like opening the window blinds and letting in the light.

I fully expect that the next three years will be just as challenging, and just as rewarding.

8

Newark Brings Its Municipal Government Online

Sharpe James, Mayor of Newark, New Jersey

Getting a traffic ticket is always an annoying experience. In the city of Newark, we believe that paying it should not be.

Municipal courts play a critical role in the administration of all cities and towns. They oversee the collection of parking and traffic fines and sit in judgment on housing, fire, truancy, and health-code issues. The courts provide a forum for residents to contest summonses and complaints. They see and insure that justice is done on issues that affect the lives and safety of every resident and visitor.

The collection of fines is often seen as a process to provide municipalities with more revenue. Fines do indeed produce revenue, but that is not their purpose. Like all cities, we impose fines to punish those people who violate our ordinances. They serve as a deterrent, punishment, and warning to adhere to laws that are designed to protect the safety of all of our residents and motorists. Just as importantly, we are determined to make the punishment fit the crime so as not to be cruel or draconian. And, in all of our municipal agencies, we have placed great value on technology and friendly, efficient, and professional customer service.

Newark's municipal court is the largest in New Jersey. It judges 17,000 defendants and processes 300,000 tickets annually. In the past ten years, demands on the court increased dramatically. The Newark Police Department doubled its personnel from 1992 to 1998. In the last six years, the department cut crime by more than 53 percent and greatly increased its enforcement of municipal ordinances, especially quality-of-life issues, which in turn increased the caseload in municipal court.

An increase in the number of uniformed officers patrolling our neighborhoods resulted in an exponential increase in the number of cases filed with the court. However, the personnel resources allocated to the court remained essentially the same during that entire decade. The weaknesses in the court's operation were also compounded by an organizational structure without an identifiable plan of accountability and delivery and by the inadequate use of information technology to handle the extraordinary increase in filing. Last year, the impact of those successes overloaded our court, creating vast ticket backlogs, long lines to pay them, and customer complaints, which garnered media attention.

To address this situation, I requested that the superior court temporarily reassign our former Newark business administrator, now Essex County superior court judge Glenn Grant, to our municipal court as acting presiding judge, with a mandate to enhance customer service and the court's use of technology. Judge Grant is eminently qualified to do both. In 1986, when I first took office as Newark's mayor, I appointed him as Newark corporation counsel. When our first business administrator left in 1990, I moved Grant to that position. His mandate was to bring Newark's municipal government into the twenty-first century by, among other things, overhauling and updating our computer technology.

Through my tenure, I have given the following strong message to our chief judge and to all of our directors and managers: Newark must work harder and smarter. We must make positive changes in how our city serves the public at the least possible cost. New technologies can help us do that.

In 1986, the city of Newark relied on mainframe computers from outsourced vendors to handle tax and payroll issues and little else. Judge Grant changed that policy. Newark is now on the cutting edge of technology use. We built a state-of-the-art police and firefighter dispatch system that enabled us to tie Global Positioning Systems into our programs, which are used to track crime and deploy personnel. We used similar technology for our Department of Water and Sewer Utilities to track sewer repairs and for the Department of Health and Human Services to partner with area hospitals to track morbidity and disease outbreaks.

We also brought in PC networks for our police, fire, sanitation, and code-enforcement officers for case processing, which eliminated using typewritten carbon paper as an instrument of policy. In recent years, we have made possible the live videostreaming of my annual State of the City address and other major municipal events. Now we dedicate more than $14 million of our annual budget solely to technology.

While we were addressing these areas, however, the court system was relying on the city's AS400 IBM computer system, which went active in 1985, to process parking tickets and other motor-vehicle violations. The city of Newark went online with the state judiciary's automated S3670 computer system in 1992. This system tracks both traffic tickets and felony and misdemeanor cases. As technology has changed dramatically in the past ten years and our caseload has expanded just as dramatically, this system has become inadequate and obsolete.

The failure to keep up with technological advances created a backlog in processing tickets, thus creating the problems we faced last autumn. Acknowledging this defect, I sought the assistance of Judge Richard Williams, administrator of the state's Administrative Office of the Courts. At my request, Judge Williams put together a committee, including Judge Grant, which sought to determine the cause of the problem and make recommendations on how to correct it. Judge Grant's temporary assignment grew out of those recommendations, and I advocated and endorsed the idea.

Judge Grant quickly identified the issues facing the court. The court maintained seven separate bank accounts. This practice violated ATS/ACS financial procedures. The court also failed to reconcile its daily financial reports of monies paid and received, to maintain finances in a secure manner, and to establish procedures for handling finances. Ticket payments received through the mail were not processed immediately. Furthermore, police officers delayed forwarding parking tickets to the court due to weaknesses in supervision and accountability.

Constituents and visitors were also very disgruntled with the court. Upon calling, faxing, or sending written correspondence to the court, they would receive inadequate information or no response at all. Couple the aforementioned issues with the fact that the municipal court of the city of Newark, the largest city in the state, was not participating in the New Jersey Municipal Courts Direct Internet Payment System, which allows constituents and visitors given tickets in the city of Newark to pay them online. Newark was not permitted to participate in this program due to its failure to meet the state requirement mandating that 60 percent of its traffic violations be filed in the system within four days.

Upon assuming leadership of the Newark municipal court, Judge Grant identified the following as key issues that inhibited the organization's ability to accommodate its constituents successfully and provide quality customer service:

- An obsolete management structure that did not promote accountability, integrity, efficiency, or customer service
- The city's lack of user-friendly technology systems that could accommodate the tremendous amount of summons, complaints, and tickets that needed to be addressed on a daily basis

Some of the following strategies used by Judge Grant attack these issues:

- Development of employee training and curricula
- Use of Parking Offender Adjudication Act funds to create and support a customer call center

- Establishment of a Customer Service Division, which included a new clerk's office and call center to provide citizens of and visitors to the city of Newark with a positive encounter with the city either through written or oral communication
- Creation of a municipal court Web page that permits users to view and pay their traffic violations electronically

Since the appointment of Judge Grant, a transformation has occurred within the Newark municipal court's procedural, physical, and technological infrastructure. Judge Grant's creation, implementation, and use of such initiatives have had a drastic, immediate, and positive effect on the Newark municipal court.

The court now maintains only two bank accounts, a general account and a bail account. This places the court in compliance with ATS/ACS financial procedures. In furtherance of Judge Grant's technological goals for the court, a proposal is in place to acquire and implement a new safe that uses electronic identification and is on a timed schedule. Ticket payments that are sent through the mail are now processed the same day. Police officers now deliver tickets to the court on a daily basis.

The most widely publicized technological advancement made by the Newark municipal court is its going online. As of March 25, 2003, it became possible for citizens and visitors of the city of Newark to pay their tickets online. By accessing the city's website (www.ci.newark.nj.us) or the state system (www.njmcdirect.com), supplying the violation number and license number of the car involved, and entering a credit card number, a citizen can avoid a court appearance. Considering that 79 percent of tickets for moving violations and 55 percent of the parking tickets in Newark are issued to nonresidents, online payment makes it easier and more efficient for violators to pay their tickets. Since the website's launch, 200 tickets per day are being paid. This number is expected to increase drastically once the public is made aware of the website's availability. Web payments provide additional revenue to the city and reduce the need for additional personnel in the cashiering and court-processing units.

Judge Grant has also established a customer-service call center and the Clerk's Unit. The technology of the new call center tracks the number of incoming calls, the amount of time a customer is on hold, and the number of calls that are lost. Verizon and Nexter 1 were the contractors for the automated system.

The Clerk's Unit uses cutting-edge technology, which permits the staff to schedule motions, look up violations, disperse information to customers who are calling, and track written correspondence through a mail-tracking software program. This technology allows the court to serve citizens and visitors in an expedited, yet friendly, manner, thus cementing the concept of technology as a means of reducing backlog, providing customer service, and generating revenue.

To address these issues, Grant decided to follow models from the private sector. "You call a bank for information about your loans or accounts, and you get it. Citizens should be able to do the same with respect to municipal court complaints and tickets."

Verizon and Nexiter 1 are creating telephone systems and software to create automated phone lines that use an automated touch-tone phone process to guide customers through their transactions. The system also tracks total calls per hour and the time it takes both computers and people to handle them, further ensuring efficiency.

Our other battle was to eliminate the backlog of tickets that had been issued but not entered into our computer system. This backlog had reached the tens of thousands; today, it is down to zero. Most people do not realize that when our police or code-enforcement officers issue a ticket, it does not automatically get entered into our judicial system. The reporting officer still has to enter the data. Before Judge Grant took over, that process was taking up to four days. However, citizen questions about tickets tend to come in within hours of the ticket's being issued, and because they did not have the information, our staff was unable to answer inquiries, including numerous faxes from residents and attorneys contesting tickets and summonses.

Judge Grant changed this by establishing the Customer Service Division in the municipal court to control the call center. He also created the five-person Clerk's Office to respond to all written correspondence from the public, including faxes. "We had no facility for that," Grant said. "So we turned Room 300 into the Customer Service Division," converting a room full of old files. "Communications are critical to maintain public trust and confidence in our ability to provide timely delivery of services," Grant said. "I insisted that we would have knowledgeable people who will answer questions and faxes." As part of these changes, Grant ordered that all faxes and letters be answered within 48 hours with a standardized, computer-generated response to ensure that residents knew their concerns had been seen and read.

Another important concern was to impose quality-assurance and integrity checks on the system. Every day, ten processed tickets are pulled at random, and those cases are phoned in to the call center to check that the person answering the phone is following procedure and that the ticket has been processed into the system.

FoxPro was used as a mail-tracking system to ensure quality assurance on the outgoing mail. Also updated were the connections with state computers to track Department of Motor Vehicle violations and driver's license suspensions and revocations. In doing so, we eliminated backlogs of unreported tickets. Once that was done, we attacked the backlogs of unpaid tickets by sending out notices and summonses. This has created a new level of efficiency in our municipal court and a higher focus on customer service.

While the municipal court has been our latest leader in electronic government, many other agencies have also jumped into the technological revolution. In 2000, the city of Newark revolutionized and unified emergency-service response by opening the Public Safety Communications Center on Washington Street. This 15,008-square-foot, two-story facility is shared by our fire and police departments, replacing two separate command-and-dispatch centers.

The building cost $3.755 million, and was delivered by its prime contractor, Kullman Industries of Avenel, New Jersey, on time and under budget. It was built using modular construction, which means that the building is essentially a jigsaw puzzle of pieces that have been put together. It was first assembled on Kullman's property in Avenel, which enabled police, fire, and engineering officials to do a walk-through. After they signed off on the project, Kullman dismantled the building and reassembled it on site. Although the 14′ × 20′ modules were brought to the site over a three-day period in late July 1999, it took six months to construct the building's 28 modular sections.

The communications center's heart is the combined Call Taking/Dispatch Center, a 3,153-square-foot room, which answers and tracks all 911 calls and other emergency calls. In an air-conditioned environment, fire and police communications officers take calls and key the information into their computers. Calls and assignments are tracked on large screens, which show computer-generated maps of Newark. With Global Information System (GIS) maps, senior fire and police officers can track response times to calls and the length of time assigned units are at a given location. This process also simplifies the job of logging and recording 911 calls and responses. The building draws its power from the city grid, but also has a 125 KvA source that will kick in immediately in case of a power failure, providing 56 minutes of power.

Security for the communications center is also high tech. The building has bulletproof glass, video cameras, and is tornadoproof. Furthermore, 23 thumbprint-reader-guarded doors control entry to the building's rooms. The building also includes a conference center/briefing room, which functioned as the city's emergency command center on September 11, 2001. Representatives of city, county, state, and federal agencies responding to the terrorist attacks on America set up their laptops and computer equipment in the briefing room and connected them to modems and dedicated phone lines. We have also used this room efficiently for snowstorms, antiterrorist drills, training classes, and even press conferences.

The Public Safety Communications Center has been a success since its opening in early 2000. The building's use of sophisticated computer technology in a secure environment has enabled our emergency-response agencies to slash response times significantly. In the late 1970s, our police department had response rates of up to 18 minutes per a call, and some calls were never answered. Now our response rate is down to 3 minutes, and we do not miss a single call!

The tracking system also enables our police and fire departments to identify crime and arson trends. We can record and track activity and incidents on our GIS maps and put them on a large screen at the weekly COMSTAT meetings of the Newark Police Department's senior officers. At these meetings, using the generated maps, senior officers can see developments at a glance and work out response and prevention strategies.

The success of this program has been demonstrated by our public-safety team's hosting of numerous police and emergency-response agencies from across the nation and from as far as Portugal and India, who are studying our communications center as a model for their own facilities.

The city's use of GIS mapping is not limited to tracking crime and fires. During the last decade, we have used GIS to assist in our numerous infrastructure projects for the Department of Water and Sewer Utilities, the demolition of outdated housing projects, and roadway maintenance improvements. We have also incorporated our citywide GIS into epidemiological tracking by our Department of Health and Human Services to track morbidity trends.

The use of new technology has also impacted our housing-code enforcement officers. Last year, Newark unveiled CERTS hand-held computers for our Department of Neighborhood and Recreational Services' Division of Housing Code Enforcement. This division is responsible for enforcing Newark's vital housing-code ordinances and makes regular inspections. Failure to obey our codes can lead to municipal court summonses and hefty fines. The heavy development that is going on in all of our neighborhoods has placed an increased burden on our inspectors, and the use of the CERTS computer is an attempt to help relieve that burden.

CERTS hand-held computers are Palm Pilot computers issued to our inspectors and linked by wireless phone to their supervisors' computers. As housing-code enforcement officers make their inspections or answer complaints, they can file reports by punching buttons to fill in forms on their Palm Pilots' screens. Personnel can punch in the data from their inspections and update the files to reflect whether or not the landlord has abated the violation. They can enter new complaints from their sectors and process them on the spot. At the start of the day, housing-code enforcement officers can also receive their day's assignments and itineraries through the computers. At the close of the day, supervisors at their offices can download and print out the day's transmissions from officers in the field.

Supervisors can look over the complaints on screen, make notes on them, and print them out for signature and mailing. This cuts down on the time spent processing and mailing complaints; now it only takes one day. If we file a complaint on Monday, we mail it on Tuesday.

Each of the personal Hewlett-Packard Personal Data Aide hand-held computers costs about $700. The CERT program was first proposed in 1999, and after studying various computers, Hewlett-Packard was chosen for a test. Phillip Spears, a housing-code enforcement officer, was sent into the field this year for a four-month pilot program. He recorded 1,572 complaints in that time in a number of different neighborhoods.

Armed with the CERT computers, housing inspectors can visit 30 or 40 properties a day and conduct exterior and sanitation inspections. They can then review complaints and inspections, fill the forms out, and file them in two minutes online. The CERTS program, which was designed for Newark, also enables code-enforcement officers to report sanitation, health, fire, and other violations that could require referral to other agencies.

Thus, we are taking a holistic approach to using modern technology in Newark. We issue hand-held portable computers to our code-enforcement officers in the field. We provide our communications clerks with computer technology so that they can answer requests from the public. We provide our supervisors and managers with computer technology so that they can maintain quality, provide customer service, and effectively plan for the future. A comprehensive approach! A holistic approach! Here in Newark, America's third-oldest city!

At all levels, in every neighborhood, in every department, Newark's municipal-management team is leading the way, finding new methods and new technologies to answer the question that has faced every city since ancient Babylon: how can we serve the public most efficiently and for the least cost?

In Newark, New Jersey, I am proud to say that we are working to answer that question.

9

GIS in San Francisco

Willie Brown, Mayor of San Francisco, California

The landscape and geography of San Francisco, California, are among the most recognizable in the world. At the tip of a peninsula stretching northward, the city commonly called the "Gateway of the West" brings fond memories to those who have visited and smiles to those who call her their home. The vision of San Francisco is one of undulating hills, of tightly packed homes, of skyscrapers and bridge—a city where not only do bay and ocean meet but where cultures, landscape, and economies come together to form a true melting pot that exemplifies America.

With a population of 776,733 in its 47 square miles, San Francisco is one of the most densely populated urban centers in the United States. Like most comparable European cities, San Francisco's age and unique landscape create a challenging opportunity for city management. With utilities, streets, and buildings in excess of 100 years old; a variety of mechanisms for travel (automobile, bus, subway, light rail, cable car); and unique parks, geology, and waterways, San Francisco's beauty requires diligent and meticulous oversight.

It seems no coincidence that the technology revolution finds its home in the San Francisco Bay Area, where these advancements in science have enabled city government to protect and foster these valuable assets. In particular, the use of geographic information via the development of geographic information systems (GIS) has been integral in organizing, managing, and analyzing how San Francisco supports and protects its citizenry and businesses.

GEOGRAPHIC INFORMATION SYSTEMS

GIS is essentially an organized collection of computer hardware, software, and geographic data that is designed to efficiently capture, store, update, manipulate, analyze, and display all forms of geographically referenced information. Over the past decade, San Francisco has worked to leverage this type of information not only to streamline its business processes but ultimately to increase its ability to provide essential services to its employees and the public at large.

The city and county of San Francisco have been using GIS within individual departments to enhance both operational and analytical functions since 1992. The Department of Public Works (DPW) was also the initial creator in 1994 of spatial "basemap" information, which consists of essential cadastral map information that all other location-based information can be referenced to.

Over the past five years, DPW has developed and maintained the city's basemap efforts. However, the overall GIS environment has lacked centralized promotion, thus hindering the full potential of GIS within the city as a whole. Lack of coordination and funding for projects has additionally allowed departments to use more antiquated maps and systems to meet their own specific needs.

In an effort to resolve these types of issues, the Department of Telecommunication and Information Services (DTIS), with the support of the mayor's office, has taken the lead in developing a centralized, citywide GIS model. The intent of this strategic plan is to outline DTIS's vision for this enterprisewide GIS service, including management and organizational structure, resources, and implementation timelines. DTIS classifies GIS as an essential enabling technology.

The full realization of the city's GIS plan will enable departments to use better information and tools for analysis; to streamline and improve planning efforts; to foster productive sharing of information between departments; and eventually to provide the public with timely, accurate, location-based information.

Background and History of Geographic Information in San Francisco

Over the past ten years, many government agencies throughout the country have developed GIS in the departments that have had the most immediate need for this technology. Typically, departments within organizations, such as public works (which has the need for engineering design and management tools), finance (which finds it easiest to acquire funds for GIS), or planning (which has the need for zoning and planning information) have taken it upon themselves to initiate GIS programs. As other departments have begun to see the advantages of using GIS within their own work processes, organizations have reevaluated which department is best suited to house their GIS programs. The majority of organizations that have gone through this process have identified their information technology departments as the obvious choice for managing, implementing, and maintaining GIS.

In San Francisco, the DPW has historically taken on the role of GIS data creator and distributor of citywide spatial information (i.e., basemap layers). The Office of Geographic Data Services (OGDS), a division within DPW, was created specifically to maintain and manage this basemap information.

As basemap development and maintenance continued throughout the late 1990s, OGDS was viewed as the sole source of GIS expertise in the city. With an immediate need for GIS functionality but no mechanism to provide it, OGDS unofficially took on several roles, including the following:

- Provider of GIS application services to other city departments
- Distributor of GIS basemap information (via CD-ROM or the city's intranet)
- Maintainer/integrator of spatial data for other city departments

In December 2000, under the direction of Mayor Willie L. Brown, DTIS took on the role of developing San Francisco's first true Enterprise GIS program, with the following mandates:

- *Enterprise access to standardized data sets:* Organizing and maintaining GIS data (in an enterprise fashion) from all contributing departments creates a mechanism to allow standardized, dynamic access to spatial and other related attribute information.
- *Cost sharing:* Centralized GIS information allows costs that were originally spread out over many departments to be structured in one area. Duplicate efforts and spending can be reduced.
- *Use of expert resources:* The current approach to GIS is to develop interdepartmental expertise. Our approach follows the same model applied to all information services within the city: by centralizing data dissemination and application development, the city is able to share in the costs and overhead needed to develop complex information-technology architectures, such as GIS.
- *Data sharing:* The current method of data analysis, with regards to GIS, is to use interdepartmental data sets to come up with the prescribed results. If departments need information that may be located in a different department, they must take the initiative themselves to attempt to acquire such information. Our approach would be to consolidate this effort within DTIS. Serving as the data provider for the city, DTIS's responsibility would be to collaborate with all city departments and integrate their data into an overall data repository, from which all city departments could access information, following a standardized methodology.

- *Refined and more efficient management-vendor partnerships:* Currently, city departments manage and maintain their own relationships with GIS vendors that supply software and expertise for specified projects. While this plan recognizes the need for departments to maintain aspects of independence, the ability to consolidate our approach to software maintenance, licensing agreements, and contracts regarding GIS enables the city to manage and maintain these relationships more efficiently.
- *Integration of GIS technology with future systems:* Future needs to integrate GIS technology with peripheral systems (e.g., the police's 911, RMS/CAD systems; Department of Building Inspection's permitting system) will be streamlined if the city has an integrated, enterprisewide approach to GIS.

In addition to the above, Enterprise GIS provides several key advantages:

- Sharing datasets provides departments with more information to make better decisions.
- Standardizing data distribution enables departments to look to one source for all citywide GIS data, eliminating the need for employees to assemble GIS information on their own.
- The need to duplicate GIS data sets throughout the city is eliminated.
- It provides dynamic, online access to GIS data.
- Departments can pool resources and share the benefits in negotiating GIS contractual services, maintenance agreements, and so forth. The converse is for individual departments to perform these functions on their own, often times in parallel to other departments.

While there are substantial uses for GIS on a departmental level, the deployment of this technology on an enterprise basis clearly has numerous benefits. In the broadest sense, Enterprise GIS has provided San Francisco with a more consistent and reliable location-based information structure for city employees and the public, in a manner that is efficient and productive for all. More information can be reviewed on our website (www.sfgov.org/gis).

How Does San Francisco Use GIS?

Currently, several departments throughout the city use GIS:

- *Public works:* street maintenance, facilities management
- *Public utilities:* water infrastructure management
- *Parks and recreation:* facilities management, natural-resource analysis

- *Real estate:* parcel-information queries, real estate analysis
- *Public health:* health statistics, disease monitoring
- *Planning:* zoning, permit management

Each of the departments listed above has used GIS to better maintain and manage its location-based information. There are some clear, documented advantages to using GIS technology:

- For city employees
  —Increased speed of work because there is easier access to commonly hard-to-assemble information
  —Increased access to information for better decision making
  —Increased ability to manage and maintain facility infrastructure
  —Departmental ability to analyze location-based information for predictive analysis
- For the public
  —Allows better access to government services
  —Provides improved government services and government response
  —Provides new information available in easy-to-understand format (i.e., a map)

GIS and Interaction with Citizens

San Francisco's efforts to involve its citizenry in all aspects of government have been paramount. In many ways, geographic information is the "glue" that can bring government, the public, and businesses together with one common premise. Over the last two years, San Francisco has attempted to bring this ideal to fruition in several ways.

Making Geographic Information Available over the Internet

Over the past several years, San Francisco has attempted to make much of its nonsecure GIS data available to the public, either through directly viewing the information via a Web browser or by actually downloading it. The former effort (viewing maps through a Web browser) has been a key focus, with several mapping applications currently available:

- *SFViewer:* San Francisco's basic mapping portal is accessible from the city's homepage or from www.sfgov.org/sfviewer.
- *SFParcel:* San Francisco's assessor, Mabel Teng, has recently made property assessment information available over the Internet (go to www.sfgov.org/assessor, then click on "Parcel Information") through

the efforts of DTIS. Users can view property information based on an address, as well as view the actual block map that was previously only available by walking into city hall.

- *SFProspector:* SFProspector (www.sfprospector.org) is San Francisco's first dynamic economic-development mapping site. This portal is described in greater detail later in this chapter.

Celebration of GIS Day

GIS Day, which is internationally celebrated every year during Geographic Awareness Week (the third week in November; sponsored by the National Geographic Society, the U.S. Library of Congress, and the U.S. Geological Survey), has been a great opportunity to show San Franciscans how the city is using geographic information.

Key Focus: Geographic Information and Economic Development

The use of GIS for economic development is not a new concept, with several U.S. cities and counties leveraging technology in this capacity, including Tucson, Arizona; Kansas City, Missouri; Vallejo, California; and San Mateo County, California. However, San Francisco's use of GIS, particularly for improving its business economy, is of particular interest for several key reasons.

- *Review and analysis of economic indicators.* San Francisco not only relies heavily on its own citizens for workforce support but additionally uses individuals from the Bay Area in general. Understanding where our workforce lives, as well as how this affects incoming businesses, is critical for improving our economy.
- *Large base of technology-literate citizens and businesses.* As is normally the case, San Francisco was recently ranked as the number-one "wired city" by *Yahoo Magazine* (2002). With its close proximity to Silicon Valley, as well as previous influxes of dot-com businesses throughout the 1990s, it is no surprise that over 70 percent of San Franciscans have an Internet connection. Additionally, broadband (Internet connectivity 384K and above, e.g., DSL, cable) use throughout San Francisco is very high.
- *Density and variable factors of San Francisco landscape.* As mentioned previously, San Francisco's density and small area (47 square miles) make it somewhat comparable to one of New York City's boroughs. Yet, with its population of 768,000 and a plethora of unique businesses, citizens, services, and the like, the use of GIS for planning and management becomes all the more important.

San Francisco approached leveraging GIS for economic development by implementing SFProspector, a website that allows users to identify available commercial property in San Francisco. The site also provides data including workforce demographics, zoning data, business, and tax-incentive information. The data is displayed using a Web-based GIS that combines layers of information to enable a better understanding of the comprehensive details about a specific location.

Any commercial broker, property owner, developer, or similar real estate entity can list available commercial property at no cost. The site acts as a dynamic and comprehensive listing system for brokers and interested companies, where visitors can contact the respective brokers directly about specific properties. Linked to the city's frequently trafficked website—which receives a minimum of 1.5 million visitors per month—SFProspector promotes the properties listed by brokers, and provides critical business data, which gives enormous exposure to listed properties and brokerage firms.

SFPROSPECTOR

One of the key components to leveraging geographic information, especially in its use for the public at large, is ease of use. This was a primary consideration in the development of the SFProspector project.

If a broker wishes to participate, he or she initially contacts the SFProspector staff to obtain an individual, secure, company login and password. The brokerage company's designated listing administrator then begins entering data directly into a user-friendly Web form. As it is entered, users can instantly see all data entered on the property, including available square feet, rates, and photographs.

Businesses that are actually looking for an available property for lease, rent, or sale can view and use SFProspector by visiting www.sfprospector.org. The easy-to-use, browser-based format lets anyone with an Internet connection access SFProspector's maps, properties, and GIS-based data.

The broker's contact information, which is entered by the broker, accompanies each property listing. After entering the listing, along with any additional information (such as photos of the building), the broker can then update the information, which immediately places the listing on the map.

Commercial brokers can update their data 24 hours a day, 365 days a year, so the inventory of available properties constantly remains current. San Francisco annually updates census data, detailed city data—including current information on planning codes, enterprise zones, businesses in San Francisco, and transportation data—as changes occur. Additionally, SFProspector offers site location data and demographic information for the entire city. The asking price, square footage, property description, zoning classification, brokerage company and realtor contact information, in addition to other vital information will be listed with each property. When considering a specific property, users can also query the transit accessibility, neighborhood demographics, workforce data, and existing market competition in any radial vicinity of the property. Individual brokers can include any pertinent information; it is completely up to them.

As mentioned previously, several other municipalities are leveraging GIS to assist in economic development. However, San Francisco's approach is quite unique, considering the interactive aspects of the project. In addition to the commercial property listings and the current-year demographic and economic information that are available, SFProspector offers access to a breadth of city and county of San Francisco data that is critical to relocation or expansion decisions. Data provided includes business data from the Treasurer/Tax Collector's Office (registered businesses), data on enterprise and other incentive areas, zoning information from the planning department, transit information from the San Francisco Municipal Railway, as well as traffic counts and city parking garages from the Department of Parking and Traffic. These city departments have truly stepped up to show how municipal government can work together to assist our community with the aid of cutting-edge technology.

The city recognizes the importance of expanding and sustaining its business community and is therefore committed to making "doing business" as easy as possible. With roughly 87 percent of businesses saying it should be a priority for government to invest in making more information and services available over the Internet, as well as with the growing number of people who conduct business on the Web, SFProspector provides an invaluable, real-time service for many businesses contacting the city regarding site-selection information.

As mentioned previously, users can get to SFProspector through its direct website (www.sfprospector.org) or via the city's website (www.sfgov.org/sfprospector), which attracts approximately 1.5 million visitors per month. With links to other frequently trafficked sites, such as the San Francisco Chamber of Commerce and the San Francisco Center for Economic Development, the mayor's office and its partners will continue to promote SF-Prospector for use by all.

CONCLUSION

San Francisco's efforts (both city and county) to increase vitality and economic development through the use of technology have been extremely successful. In particular, the integration of city information geographically has streamlined efforts and increased efficiencies in several areas, including homeland security, criminal analysis, business and economic development, taxation, public works coordination, and social services.

More specifically, our focus on the use of GIS for economic development via the Internet has been extremely beneficial, with over 600 commercial listings posted by over 20 realtors. In addition to the tremendous value this service provides to potential new businesses, our SFProspector portal is an amazing tool for existing businesses within San Francisco. With many companies, organizations, and individuals using this technology for purposes other than site selection (e.g., demographic analysis, neighborhood studies), the value and cost efficiency of using the Internet to communicate complex governmental information becomes readily apparent. To a greater extent, the ability to convey such information visually extends this value even more. With the city's and county's technology objective of "serving our citizens through technology," San Francisco's efforts such as those described in this chapter are literal examples of how our government is living up to this motto.

10

High-Tech Communications Trailer: Enhanced Public Safety

Neil Giuliano, Mayor of Tempe, Arizona

Tempe, Arizona, is known as a premier special-events host. With an abundance of sunshine year-round and several outstanding indoor and outdoor public venues, the city is the site for hundreds of local, regional, and national events each year. We have hosted a Super Bowl, a papal visit, and two college football national championships.

In October 2004, the final presidential debate took place on the Arizona State University campus, near the heart of downtown Tempe. In January 2004, we played host to the Rock 'n' Roll Marathon. We are in our second year as an Association of Volleyball Professionals tour site, and we are slated to be the site of an Ironman triathlon qualifying event in 2005.

Of course, I would be remiss not to mention our annual Tempe Tostitos Fiesta Bowl New Year's Eve Block Party, which draws more than 100,000 partygoers and has been listed by *USA Today* as one of the Top 10 places to ring in the New Year. When I was elected mayor of Tempe in 1994, I did not foresee how these events would strengthen our community pride and our status as a destination location.

I also could not have foreseen that keeping the public safe at these events would evolve into an issue of national security. Preparing for an occasional fistfight and ensuring that appropriate fire lanes are clear has been replaced by the reality of protecting against, and always being prepared to respond to, any level of terrorist activity. The tragic events of September 11, 2001, require that communities all over the nation take public safety to another level.

In Tempe, we have broadened the scope of how we view the protection of our water sources, our buildings, and our high-profile events. We have heightened our awareness of threats to specific cultural populations whose members have been targeted in antiterrorist hate crimes. We are learning to live in a different world. Finally, we are examining and inventing new ways to ensure that the members of and visitors to our community are safe in that new world.

HITCHING UP THE TRAILER

For many years, even prior to September 11, staff in the city's information technology department contemplated building a mobile-communications trailer to use at the block party, the Fiesta Bowl football game, and other ancillary events. The idea was to facilitate communications among multiple public-safety agencies. Instead of having numerous organizations communicating on different frequencies, on different bands, and in different formats, the idea was to tie them together, centralizing communications on one channel and allowing all dispatches to be made by a single individual.

What evolved was a high-tech, nonmilitary, communications-interoperability platform housed inside a custom-built, 18-foot trailer. The technology is a specialized cross-connect system previously available only to the military. Known as the ACU 1000, developed by JPS Communications, the technology translates the communications of dissimilar systems, allowing the city to patch one or more agencies' radio signals to another agency's receiver. In other words, officials of the Tempe Police Department can talk to the Tempe and Phoenix fire departments, who, in turn, can communicate with the Federal Bureau of Investigation; the Bureau of Alcohol, Tobacco, Firearms, and Explosives; the Maricopa County Sheriff's Office; or any number of agencies, depending on the situation.

The system can tie together three 800-MHz trunking systems, three VHF radio systems, two UHF radio systems, and a ham radio band. Additionally, thanks to the addition of spread-spectrum wireless technology, we can support the use of long-range cordless phones that have two-way radio capacity and text messaging. Moreover, they work indoors, unlike satellite phones, which only work outdoors.

Thankfully, the unit has not been used or needed during a serious emergency. However, during events like the block party, the July Fourth celebration, and the Fiesta Bowl, it has proven to enhance the response time of our public-safety personnel. This is vital for situations that require prompt police and medical attention. In the past, a police officer might have placed a request for paramedics through one dispatch location, which would then call a separate location, which would dispatch personnel to the scene. Now, with a "one-stop shop," personnel are used more effectively and efficiently than ever before.

Multiple Uses

While the unit performs well for special events where streets are blocked and multiple agencies are involved in a large but confined area, it also has value during other exercises. From Thanksgiving through Christmas, the police department uses the unit for its driving-under-the-influence (DUI) task force activities, which involve 16 agencies from several cities and the county's Department of Public Safety. The communications trailer is placed in a large parking lot from which officers are "commanded" in the field. The unit allows the task force to operate without interfering with regular radio network traffic.

Additionally, the unit has been helpful to police as a backup to SWAT operations and to the fire department for communication with multiple agencies during two-alarm fires. The communications trailer also has value for nonemergency situations. Recently, when a city building temporarily lost its communications system due to an electrical storm, the information technology staff brought in the communications trailer and kept affected departments functioning until regular service could be restored.

The Next Step

The strength of technology lies in its ability to evolve and improve consistently. Often, items become obsolete almost the minute they hit the market. Our information technology department continues to explore ways to ensure that the communication vehicle is up to date and equipped with the latest technology.

Future plans include adding the ability to activate a wireless local-area network so that police officers and other personnel can use their laptop computers anywhere within 300 feet of the mobile unit to access the Internet or the city's network to pull up maps, photos, fingerprints, and other data that are helpful at a scene. The ability to connect officers in the field to a host of resources locally, regionally, nationally, and internationally can lead to solving crimes and apprehending suspects more expeditiously. In the case of a hazardous materials spill, it can help officials assess the impact on nearby neighborhoods or surrounding areas more quickly.

The Maricopa County public health department is interested in the trailer's capabilities for providing assistance should outbreaks require countywide inoculations of large populations.

For communities considering similar mobile-communications capabilities, it is important to involve your police and fire departments in the deployment and setup of the unit during events and training exercises. The need for this becomes obvious when an actual event or exercise is taking place and orders are being given to and received by on-scene commanders. A radio technician has no authority in this situation and is not the best person to be making decisions about who should be dispatched into what systems. It is critical for police and fire departments to have trained personnel who can operate the equipment in the trailer.

CONCLUSION

Tempe will continue to explore effective ways to use the communications trailer on a more regular basis. As more people are trained and more agencies become aware of the unit's capabilities, we will discover more innovative ways to expand its use.

In the meantime, Tempe can already see the value of having such a tool available to preserve and protect the community. Public officials cannot put a price tag on safety. However, the $80,000 investment in the mobile-communications trailer has already paid dividends.

And the peace of mind is priceless. While the unit does not get a lot of use in normal, day-to-day operations, it is there when and if it is needed. We view it as an insurance policy: one more strategy for responding to the needs of the community and for protecting it from harm.

Part III

FACILITATING GOVERNMENT-TO-BUSINESS INTERACTIONS

11

The Commonwealth and eVA: Improving Government Efficiency

Mark Warner, Governor of Virginia

The Commonwealth of Virginia, like other states, has been confronted by one of the most difficult periods in its modern history. A revenue shortfall reaching more than $5 billion and the resulting fiscal challenges facing us have provided both the opportunity and the necessity to examine how we do the business of government. One essential path to that improved performance is a smart, business-focused use of technology.

A model case is eVA, Virginia's statewide electronic-procurement system. Introduced in March 2001, eVA is providing a better way for the commonwealth and its private-sector suppliers to do business. Through a seemingly simple Web portal, eVA effectively makes more than 300 different, independent purchasing systems across state government act as a single, virtual system. It also provides suppliers with one location to market their goods to government agencies in Virginia. As one of the nation's premier public-sector Internet purchasing systems, eVA was recognized by the national Center for Digital Government as "Best of Breed" in the electronic-commerce and business-regulation category in its 2002 Digital State Survey. It is a prime example of the core concept that changing culture and business processes goes hand-in-hand with the use of technology to improve government performance.

The development of eVA didn't happen overnight. Gov. Jim Gilmore issued an executive order in May 2000 that laid the groundwork for building eVA as a prime element of a broad e-government vision. The Department of General Services (DGS) had been gathering public comments on what an electronic-procurement system should do for both buyers and suppliers. In June 2000, it issued a solicitation for eVA's development. Among the solutions proposed by various vendors, DGS selected American Management

Systems (AMS), a Virginia-based business and information technology (IT) consulting firm, as offering a product set that could best provide the functionality envisioned for Virginia's electronic-procurement system. Partnering with AMS, the commonwealth developed and launched eVA in March 2001. Since then, Virginia has made great strides in building use of eVA among state agencies and suppliers and in further refining the system.

WHAT WAS LIFE LIKE BEFORE EVA?

Like many governments, the ability of the Commonwealth of Virginia to purchase goods and services efficiently was hampered by a decentralized procurement model. Before the commonwealth built and deployed eVA, selling to and buying on behalf of government was a daunting task.

As an example, consider a supplier who wanted to sell office supplies to the commonwealth. In order to market goods to possible buyers before the advent of eVA, the supplier first had to figure out where to find the purchasing offices of more than 170 state agencies and universities. It then had to travel to these offices to register as a vendor and find out about available business opportunities. For an annual subscription of $75, vendors could receive a periodic paper publication of solicitations. However, it listed only the opportunities valued at over $30,000, so the smaller opportunities weren't apparent. Because mail delivery of the paper publication often lagged, suppliers sometimes found they couldn't make a timely response to a state solicitation.

After submitting a bid, suppliers again had to travel to the state purchasing office to find out if the bid was accepted. The vendor who won the contract for office supplies then faced another expensive proposition: sending out a paper catalog to the possible buyers. If prices on a particular good changed, the supplier had to send out price-sheet updates to the more than 170 state offices, and sales reps had to make sure that buyers used the right price sheets.

Before eVA, the format and information on state purchase orders often varied among agencies, so suppliers made mistakes when determining what an agency was ordering. As a result, there were frequent returns and order corrections. Because the whole process was conducted on paper, suppliers couldn't automate their supply chains for delivery. All of the rework and back-and-forth communication had the potential for phenomenal delays in supplying agencies with what they needed—and in finally getting payment for the goods.

With the old system, a buyer in a state agency trying to purchase supplies had the same experience from the other side. Agencies faced a multitude of price lists, returns due to errors in product or pricing, and time-consuming paper-based processes. Overall, state buying patterns were characterized by a lack of knowledge: not knowing all of the items available on the multitude of paper contracts and catalogs, not knowing whether the vendor next door was the best supplier for something needed, not knowing if some other agency had found a better way to make purchases or had gotten a better price.

In short, the situation in Virginia produced a dependence on the personal relationship. Suppliers sold only to offices they knew, and small businesses had limited access to the market if they didn't have the resources to build a broad set of these types of personal relationships. Because each state purchasing office operated as its own business, even down to the different satellite offices of a single agency, the system abounded in missed opportunities to leverage buying power.

THE SOLUTION: STATEWIDE ELECTRONIC PROCUREMENT

A new way of doing business through a single electronic-procurement system for the state was envisioned as a way to resolve the inefficiencies of the old system. Fundamentally, eVA is an end-to-end, government-to-business network that streamlines the commonwealth's purchasing processes. It provides electronic purchasing through a website for all Commonwealth of Virginia agencies, local governments, and institutions of higher education. It funnels this purchasing through a single electronic portal that is capable of managing the unique needs of a diverse group of state and local agencies and suppliers. eVA does this by automating workflow; by utilizing common, auditable business rules that apply to all users, while also supporting unique rules for each buying organization; by providing data capture and aggregation of procurement information and activity; and by securely transmitting transactions and data.

For suppliers, eVA offers the advantage of one standard way to access business with the commonwealth. It offers a single face of government to suppliers using one electronic standard, regardless of the multiple systems that different agencies use. Suppliers no longer have the frustration and additional cost of connecting their order-management systems and business processes to government in multiple ways to sell goods and services to the commonwealth.

eVA also provides suppliers with a self-service tool to register across multiple government agencies. Suppliers can enter their own demographic information and confirm its accuracy, thus increasing the quality of the supplier data. Through vendor self-service, agencies avoid the time and resources needed to manage these processes.

Registered vendors can conduct Web searches for, view, and electronically bid on solicitations. eVA also offers reverse auctions, in which vendors can anonymously post bids to an open forum and then compare their bid to the lowest one submitted. Vendors can then resubmit their response at a lower bid, providing real-time competition for the buyer.

eVA uses technological tools to share information with suppliers regarding contract opportunities, historical contract and bidding information, and government news and information. Suppliers who have joined eVA report that participation has given them visibility in a market that they couldn't have accessed under the old methods of paper-catalog mailing and site visits. Their electronic catalogs are now visible to a marketplace of more than 5,000 government buyers that is dynamically expanding. For small, minority, and women-owned businesses, eVA has taken the concept of a level playing field for market access to a much higher level than ever before. One reported, "We have received many new orders and established a number of new accounts from outside our traditional market area. That never would have happened without eVA."

For government agencies, eVA offers as many advantages as it does for suppliers. First, shoppers can easily connect to eVA through a Web browser directly from their desktops. From there, they can access and search online supplier catalogs and place electronic orders for goods and services.

If a solicitation is required, the necessary documents are created through predefined libraries of information and published on the Web. Recipient vendor lists are also created electronically so that as solicitations are published on the Web, registered vendors are automatically sent e-mail notifications of, and hyperlinks to, the impending opportunity. Procurement documents are also distributed electronically.

The entire bid-evaluation process can now be handled electronically, from posting submitted bids on the Web to submitting and compiling team evaluations. eVA provides the buyer with a summary of the team's evaluation, an assessment of the vendor's responses to evaluation criteria, and an electronic-bid evaluation of prices by item and by vendor. When the buyer is ready to issue an award, document delivery and publishing requirements are selected, and award results are posted to the Web for public review.

eVA supports the creation, modification, and distribution of contracts, master agreements, and purchase orders to vendors. eVA also sets the stage for automated payment processing by matching goods or services received to outstanding purchase orders. It can track partial orders as well as overages. eVA provides robust tracking and reporting capabilities so that users can track and audit procurement progress, activities, and history. Invoices, both electronic and paper, are supported by the system. In the future, these invoices may be passed electronically to agency financial systems, which will allow electronic payment authorization and take advantage of another of the commonwealth's technology successes, electronic funds transfer (EFT), or bank-to-bank transfer.

In sum, eVA cuts down on paperwork, allows the commonwealth's purchasing agents to compare prices, and lets online purchasers benefit from cooperative buying and volume discounts. At the same time, government agencies retain their unique business rules. Effectively, eVA offers management of the complete procurement life cycle to all of the state agencies, colleges, and universities—as well as local governments—that participate.

FOCUS AREAS TO CREATE CHANGE

Many large technology projects in government fail; eVA has not only proved to be successful but has also become a model for how we implement technology solutions in Virginia, as well as for other states seeking similar success. Virginia's eVA project team focused on six areas that form the basis of the system's successful results. These focus areas are (1) an innovative project-funding model, (2) respect for decentralization, (3) executive sponsorship, (4) stakeholder collaboration, (5) project marketing, and (6) training for users. Any large technology solution that's intended to change fundamentally the way that government does business must consider these important facets.

Innovative Funding Model

eVA uses a reverse-funding model that has eliminated the need for up-front appropriations, which has been critical to Virginia's ability to continue its development despite intense budgetary constraints. Rather than the commonwealth's paying for the implementation of the eVA system, the reverse-funding model makes use of two funding streams: suppliers pay a 1 percent transaction fee, capped at $500 per order, and an annual registration fee. This model was developed through focus groups with large and small suppliers who were asked what they would be willing to pay for value-added electronic-commerce services like those offered through eVA. Although a few suppliers initially resisted the idea of paying a fee, they quickly saw that the vastly larger customer base and increased order accuracy generated opportunity and efficiency that would quickly compensate them for the fees paid.

The challenge inherent in this reverse-funding model is that government must be committed to building a large user base of both buyers and suppliers. Without an active and large buyer base, suppliers won't participate—and the revenues from fees won't materialize. Without a large number of registered vendors and the resulting availability of competitive pricing, many state agencies won't be willing to change to a new procurement system.

Reverse funding also requires a private-sector project partner who's willing to make the up-front investment to fund system development until the expected revenues are realized. eVA's development was assured with the inclusion of a minimum-payment guarantee in the contract with AMS, which forced the commonwealth to focus on encouraging eVA adoption by agencies and suppliers to reach the payment threshold. This approach drives both the commonwealth and AMS to remain committed and engaged because both are working to earn project revenue.

Unquestionably, a reverse-funding model requires a committed partnership that is outside the standard approach of a technology-consulting firm that delivers a project, collects payment, and departs. Therefore, any use of this model requires that government choose its business partner carefully.

Decentralization within an Enterprise Approach

One critical element of eVA's development and implementation was recognition of Virginia's highly decentralized approach to procurement. In Virginia, agencies hold their "local autonomy" dear, and any threat to it is a sure recipe for failure of an enterprisewide system.

An early key decision for eVA was the choice of a solution that most effectively supported decentralization of business rules and activities (local autonomy), while creating enterprise data and delivering efficiencies to all users (central collaboration). eVA's technology centralizes the catalogs that compose the online marketplace, and it standardizes the ordering process. However, it permits each purchasing office to have unique business rules for purchasing, as well as unique financial rules for how eVA communicates with the office's financial system. This technological feat, accomplished by a combination of table-driven rules and data entry, entirely supports the independence of buying entities, while leveraging the benefits of acting as an enterprise.

Convincing agencies that eVA would support decentralization required an early communication campaign targeting the highest levels of the purchasing organizations. The eVA team, which anticipated the concerns of state agencies, was direct and open about what the system would and wouldn't do and demonstrated that adhering to systems standards wouldn't decrease their organizational ability to manage their own businesses.

Executive Sponsorship

A project as complex as eVA—with its number of stakeholders, the amount of business process and cultural change required, and the implementation time frame—requires visible executive sponsorship and personal involvement to reach its full potential.

When I took office in January 2002, the eVA project was clearly a pioneer, but it was underutilized and didn't have much visibility. Not enough of Virginia's state agencies were using eVA routinely for their purchasing, and its registered vendor base didn't include many of the companies who regularly sold goods and services to Virginia agencies. We quickly recognized the potential of eVA to serve as a symbol for "government done right" and its value as a tool that uses technology for better government performance. As such, we took steps to raise its prominence as a key component of Virginia's program for better government business practices.

First, I used public forums to talk about my belief in the potential of eVA to be more than just a project or a system. Instead, it should become the strategic lynchpin for the way in which the commonwealth manages and expends funds. In a business, purchasing is a strategic activity: what we choose to buy and how we get the best price for the best value are critical decision points. For an enterprise the size of the Commonwealth of Virginia, effective purchasing decisions and methods are essential to stretch the value of our dollars and to increase government operational effectiveness. I wanted everyone who would listen to understand that using eVA would become the way in which Virginia would do business.

Second, cabinet secretaries were made aware of the strategic nature of eVA and the importance of its continuous use in state agencies. Using eVA's data warehouse of purchasing activity, quarterly report cards were issued on the volume of spending and frequency of use by agency. This information was made available on the Web and was discussed at quarterly cabinet meetings. Executive agreements with state agency heads were revised to include performance standards on the use of eVA.

This sort of performance accountability brought focus and attention to purchasing from state-agency leadership, which has actively removed roadblocks and found ways to facilitate the use of eVA. As a result of these and other efforts, Virginia has seen a surge in eVA use in recent months. Over 85,000 purchases and $525 million were processed through eVA in about 15 months, the largest volume through any system of this type in the nation.

Third, an executive oversight committee was created to provide senior support for the already strong eVA project team. This committee, chaired by the secretary of administration and including executive managers from the commonwealth and AMS, meets at least quarterly to review the project. The eVA project managers advise them of areas where executive-level support is necessary to overcome roadblocks, and the committee provides strong advocacy for the project.

Fourth, but not least, some of Virginia's cabinet secretaries and agency heads became personal and public advocates of eVA. The secretaries of administration and technology, in particular, took on roles as visible proponents of the efficiencies and economies of the system. They continue to take this message to many audiences, including the Virginia legislature. They work to build knowledge of and awareness of eVA's benefits with legislative stakeholders. This ensures that legislators understand the value of eVA's efficiencies and its creative reverse-funding structure in these constrained economic times. The secretary of education has also been a strong advocate with public colleges and universities.

Collaborating with All Stakeholders

If one thing has made the eVA project a success, it's been the strong teamwork shown by the eVA project team, which includes members from three separate disciplines: procurement, technology, and finance. These members have worked closely together to support each other and the project, and the results have been remarkable despite their limited resources. The business leaders determine the needs and drive the project, but they're simultaneously in lockstep with technology and finance to make these needs a reality. Members of the team are free to provide their insights into any area, whether within their own discipline or another. This kind of interactive exchange of information and mutual respect by every member for the insights of the other members has resulted in a formidable team that has overcome many challenges.

Another important factor that has contributed to the success of eVA has been consistent collaboration with all key stakeholders, across all of the stages of project development, from the very beginning design stages to implementation. When the eVA project team was still conceiving the concepts for e-procurement in Virginia, it held brainstorming sessions with both suppliers and state and local government buyers across the commonwealth. The team solicited ideas and feedback on the concept of operations and on the reverse-funding model, which was a new idea in many quarters. This proof-of-concept tour helped to build consensus and a sense that their ideas could affect the project's direction, particularly among government participants.

Next, a cross-governmental design team took the initial concepts and the group-session results and turned these into a detailed request for proposals (RFP). The design team comprised recognized leaders in the state- and local-government and higher-education procurement communities; fiscal oversight members from the Department of Accounts, the Department of the Treasury, and the Department of Planning and Budget; and DGS fiscal, procurement, and IT staff.

The benefits of an interdisciplinary design team went beyond the obvious need to ensure that all stakeholders had a voice. Team members advocated for the business needs of vastly different environments across state government. For example, the needs of the Virginia Department of Transportation in purchasing for road building across the state are very different from the needs of Virginia Polytechnic Institute in buying educational support materials. As a result of the interdisciplinary design team, Virginia developed demanding requirements that the new electronic-procurement system work for all possible users. Because the design required the new system to reflect the myriad facets of purchasing in Virginia government, eVA is able to meet these disparate needs.

Virginia carried the interdisciplinary approach through the implementation phase, retaining the design team as a steering committee so that it could offer feedback on specific concepts when important decisions had to be made. This forum helped iron out problems and offered cross-functional thinking, producing better solutions than a single business orientation would have. For example, the steering committee developed a new approach to the commonly used, state-issued purchase card (Pcard), typically used by state agencies for immediate purchases and carrying a low dollar threshold for approved purchases. The committee developed an idea to leverage the Pcard as a gold purchasing card: if agencies used the card to purchase through eVA, they could receive higher spending limits. This encouraged Pcard and eVA use, both of which bring efficiencies to the commonwealth's purchasing practices.

The collaboration mechanisms that Virginia established early on continue to function even now, as eVA goes into its third year of operation. One current issue is the need to move data between eVA and the more than 40 different enterprise resource-planning (ERP) systems in Virginia's decentralized state agencies. The technical staffs from design-team agencies came together to figure out how to design interface engines and a message broker to translate data from one system to another. The work of these technical staffs has reaped a huge dividend for state and local governments because the investment of time and energy won't be made multiple times to solve the same problem.

A final critical area of collaboration is Virginia's work with our private-sector partner, AMS. Because the state's technical staff could brainstorm and whiteboard problems with AMS staff, rather than simply receiving a technical design that was prepared according to RFP specifications, we produced a more flexible result. Virginia worked out the functional issues of eVA in tandem with AMS, holding prototype sessions with real buyers and sellers to test out designs and jointly solve problems identified.

Marketing to Win Support

As Virginia implemented the newly developed eVA system, we learned that it's critical to market the use of the system to both suppliers and buyers. Marketing is essential to build excitement and a core understanding of the system's outcomes and benefits.

Creating an appropriately scoped marketing program is a challenge for most governments, which are typically unfamiliar with marketing principles and practices. Virginia hired a marketing firm early in the project to help create marketing materials and a brand identity for eVA. The materials explained what eVA is, what its benefits are to both buyers and sellers, and how the funding model works.

Because Virginia had no central data repository of purchasing activity from which to identify the most common suppliers and the extent of their business relationship with state agencies, Virginia began by marketing eVA to 28,000 suppliers identified through the financial information of several state agencies and universities. The state made individual one-on-one pitches to suppliers and, in this way, registered the suppliers that agencies use repeatedly and built a base on which agencies could begin electronic shopping. This initial effort gave eVA over 9,000 registered vendors. Those vendors who quickly grasped the value of eVA registered and posted an electronic catalog have reaped benefits from early exposure.

Given the number of suppliers actually doing business with the commonwealth, achieving widespread eVA vendor adoption has been slow and has required a great deal of effort. However, eVA's data warehouse has recently "gone live" and promises to yield exactly the supplier information needed to increase the number of sellers participating in the marketplace. By matching eVA data to purchasing files from agencies, we've been able to create agency report cards that detail the suppliers used and the volume spent outside eVA with non-eVA-registered vendors. These report cards illustrate to agencies how much they could potentially save by doing business in the eVA marketplace, and they identify for the eVA team nonregistered suppliers to target. This kind of matching wasn't initially available for many agencies because they weren't able to supply purchasing data from their various back-end ERP systems. However, eVA's new system interfaces will enable more agencies to provide this data and participate in such analysis over time.

The eVA team's latest marketing strategy is to hold vendor workshops with individual state agencies, which invite their historical suppliers to attend. Suppliers participate in order to support the goals of their customer, the buying agency, and the eVA team is able to recruit these suppliers directly and help them register on-site. The eVA team also recently developed a supplier-recruitment kit and trained agencies to manage their own workshops with consistent, clear messages about the benefits to suppliers of participating in eVA.

There's still resistance to change from some suppliers who do business with the commonwealth, but continued outreach, marketing, and policy support for vendor registration will facilitate change.

Training for Users

At the same time, Virginia has learned that marketing alone can't achieve everything. Rather, marketing to build awareness and convince an audience of the business value of an e-procurement system is not a substitute for training. User training focused on developing user competence is essential in any technology implementation. On a procurement project such as eVA, the training challenge extends to both government purchasers and private-sector vendors.

For government purchasing organizations, Virginia's first eVA training was a classroom-based "train-the-trainer" approach, which proved unworkable in producing the competencies required. What was really needed was deeper cultural change. So, the commonwealth retained some classroom opportunities but moved to a mentorship model of eVA training. Each of the 175 separate state purchasing offices across Virginia was assigned to one of eight DGS mentors, who repeatedly visited offices personally and worked side-by-side with buyers to walk them through transactions. One-on-one mentoring has helped purchasing organizations in state and local government learn to use the system and has dramatically improved eVA's adoption rate. This consultative approach provided a realistic response to the challenge of creating cultural change by helping people change, at whatever level of participation they required.

After two years of mentoring state agencies, the eVA team was able to return to the train-the-trainer model in state agencies and higher-education institutions as they brought more buyers and offices online. Because eVA has been operational long enough to spark interest in local governments, Virginia has now assigned a local-government mentor to work with all municipalities.

On the supplier side, the eVA team offered online materials and targeted training. This worked well enough to build the base of 9,000 vendors who provide about 80 percent of the goods and services that the commonwealth purchases. To broaden the supplier base for the benefit of both government buyers and the suppliers themselves, the eVA team is currently gearing up to offer vendors regional classroom training and immediate, on-site vendor registration.

One training lesson the commonwealth learned from the rollout of eVA is the necessity of being flexible and responsive to the needs of the customers who use the system. Greater success was achieved with eVA once Virginia recognized the need to move to a consultative mentoring model.

eVA AS E-GOVERNMENT INNOVATION

Three principal areas of fundamental innovation in eVA point toward the maturing of e-government from a static website to a business model for government service delivery. These include (1) business innovation, (2) the supporting technical innovation, and (3) a fundamental shift in thinking towards responsibility to act on behalf of the entire government enterprise.

The business innovation of eVA was to conceive of the purchasing function of government as more than simply the buying side. Instead, it's the entire realm of materials management, enhancing the business capabilities of both the buyer and the seller.

eVA allows buyers to obtain the best product at the best price in the most efficient way. With Pcard usage, linkages to financial systems, and the potential to tap into EFT, it also allows agencies to automate payment for the product. And it will further motivate buyer satisfaction with supplier performance.

For sellers, the eVA perspective is one of suppliers, as partners who have business needs that should be supported by the system. eVA can feed directly into a supplier's automated supply-chain management, allowing the supplier to reduce the number of sales reps, cut supply times, and save costs. This can build huge economic gains for the supplier community, thereby building up the business climate of the commonwealth.

Furthermore, eVA has achieved several technical innovations. First, Virginia can claim position as the first government entity to create a seamless procurement environment for all stages of public purchasing. Although eVA appears to the supplier and the buyer as one common product set accessed through a single sign-on to all functions, the functions are technically produced by different products and were integrated to allow user credentials to move from module to module, while appearing to be seamless.

A second technical advance is eVA's multijurisdictional capability. Every agency using eVA has its own workflow, approval levels, and accounting requirements—and each entity can maintain this autonomy because each has its own view of eVA. This customization can occur because the business rules for each entity are table driven, so settings in tables can change as rules change—without need for software-code modifications. Additionally, the business rules that regulate the activities of a particular user are called on by the data that the user enters. For example, a user's agency may require an additional approval stage for purchases over $500; when the user chooses the commodity to be purchased, the value field triggers the workflow for the second approval.

However, this customization doesn't prevent eVA from taking all of the purchasing information that state agencies and local governments generate and automating the process for requisition and order through a common point. The data are normalized using the international XML standard and is easily taken into eVA for order delivery and data-warehouse reporting. Even if agencies use the procurement module of their ERP systems to manage their procurement process, eVA's interface engines and message broker offer them an electronic order delivery capability and participation in the statewide procurement data warehouse.

Another technological advance of eVA is that all of its functions require only a Web browser for use. No other system presently operational in the nation uses only a Web browser for every action, from user administration to agency business rule setup to complete deployment to report development against the data warehouse.

A final technology first is the means by which eVA is delivered to the commonwealth—as a service owned and hosted by a third party. AMS performs all of the software, customer support, and data-center management. Virginia owns only the data and the business need and purchases the e-procurement service from the experts. This is a tremendous e-government transformation. Under older approaches, the government would bear the cost and responsibility for all aspects of the solution. This application service model allows the DGS Division of Purchases and Supply to remain focused on its mission: establishing and promoting effective government procurement practice.

Finally, eVa began "thinking for the enterprise." While the traditional technology project approach typically focused closely on the single mission to be achieved and its related business processes, the technology now available for projects like eVA enables project participants to consider all of the ways in which opportunities for extended e-government are possible. People who drive such projects must think about how broadly the opportunity can be applied for the benefit of government, especially in an age of such limited resources.

eVA designers have taken this principle seriously. For example, when they developed the model for vendor data, they considered all of the ways in which a vendor must interact with the state—to get licensed, to get certified as a small or minority business, even to receive payment for goods and services. Rather than capturing only the data elements needed for the purchasing function, the team built a model that enables capture of all the data needed to support licensing, minority certification, even electronic funds payment. These functions are outside the DGS's scope of responsibility and are performed by three entirely different agencies. When these agencies are prepared to use the information to improve their own business functions, the eVA data architecture will allow gathering of this information to support them. Suppliers will thus have a far superior interaction with state government because they'll begin to have the one-stop experience that has long been the promise of e-government.

This enterprise thinking is at least as important as technological innovation. It sets the stage for better technology adoption throughout government. When people think in terms larger than their own functional responsibilities and instead feel ownership of the enterprise, creative ideas and fundamental changes in government performance are possible.

Benefits of eVA

There have been obvious performance benefits as a result of eVA's implementation, and we anticipate more of the same as the system continues to be developed over the next two years. We see significant cost savings to state agencies through more competitive contracts and creative supplier offers to cut costs through bulk buying and other cost-saving measures. There's greater internal efficiency for both buyers and sellers because the process is quicker and generates less paperwork. Certainly, the broader purchasing base has opened business opportunities, especially for small, woman-owned, and minority businesses. And government buyers are able to make better decisions through the real-time management of newly visible performance and spending information.

A subtler, but no less exciting, benefit has been the change in the role of DGS's purchasing division and the eVA team. The purchasing division is charged with ensuring compliance with the Virginia Public Procurement Act—but through eVA, these employees have been able to become active mentors and enablers of effective procurement practice in the commonwealth for both buyers and sellers. This is an exciting transformation in government service in Virginia

eVA's emerging success is the result of the blending of a talented, dedicated project team, a strong commitment from our private-sector partner, and continued support from the top leadership of Virginia government. We all see the potential of e-procurement to advance our common goal of more efficient and effective government for all of the citizens of the commonwealth.

12

Making Government Work

Jeb Bush, Governor of Florida

Since 1999, when I took office, Florida has embraced the concept of e-governance and the possibilities that it holds for enhanced productivity and service delivery in state government. It's an integrated part of our vision to provide a smaller, more efficient state government.

We've embraced e-governance through several initiatives. The State Technology Office provides direction for achieving efficiency, multiagency coordination, and a state electronic portal for e-government services. MyFlorida.com has been established as the state portal, or single point of entry, for state of Florida information. Simultaneously, a help desk has been created as an integrated service-delivery model for all state agencies, and technological improvements in child-support enforcement have increased collections.

A good example of how technology has improved programs provided by the state of Florida is the new Business and Professions Online Licensing System.

MyFloridaMarketPlace (e-procurement) is an initiative to streamline state purchasing operations and reduce cost. Furthermore, by collaborating with the Florida legislature, we have created the Office of Information Systems, which provides leadership and coordination for cybersecurity. These initiatives are part of my administration's ongoing plan for an integrated enterprise-level system.

STATE TECHNOLOGY OFFICE

The State Technology Office is the agency charged with bringing my vision for information technology (IT) to reality. The State Technology Office works closely with Florida leaders in both the public and private sectors to integrate IT systems and eliminate unnecessary duplication of IT hardware and software purchases by state agencies. By developing and purchasing IT on a volume basis, the entire process of IT integration and standardization becomes easier and costs less than if agencies went their own way.

"Build it once and use it many times" is a goal of the State Technology Office. With the support of my administration and other key decision makers, the State Technology Office will make best use of tax dollars by using an enterprise business model to drive the development of the state's major technology and information components. All of this is necessary because the majority of Floridians expect IT to improve government services dramatically. Through these concerted efforts, the state will deliver services to taxpayers with unprecedented efficiency.

I intend to build on the commitment that I made to transform Florida's IT infrastructure into an integrated, efficient system. This system will serve the citizens of Florida by getting critical information where it's needed, when it's needed. The State Technology Office is continuing to implement the strategic initiatives contained in its business plan. Some of those initiatives are highlighted below.

State Portal

The State Technology Office has established MyFlorida.com as the single point of entry for information about the state of Florida. MyFlorida.com provides increased access to information, products, and services. The portal is reliable, secure, and customized. It also has a powerful search engine, external content, and integrates state and local government applications.

Enterprise Help Desk

The State Technology Office's help-desk initiative incorporates an integrated service-delivery model for all state agencies. This consolidated approach allows for IT problems and their solutions to be shared, thus maximizing customer service and productivity. Due to the rapidly changing and growing needs of IT customers, it's important for agency help desks to be able to share and transfer data. An enterprise-based help-desk system will result in increased cost savings and efficiencies by allowing for the exchange of trouble tickets among agencies, providing a monitoring element for common systems or networks, increasing the ability to engage in network-security monitoring, and coordinating all of these efforts through a Web interface that will provide information to users.

Child Support Enforcement Automated Management System

The Department of Revenue consistently searches for innovative strategies to improve delivery of child-support services to families. In addition, the department keeps pace with changes in federal requirements for improved performance, functionality, and reporting. State and federal demands create short- and long-term performance challenges when the tool available is a rigid mainframe computer system, which is operated by another state agency. An early feasibility study revealed that building another comprehensive technology solution would be complex and very costly to support, presenting another challenge to improving service delivery and performance.

The department solved this problem through interchangeable technology with a pay-as-you-go financial plan. The new Child Support Enforcement Automated Management System is expected to deliver significant results even in the early stages. The department projects that the system will increase collections by $735 million, reduce operating costs by approximately $24 million, and increase earnings by approximately $14 million over five fiscal years, beginning in fiscal year 2003–2004.

Business and Professions Online Licensing System

The Department of Business and Professional Regulation provides customer service to the nearly 1 million (1 out of 16) Floridians who must obtain licenses from the state of Florida. To increase efficiency, the agency engaged a private corporation to develop an online licensing system. This system will dramatically improve business operations, significantly enhance customer responsiveness, and centralize key customer-service functions. The project uses a licensing software system, Internet services, and a centralized service center.

With the new system, Floridians will be able to update license information 24 hours a day, 7 days a week by phone or on the Internet. They can also obtain a new license online. A reduction in forms and correspondence will dramatically decrease processing times. For example, the agency will have a single point of contact instead of 200 published phone numbers. Personnel will be cross-trained and gain skills in new areas. A customer-service agent will speed the interaction with customers, including "Web chat" and "co-browsing," where the customer-service agent can assist the customer in completing Internet transactions. These benefits reduce operational costs, improve efficiency, and provide for a more responsive agency.

Since implementing new technology in July 2001, this department reports that almost 477,000 phone calls were received at the Customer Contact Center as of June 2002. Of these calls, 177,000 were handled through customer self-service (Internet services or interactive voice response). The answer rate in the center is more than 95 percent compared to 66 percent before the new technology was implemented. In addition, 75,000 online accounts and more than 20,000 online renewals have been activated (representing 30 percent of those in the current renewal cycle). With these enhanced services, licensees and the general public will have instantaneous access to information that under the old system was difficult to retrieve. As a result, the public can make more informed decisions about the businesses and professionals it engages for services.

E-Procurement via MyFloridaMarketPlace

As part of my administration's vision to create a more efficient and effective government, Florida is embarking on an exciting initiative to design, build, and operate a Web-based procurement system. This new "e-procurement" system, named MyFloridaMarketPlace, is designed to streamline vendor interactions with state government agencies that purchase their goods and services. This new system will provide a user-friendly Internet portal to allow business owners to register, receive information on upcoming bids, post information on their products and services, and receive purchase orders electronically.

MyFloridaMarketPlace will provide a centralized source of procurement information for the Florida business community and enable vendors to communicate to a broader buying audience. Key benefits for vendors include

- *Single point of registration:* Vendors will register once, and their information will then be available to all buyers using the system.
- *State-of-the-art tools:* Electronic, Internet-based transactions will provide a consistent and more efficient way of doing business with the state.
- *Increased access to buying entities:* Registering with MyFloridaMarketPlace will provide vendors with access to all buyers using the system.
- *Enhanced economic-development opportunities for small business:* MyFloridaMarketPlace will enhance economic development opportunities for small business by increasing access to the "state" marketplace.
- *Reduction in administrative burden:* Using MyFloridaMarketPlace will reduce the administrative burdens of processing paper, remittance processing, and other paper-intensive procedures.

MyFloridaMarketPlace will be implemented in a phased approach starting in May of 2003. The Department of Management Services and the Department of Transportation will participate in the initial rollout. Subsequently, the system will be implemented in other executive branch agencies, then made available to public schools, universities, community colleges, and local governments. All purchases made by these agencies will be completed using MyFloridaMarketPlace.

CYBERSECURITY

Technology security for Florida's IT infrastructure was already under development when the events of September 11, 2001, occurred. Since that time, the importance of protecting the state's technology assets and information has risen to a new level. Working together with the legislature, we created the Office of Information Security to provide leadership and coordination for the following statewide activities: agency information-security audits, training for information-security managers, the use of firewalls and the security of various state systems, background checks on technology staff, enterprise-level IT security policies and procedures, and IT disaster-recovery plans. My most recent budget recommendations included funding for the continued implementation of this important initiative.

MOVING FORWARD

Florida is proud to be a leader in e-governance. Technology is a key component of efficient management in the information age, and our constituents expect service and convenience on par with what they have come to expect in the private-sector digital marketplace. We plan to continue embracing e-governance within the overall context of providing a smaller, more efficient government for all Floridians.

13

The District's Business Resource Center: The Best in E-Customer Service

Anthony A. Williams, Mayor of Washington, D.C.

When I took office as mayor of the District of Columbia in January of 1999, I was determined to join the mayors all over the country who have helped to make our cities places where people want to live and where businesses want to locate. In 1999, Washington was already a great city, rich in resources. Not just the home of the federal government, it was a place of beautiful, tree-lined neighborhoods, cultural attractions, historic architecture, and a talented, diverse population. Nevertheless, there were formidable obstacles to our urban renaissance. The District's declining services and much-publicized fiscal woes of the 1990s had driven residents away and undermined the confidence of businesses. We had to harness every resource to bring residents and businesses back, and we turned to technology, our newest resource, to help.

E-government has played a major role in our effort to bring people and businesses back to the District of Columbia. By offering residents and businesses a new way to obtain city information and services, at times and places that suit their convenience, e-government has contributed to the turnaround in customer service that is a hallmark of my administration. One of our most successful and innovative e-government initiatives is the District's two-year-old online Business Resource Center (BRC).

PROJECT SUMMARY: THE DISTRICT OF COLUMBIA'S ONLINE BUSINESS RESOURCE CENTER

The District of Columbia launched its online BRC (www.brc.dc.gov) in August 2001 to provide the District's 95,000 businesses with a one-stop shop for business information, business assistance, and online transaction processing. The BRC offers comprehensive resources for firms of all sizes and types—from the sole-proprietor nail salon to the nationwide nonprofit or Fortune 500 company.

THE ROAD TO THE BRC

Laying the Foundation

The District traveled a long road to the opening of the BRC. Four years ago, the District lacked the technological foundation to support a simple online transaction, much less a complex e-government initiative like the BRC. In fact, our technological resources were in disarray as the result of over a decade of disinvestment in information technology (IT). The District had 370 separate, unlinked, often redundant computer systems, few automated government processes, no wide-area network (WAN) for e-mail and Internet access, and an inventory of hopelessly outdated hardware and software. We had no online services, not even a website for basic government information.

Four years later, we have modernized hardware, software, and communications equipment, automated hundreds of previously manual functions, and built a citywide technology infrastructure, including state-of-the-art central data centers, a citywide e-mail system, a broad-bandwidth citywide WAN, and a central Web portal that is the gateway to single-agency and multiagency websites. In short, we have the robust technological foundation necessary to support the most powerful and innovative e-government initiatives. The first step in this transformation, and a vital first step on the road to the BRC, was a political one. For the first time, the District centralized management of technological resources and leadership of major technology initiatives with the creation of a single, cabinet-level agency, the Office of the Chief Technology Officer (OCTO). Centralizing technology management made it possible for the District to eliminate redundant IT resources and costs and to build a common citywide technology infrastructure for all 68 city agencies, including a central Web portal capable of hosting multiagency initiatives like the BRC.

Centralizing technology management was vital not only to building the technology infrastructure needed for e-government but also to providing the leadership necessary for broad multiagency initiatives. OCTO's implementing legislation authorizes it to manage District technological resources and charges the agency with delivering technology solutions for all District agencies. So, when we confront broad challenges, such as how to use technology to help bring businesses back to the District, OCTO leads the development of broad-based solutions.

Defining the Solution

Our challenge was to determine how to use technology to help improve the relationship between District government and the business community. To design the solution, we considered two broad questions:

- What do District agencies need to serve and regulate businesses more efficiently and effectively?
- What do our businesses need to prosper in the District?

To answer these questions, OCTO gathered representatives from relevant District agencies and a variety of local business groups, forming a broad-based partnership to design a comprehensive solution. District agencies identified an extensive list of needs that could be met, at least in part, through e-government.

The District's Department of Consumer and Regulatory Affairs (DCRA) is responsible for business registration and licensing, as well as for administering most of the city's business economic, health, and safety regulations—from rental housing codes to restaurant health ordinances. To encourage and expand compliance with licensing and registration requirements, DCRA wanted an online business-registration and business-licensing system that would make it fast and easy for businesses to understand these requirements and to fulfill as many of them as possible online. In addition, to help improve compliance with other regulatory requirements, DCRA wanted a one-stop shop that would present and organize compliance information in an accessible, easy-to-understand way.

The Office of Tax and Revenue (OTR) collects all District taxes, including business property and income taxes. OTR wanted to increase business tax compliance with a system that would make it easy for businesses to identify and track business tax requirements and make payments online. Like DCRA, OTR also wanted to encourage business registration to compile a more complete database of businesses that might owe taxes to the city.

The District's Office of Planning (OP) is responsible for urban planning and economic development. Like DCRA and OTR, OP also wanted to expand business registration so that it could identify the District's businesses and their locations to conduct effective planning to meet their needs.

The Office of Local Business Development is responsible for conducting outreach to local businesses, particularly small and disadvantaged businesses, to help them maximize participation in District contracting opportunities. The Office of Partnership and Grants Development (OPGD) is responsible for identifying opportunities for the District to participate in grant programs and public–private partnerships and for helping District agencies pursue those opportunities. These agencies wanted a new forum with a broad reach to publicize their initiatives.

Local business-development coalitions (including D.C. Agenda and D.C. Marketing), neighborhood groups (such as the Georgia Avenue Business Resource Center), academic centers (including Howard University), national interest groups (such as the National Association of Women Business Owners), and small-business owners throughout the city contributed to the development of the BRC. They agreed that businesses would benefit from online information about District licensing, tax, and regulatory requirements and contracting opportunities, and that an online transaction system would encourage businesses to meet regulatory requirements and pay business taxes. These groups also pointed out another critical need, particularly for the District's extensive small-business community, which was for basic information and assistance in all aspects of running a business.

Many new and small business owners have expertise in the goods and services they plan to offer but lack the basic business skills to transform this expertise into a profit-making enterprise. Few new or small business owners can afford to take the time to learn how to create a business plan, get financing, or keep the books. When OCTO launched planning efforts for the BRC (and, in fact, when the BRC opened in August 2001), no state or local government business website offered this kind of assistance. If the District could provide basic business help online, it would help businesses grow and prosper in our city, and help win back the business community's confidence in the District government.

Summary

Our multiagency, public–private planning effort identified the following broad components of a business website for the District:

- Clear and concise online information about District licensing, registration, regulatory, and tax requirements
- Online transaction processing for licensing, registration, and fee and tax payments with guidance to make transactions simple and fast
- Online information and tools to supply basic business expertise for firms of all types and sizes

PROJECT DESCRIPTION

The website that resulted from our broad-based planning efforts contained more than 3,000 pages of information, transactions, and business tools. I encourage you to visit www.brc.dc.gov and see it for yourself.

Needs-Based Gateway

The BRC is a gateway that guides firms through every process necessary to starting and running a business in the District. Its overall structure is needs based, on the theory that online government services are easiest to use and most likely to gain acceptance if they are geared to the needs of the user, rather than organized hierarchically.

A business owner or manager enters the BRC site either directly (www.brc.dc.gov) or through the District homepage (dc.gov), where the BRC can be reached via the link "Doing Business in DC." The BRC's home page offers three entrances to the site, each designed to fit a particular set of needs.

The "What Do You Want to Do" menu is aimed at first-time visitors and those who want to explore every resource the BRC has to offer. It provides a comprehensive list of links covering all events in the life cycle of a business. The menu identifies each business event and outlines the services the BRC provides in connection with that event.

The left navigation bar serves as a second gateway, designed for the visitor with a limited purpose, such as fulfilling licensure and tax obligations. This gateway links to a menu of four services: obtaining a business license, registering a business name, and filing and paying taxes.

The third gateway, "Market Information," is designed for business visitors who want to acquaint themselves with the District business environment. This gateway offers links to D.C.-specific information, including community development, city maps, lending institutions, local business-development assistance, and market facts and statistics.

Comprehensive Business Resources

Whichever gateway is chosen, the business owner gains access to a wealth of information, resource guides and links, online transactions, in-depth management tools, and downloadable forms. These resources include the following.

Guidance through the Entire Business Life Cycle

Consistent with its need-based orientation, the BRC's information resources include extensive tutorials organized according to the life cycle of a business. These tutorials guide the visitor step by step through all functions in the business life cycle, providing both generic business assistance and District-specific information for each phase in the cycle. These tutorials cover the following business functions, among others:

- Starting a business
  - —Choosing a business form (e.g., partnership, corporation)
  - —Deciding on a business structure
  - —Developing a business plan
  - —Obtaining a tax identification number
  - —Registering the business with the District
  - —Obtaining a certificate of occupancy
  - —Identifying the type of license required
  - —Registering the trade name of the business
  - —Applying for a business license
- Starting a nonprofit business
  - —Determining the federal 501(c) category for a particular type of business
  - —Establishing a nonprofit board of directors
  - —Developing nonprofit bylaws
- Financing a business
  - —Identifying and organizing financing resources
  - —Evaluating resources
  - —Obtaining additional resources, including loans, grants, venture capital, and public equity financing
  - —Obtaining a credit report
  - —Completing six key financial statements
- Continuing a business in the District
  - —Filing required reports with the District
  - —Renewing business licenses
  - —Filing franchise tax returns
- Relocating a business in the District
  - —Obtaining business-relocation assistance from local and national sources
  - —Obtaining market-research statistics
  - —Taking advantage of the wide variety of incentives to locate a business in the District and in special tax-favored enterprise zones within the city
- Dissolving a business
  - —Filing the articles of dissolution specific to the business type

Many of these tutorials draw on information from sources outside the District, such as the federal Small Business Administration (SBA), Department of Housing and Urban Development, and Internal Revenue Service; private credit-reporting agencies; and local and national business-development groups such as the Digital Capital Alliance, the Greater Washington Board of Trade, and the U.S. Chamber of Commerce. All source identifications provide links to explanations and the homepage of the source.

Resource Links and Guides

The BRC ensures that a current or prospective business proprietor has access to, and guidance through, virtually every business resource available in the District, including the following, among others:

- How to obtain bank loans from local lending institutions, including contact information for and site links to over 20 local lenders, as well as a step-by-step guide to the loan process and developing an effective loan presentation
- How to initiate a public stock offering, consistent with applicable federal regulations
- How to obtain startup and venture capital using the resources of the National Business Incubation Association
- How to obtain financial assistance from the SBA
- How to participate in DC Business Connections, a local business-outreach program
- How to obtain land-development assistance and bond financing through the National Capital Revitalization Corporation
- How to take advantage of District and federal tax and development incentives, such as Community Development Block Grants, technology-oriented incentives, housing-development assistance, and employment-training tax credits
- How to participate in local business networks such as the Digital Capital Alliance, the Greater Washington Board of Trade, and the Chamber of Commerce
- How to do business with the District government, including guidelines on how to qualify as a District contractor and how to navigate District procurement procedures, as well as a searchable index of all contracting opportunities available with the District government

Online Transaction Processing

The BRC, either directly or through links to the District's online eTaxpayer Service Center, offers online transaction and payment processing for virtually all transactions a business needs to conduct with the District. Online transactions and payments include the following:

- Business registration
- Registration-fee payments
- Business-name registration
- Obtaining a business license
- License renewal

- License-fee payment
- Uniform Commercial Code filings
- IRS employer identification number application
- Business tax registration
- Business income-tax payments
- Franchise-tax payments
- Real-property-tax payments

Payments are processed using a secure payment engine. A recent comprehensive revamping of the District's entire Web portal redesigned all transactional applications, including those of the BRC, to ensure that all essential details about a particular transaction were provided; the information was clear and free of "bureaucratese"; and possible questions and ambiguities were addressed through definitions, links, and pop-ups.

Most importantly, the application redesign restructured transactional applications to let visitors determine at the outset whether they are eligible to conduct the transaction online, then to lead visitors through each transaction using wizard technology. The wizard-based methodology provides a step-by-step outline of each transaction on the application's top page and numbers each successive step so that the visitor always knows how many steps remain in the transaction.

The path through each transaction also allows the visitor to download forms so that if he or she is ineligible to conduct the transaction online or wishes to complete one of the few transactions that we don't offer online, the visitor can save time on an in-person visit by completing forms in advance. At the end of each transaction, the visitor may also download summaries of the other compliance requirements that apply to his or her particular type of business.

Management Tools and Online Consulting

The BRC takes a giant step beyond most e-government business sites by offering business owners a variety of how-to's and management tools. These services are tailored especially for sole proprietorships and small businesses, which predominate in the District, but also offer useful management aids for businesses of any size. These tools include the following:

- A complete set of instructions for preparing an effective business-loan presentation
- Numerous spreadsheets—complete with embedded calculation formulas—to help businesses identify and calculate financial resources
- Spreadsheets, including embedded formulas, for the six basic financial statements (e.g., balance sheet, income statement, statement of uses and sources)

- Side-by-side comparisons to aid decision making on subjects such as which business form to choose and which financing option to select
- Additional comparative evaluation tools that identify the advantages and disadvantages of a variety of key business choices
- A step-by-step guide to the creation of a business plan (provided separately for for-profit companies and nonprofits)
- A step-by-step guide to the creation of a marketing plan
- Checklists that summarize numerous requirements and functions, from starting a business to complying with various licensing and tax requirements
- A consolidated timeline of all required business filings and payments (e.g., registrations, licenses, and fees) for each business sector and structure, available in two views—schedule and calendar

Together, the BRC's 3,000-plus pages of online information, resource links, transaction processing, tutorials, and management tools provide businesses of all sizes far more than mere convenience. The BRC is the equivalent of a multifaceted management-consulting team, including a business strategist, an accountant, a marketing consultant, a District procurement officer, and an economic-development and economic-planning expert.

Help Line

No online service can be all things to all people or anticipate every possible question a site visitor may have. In addition, recent studies of automated services, including online services and other applications like automated store checkout, reveal that customer acceptance grows more rapidly if consumers know that assistance from a real, live person is close at hand. Accordingly, we support the BRC with a telephone help line that's available during business hours.

Translation

Washington, D.C., is one of the most cosmopolitan cities in the world, with fast-growing communities of residents born in Europe, Asia, Africa, and South America. Many of these residents, and the numerous small-business owners among them, speak English as a second language. Our comprehensive District Web-portal-redesign effort added translation services for all sites, including the BRC. To avoid the kinds of translation gaffes that can lose hundreds of customers with one inappropriate phrase, we used native speakers to screen machine-translation services and installed only those that withstood rigorous scrutiny. The BRC now offers machine translation of all website content in Dutch, French, German, Greek, Italian, Portuguese, and

Spanish. We'll continue to evaluate new translation products as they mature but will add only those languages that meet our tough "native-speaker" test.

Outreach and Assistance Program

As critical to the success of any e-government initiative as the quality of the site itself are two basics of customer service and e-government: awareness of the initiative and Internet access. Real Internet access means not only access to a computer with Internet service but also accessibility of the site itself for handicapped residents. To ensure awareness, access, and handicapped accessibility, the BRC is Section 508–compliant and is supported by a multifaceted outreach and assistance program.

Several of the District agencies that collaborated in developing the BRC—the Department of Consumer and Regulatory Affairs, the Office of the Chief Technology Officer, the Office of Planning, and the Office of Tax and Revenue—conduct 16 outreach workshops per calendar quarter, 2 in each of the District's eight wards. These workshops inform residents about the BRC, demonstrate how to use it, and identify all of the free Internet access sites in the ward. In the near future, workshop leaders will distribute at each workshop a comprehensive list of all free Internet access sites in the city.

In addition, the BRC offers its own free Internet access site, an office maintained by the OPGD, which business owners and managers can use during business hours. Because the District's business community includes a sizeable sector of small, nonprofit businesses—including many startups and others chronically in need of resources—our Internet center is reserved for use by nonprofit enterprises.

The BRC also offers an online newsletter, the *BRC Alert*, to help businesses stay abreast of important developments, such as changes in tax and business-licensure laws, new development incentives, and new District contracting opportunities. For example, the most recent issue of the *BRC Alert* (Volume 2, Issue 7, July 1, 2003) informs businesses about ten hot topics, including an upcoming small/disadvantaged business conference, new funding for neighborhood-improvement activities, and the District's initiative to attract new residents.

Customer Evaluation

The BRC, like all of our e-government initiatives, is aimed most broadly at improving customer service to the District's business community. The only way to be sure we're actually improving customer service is to ask our customers. We ask our BRC customers to answer that question through the "Feedback" feature of the District Web portal. The feedback option is an important vehicle for the continuous quality improvement (CQI) of the BRC.

We've found that site visitors answer early and often, typically telling us they're pleased with the site, but often advising us on how to improve it if they're not. Customer suggestions have alerted us to some technical imperfections and content problems that we might not have discovered otherwise.

PROJECT EVALUATION

We consider the BRC to be a highly successful e-government initiative. Its success is measured by the benefits it delivers to our business community, by its quantitative and nonquantitative benefits for our own agencies, and even by the judgment of our peers.

Benefits for Businesses

The BRC offers dramatic benefits for the District's 95,000 businesses:

- *Convenience:* by replacing personal visits to business-licensing, tax-collection, and grants agencies with Web access at the time and place of the customer's choice
- *Simplicity:* by distilling complex business regulations, issued by multiple agencies, into easily understandable descriptions and examples, all available from a single source
- *Speed:* by providing all necessary forms so that customers who are ineligible for online transactions can complete the forms ahead of time and speed their in-person visits
- *Resources and expertise:* by providing all businesses with the equivalent of a complete, multidisciplinary management team, giving small businesses guidance and support they could never obtain otherwise and offering even the largest companies a unique one-stop shop to meet all needs related to doing business in or with the District
- *Risk reduction:* by helping businesses to identify, track, and meet license and tax requirements and deadlines, thereby reducing the risk of noncompliance and associated penalties

Businesses' evaluations of the site, in response to the "Feedback" feature, overwhelmingly express appreciation for these benefits.

Benefits for Government

For many District agencies, the BRC provides substantial convenience and savings, helps enhance compliance, and extends community-outreach efforts.

Since the BRC went live, the volume of visits and telephone calls to service centers operated by the District's business licensing and tax agencies has dropped substantially. As a result, several agencies have reduced their customer-service positions significantly. In addition, the BRC serves as an online training and reference resource for customer-service employees, providing real-time, up-to-date information that's faster and easier to use than hardcopy manuals or classroom training courses. Online, at-your-fingertips training, provided via the BRC, improves the speed and accuracy of employee customer service and allows the agencies to reduce costs for training manuals and seminars.

In addition, by providing businesses a one-stop shop for tax and regulatory compliance information, the BRC enhances the compliance-enforcement efforts of our tax and regulatory agencies. For our planning, business-partnership, and small-/disadvantaged-business liaison agencies, the BRC creates a forum that extends the scope of their outreach efforts exponentially.

Other District agencies that receive business-related inquiries save time and resources, as well as dramatically improving their customer service, by placing their agency-specific business information on the BRC. To date, 13 of the District's nearly 70 agencies and instrumentalities are, or plan to be, represented on the BRC, and this number will grow substantially as the BRC matures. In addition, the BRC has helped to standardize the design and architecture of individual agency sites that link to it, thereby reducing site-development times and costs.

Some, although certainly not all, of these benefits for government can be captured in a return-on-investment (ROI) analysis. Because the BRC has been open for business for less than two years, we've conducted only a simplified and preliminary ROI analysis, but even this abbreviated evaluation shows significant savings. This analysis is as follows.

The District's total investment to design, build, maintain, and support the BRC has been approximately $1 million. The BRC has permitted the District's business-licensing, tax-collection, and grants agencies to eliminate over 30 customer-service positions that cost approximately $60,000 per year each in salaries, benefits, facilities, and equipment. Thus, the BRC yields annual recurring savings of $60,000 × 30 = $1.8 million. The annual cost to support, maintain, and enhance the BRC is approximately $166,000. Thus, the annual recurring savings, minus maintenance costs, yield an ongoing ROI of 163.4 percent (($1.8 million minus $166,000) ÷ $1 million = $1,634,000).

Peer Evaluation

One of the most valuable sources of evaluation for any government technology initiative is the judgment of peers in other governments. We've been honored with a strong vote of confidence from our peers across the nation: in 2002, the National Association of State Chief Information Officers (NASCIO) chose the BRC for its annual recognition award for excellence in government-to-business initiatives.

NEXT STEPS

We're proud of the BRC, but it's still a work in progress. As part of our CQI efforts, we are continuing to introduce enhancements to the site. In the next phase of the BRC, the District will do the following:

- Expand benefits in convenience and speed by adding new online transactions
- Enlarge the scope of information available on the site by encouraging more District agencies to be represented there
- Reach out to a broader group of the District's non-English-speaking businesses by adding translations as more high-quality machine translated languages become available
- Extend outreach to bridge the digital divide with our "City of Access" initiative, compiling a database and distributing lists of all sites in the District where free Internet access is available

REPLICATION

So, you want to build your own BRC? Go for it! Some jurisdictions, such as the state of Delaware, have already used our site as a model for expanded business sites, and the BRC is an easy model to follow. Other state and local governments can replicate the BRC's structure, approach, content, resources, and wizard methodology. Most of the management-consulting content and tools—such as financial spreadsheets, decision-making aids, and business- and marketing-plan guides—are generic in applicability and can simply be "lifted" from the District's BRC. Other tools, such as compliance calendars, are readily adaptable in concept and format. Similarly, our wizard technology and online transaction technology can be adapted easily to the licensing processes and tax and licensing transactions of other jurisdictions. In concept and framework, the critical outreach component can be duplicated as well.

Other jurisdictions can maximize the successes of their own BRCs by following these principles, which were key to the District's BRC success:

- *Centralize technology.* Critical to the success of our BRC was the multi-agency collaboration in its design and planning. One of the greatest obstacles you may face in launching your own BRC getting all your business-facing agencies to work together. There may be different agendas: for example, your licensing or taxing agency may want a narrowly focused project that can be launched quickly to increase compliance as soon as possible, while your economic-development agency may prefer a rich site that showcases the business-friendly climate of your city but takes longer to build. There may be conflicts as to how much each participating agency is willing to invest in the project. A central technology agency—as the only participant with no direct business stake in the project's design and with a mission to provide technology solutions equally to all other agencies—can serve as a neutral leader and arbiter of conflicts, helping to establish and maintain the multiagency collaboration that's essential to success.

- *Cast a wide net.* Invite all stakeholders—within and beyond government—to share in the goal before any development occurs. Work hard to maintain their active involvement throughout the development process.
- *Take your time.* Plan a development period of 12 to 18 months to ensure that all jurisdiction-specific compliance information is accurate, complete, and understandable and that all online transactions work consistently.
- *Buy the Cadillac.* Don't skimp on technology. Invest in best-in-class technologies like Ask Jeeves to make the site as dynamic, fast, and user friendly as possible; as our brief ROI analysis shows, your investment will pay off. (Here again, a central technology agency whose mission includes identifying the best technology solutions available can be invaluable.)
- *Maintain, maintain, maintain.* Invest in maintenance and support to ensure that the site continues to meet the high user expectations that its innovative concept and broad resources will generate at the outset.
- *Help out.* Be sure to heed the research showing that consumers want automated applications with a human touch. Incorporate a help line, staff it with the best people you can find, and invest in regular training to keep their skills and customer-service focus sharp.
- *Reach out.* Include translation from the beginning. Even though you may have only a small foreign-born business community today, demographic trends guarantee that community will grow. Test your translation products on native speakers before you buy them.
- *Get out.* Remember that an outreach program that features workshops in the community is vital to reach those businesses most in need of a BRC—the smallest firms and those operated by non-English speakers and managers without Internet access or Internet savvy. Incorporate planning for the outreach program into initial project planning so that

the outreach component is set to go on your launch date and adequately funded into the future.

- *Get a reality check.* Be sure to include a "Feedback" feature so you can get the evaluations that matter most—those of your customers.

CONCLUSION: DO TRY THIS AT HOME

Virtually any jurisdiction can benefit from a one-stop shop e-government business center. With modest funds, a spirit of collaboration, and an effective technology agency, any jurisdiction can build one. So, by all means, do try this at home! As far as we're concerned, the more copycats, the better.

Part IV

IMPROVING SERVICE DELIVERY TO THE PUBLIC

14

Digital Democracy in Alaska

Tony Knowles, Governor of Alaska,
and Fran Ulmer, Lieutenant Governor of Alaska

Alaskans like to boast that if Alaska were cut in half, Texas would be the third largest state. Simply put, we are huge.

The diversity and immense size of our landmass is a source of pride for us, but it is also a constant challenge. Because Alaska is so large (one-fifth the size of the lower 48 states combined) and our population relatively small (just over 600,000 people) we have to deliver services over wide areas without the economies of scale that can defray those costs in smaller states with larger populations.

And in the chief role of government—the delivery of services—the challenge is perhaps most daunting. How can we assure the delivery of the most basic and essential state services—education, health care, jobs, economic growth, and even matters as mundane as the registration of motor vehicles—given the immense area we must cover and the limited resources available?

The journey to answer this question took Alaska to the forefront of a new technological frontier: digital democracy.

BACK TO THE FUTURE

When we were elected as governor and lieutenant governor of Alaska in 1994, only three state agencies had websites. But Alaska had a well-deserved reputation for the innovative use of technology to connect Alaskans across its vast distances.

We have come a long way in distance delivery from 1925, when diphtheria threatened remote villages in the northwest Arctic, and Alaskans responded with the best available technology at the time—dog sleds—to relay medicine to Nome. This canine-based network for distance delivery of health services is commemorated today in the annual 1,000-mile Iditarod Sled Dog Race.

While World War II brought many improvements in communications to Alaska, our first experience in modern telecommunications came in the form of a cold war–era Air Force communications system. Called the "White Alice" system, this network of huge dish antennas placed on mountaintops and other remote sites provided then state-of-the-art communications, until it was replaced by satellite technology in the late 1970s.

The 1970s also brought great change in how Alaskans communicated with each other. At that time, the state and a telecommunications company installed small satellite earth stations in over 200 communities across Alaska. For the first time, dozens of villages had basic telephone service, which in some cases consisted of just a single phone per village and a dedicated emergency and health channel.

Public radio and television filled communications needs, especially in outlying bush communities. The Federal Communications Commission (FCC) gave special approval to allow public radio stations in outlying communities to relay personal messages. Called the "tundra telegraph" or the "muskeg messenger," this service remains a basic means for Alaskans in remote corners of the state to relay personal messages, emergency information, and, occasionally, gossip.

At about the same time, Alaska received special licensing from the FCC to install low-power television in rural Alaska. The first stations were installed in the remote Aleutian Islands and received programming by videotapes shipped from Anchorage. Thus was born the Rural Alaska Television Network (RATNET), which later incorporated satellite technology to cover most of rural Alaska with a combination of live and tape-delayed network programming. Piggybacking on RATNET's success, the state later introduced the first distance-delivery education system in the nation.

Access to state government remained a challenge with Alaska's capital located hundreds of miles and two time zones away from the centers of the state's population. Federal action in 1983 helped set the clocks straight by placing most of Alaska's population into a single time zone, but distance remained a challenge. Using a network of computers and dedicated telephone lines, the state opened a series of Legislative Information Offices that could provide copies of state reports and pending bills and allow residents to testify on legislation from hundreds of miles away, something no other state was doing at the time.

Alaska in the 1970s was at the forefront of delivering services to citizens using the most advanced technology of the day. People were able to receive information, learn, and communicate back to state government and each other using a combination of radio, television, and telephone. Alaska was a high-tech place to be.

But that didn't last.

SEEING RED

Despite the innovation of the previous decade, by the mid-1980s Alaska faced an economic recession and had fallen behind the information technology curve. Having provided basic services, Alaska was not keeping pace with rapid growth in microprocessor technology and software.

As computer manufacturers leapfrogged from 286s to 386s to 486s and began sketching the roadmap for the Internet, the network of computers linking Legislative Information Offices seemed suddenly old-fashioned. The satellite connections that had miraculously delivered dial tone to remote villages only ten years earlier quickly became outdated. Satellite delays of many seconds and distracting echoes made telephone conversations a chore.

Fortunately, Alaska benefited from a few visionaries who realized the policy implications of developing technology and telecommunications. Among these was a former Fairbanks mayor, state representative, and lieutenant governor, H. A. "Red" Boucher.

Now 80 years young, Red entered the telecommunications field as a U.S. Navy semaphore signaler on the USS *Enterprise* during the Battle of Midway. Now, he is a tireless advocate of wireless communications and networking, hosts a technology TV talk show, works as a consultant to a major computer company, and has joined forces with educators to advance the teaching of technology to children.

From the standpoint of "digital democracy," Red made his biggest contribution as the main architect and advocate of the Telecommunications Information Council (TIC).

TIC TAC TOE

In the mid-1980s, Red Boucher was concerned that rapidly evolving telecommunications technology had no policy focus and no official advocate in the state government. His solution was to sponsor a bill that created the TIC, which would act as the chief policymaking body for technology in the state of Alaska. Essentially, the TIC would serve as Alaska's chief information officer (CIO).

Chaired by the governor, the TIC consisted of each executive-branch department commissioner, a member from each house of the legislature, and a public member. The 1987 legislation that created the TIC gave it broad powers in determining policy in telecommunications and information technology in state government.

At first, the TIC dealt with issues concerning statewide architecture and made recommendations about the importance of planning, affordability, cost effectiveness, user friendliness, public accessibility, and other technology service areas. But these recommendations were not actively pursued, and the TIC fell into relative inactivity.

REVITALIZATION

Although it was inactive when we took office in 1994, the TIC offered an opportunity to further the use of telecommunications and information technology to serve our citizens. Here was a body that already had statutory authority and provided an opportunity for all departments to have a voice in technology projects and initiatives.

But the council needed a strong and active chairperson who could concentrate on the growing number of technology issues facing the world of the mid-1990s. Lt. Gov. Ulmer stepped up to the challenge and took the reins at the TIC, providing direction, organization, and staff. Her chief of staff at the time, John Lindback, was also an enthusiastic participant and leader of the TIC as he served as chair of its Technical Advisory Committee (TAC). The TAC successfully brought the tech-savvy people within state government into the process. Their buy-in to the goals of policymakers, along with their innovative ideas and expertise, were essential to the success of the project.

With the policy structure and authority already in place, Alaska was ready to take advantage of new opportunities. One of those opportunities began as a severe threat to one of the mainstays of Alaska's telecommunications services.

TAKING A SIP, BUILDING AN ARC

The mid-1990s were a time of fiscal uncertainty for Alaska, with state revenues hit by declining oil production and wildly fluctuating oil prices. In response, the state legislature sought to tighten state spending and proposed steep cutbacks for many state services, including the Alaska Public Broadcasting Service (APBS) and RATNET. During the next few years, overall state support for public television and radio was reduced by 41 percent, and funding for rural television was cut by 71 percent.

Cuts of this depth were a crippling blow to the system and a potentially lethal blow to a service that had been a valuable information link for many thousands of Alaskans. Thanks to the active leadership provided by the TIC and the lieutenant governor's office, the dedication of talented individuals from both state government and the private sector, and some lucky timing, this story became a tale of "turning lemons into lemonade."

Digital satellite delivery was just coming online and was a much more cost-efficient way to transmit programming. Technology had caught up with the service Alaska was trying to provide. The result was the Satellite Interconnection Project (SIP), funded by the state of Alaska and the federal government to convert the state-supported broadcast services to cost-efficient digital satellite delivery.

Through the SIP, public radio stations share regional and statewide channels through a system of satellite interconnections, including channels from Alaska's Interior station group, the Alaska Public Radio Network, and ÇoastAlaska, including stations within the southeastern panhandle.

On the television side of the picture, we were facing the loss of RATNET, one of the most unique broadcasting services in the world. RATNET reached homes and schools in hundreds of rural villages that otherwise could feel very remote indeed.

The product that evolved is truly remarkable today as it delivers four times the content for less money and is one of the cornerstones of Alaska's delivery of digital democracy to citizens.

First, the state's four public television stations, to meet the programming needs of the statewide audience, formed the APBS. Through the cooperation of APBS stations, four television channels were developed:

- Alaska One, the statewide public television service, originating at KUAC, Fairbanks
- Alaska Two, or Gavel to Gavel, C-SPAN-style coverage of state legislative sessions and committee hearings produced by KTOO, Juneau
- Alaska Three, a cooperative operation between the University of Alaska and the state Department of Education and Early Development, designed to transmit distance-delivery coursework
- Alaska Four, the Alaska Rural Communications Service (ARCS)

ARCS became the replacement for RATNET but concentrates more on the offerings of public television than its predecessor. Commercial programming is also offered, such as sports and state news. It is still the way most rural Alaskans watch TV.

All of these services are extremely important to Alaskans, but in the area of digital democracy, none is more so than Alaska Two, or Gavel to Gavel. This channel provides C-Span-style coverage of the 120 days of the Alaska State legislature, broadcasting committee hearings, floor sessions, and additional interview shows with legislators and policymakers. It is one of the vital ways that Alaska keeps its widely dispersed citizenry informed about, and connected with, the daily developments in the legislature.

Gavel to Gavel has also become an essential tool for people within state government or anyone else who directly interacts with the legislature. Many state offices have cable connections so that hearings can be observed or floor votes tracked. Schedules are posted onscreen between programming so that viewers can keep up with what is happening.

Like so many other services born of technology, it is hard to imagine what life was like before it. And there are no signs of the service's slowing down; streaming video of legislative action on the Web is to be fully operational later this year.

But we are getting ahead of ourselves.

First, we need to tell the story of how Alaska ended up with one of the most robust state websites in the nation.

A LONG, LONG TIME AGO, IN A GALAXY FAR, FAR AWAY . . .

It seems ages ago—before Netscape, dot-coms, dot-bombs, iMacs, iPods, and Internet Explorer—that the word "streaming" had something to do with a river, as did "Amazon." It was 1994, and in Alaska some of the first state-agency websites were beginning to take baby steps. The Departments of Fish and Game and of Transportation had basic websites that featured some press releases, photos, information about the departments, and some basic contact information.

When we took office in late 1994, we saw the Internet as an efficient way to provide our citizens with the information they needed. We believed Alaskans would respond to this new technology as a means of staying connected to government and to each other. That hunch has been confirmed—in a 2001 U.S. Department of Commerce study, Alaska ranks as the second highest state in personal computer use and Internet connectivity per capita.

We made the decision to require every state department and division to have a "Web presence." We left the term broadly defined so that agencies ready to move forward could, but departments not yet up to speed on this new technology would not be unduly burdened. We accomplished this without additional budgets or personnel. Existing employees took on the new task with enthusiasm and began building www.state.ak.us. The technical side of hosting the site fell to our Department of Administration's Information Technology Group (ITG), which set up a server designed to host all departmental websites at no additional cost to agencies.

Soon the site began filling up—with press releases, educational information, speeches, photos, and other static information that people commonly request from state government. But there was very little that was dynamic on the pages. In the beginning, it contained only outflowing information with no online business transactions or two-way communications.

That changed when we took the Division of Motor Vehicles (DMV) online.

GET ONLINE, NOT IN LINE

Once we had the beginnings of a good informational website, the TIC began examining what else could be done with this tool. The conclusion: the real value of the Internet would come when people could actually do business online. But with what agencies would this service be most appreciated? Wherever there are long lines, was the response. It is not surprising that the first place we saw the biggest line was at one of government's most notorious long-line agencies: the DMV.

Our first step was to move the DMV from the Department of Public Safety to the Department of Administration. Having DMV in the same department as the ITG made coordination easier. Within a few months, the hard work of a vendor partner and many people from both divisions came to fruition, and we implemented a vehicle-registration renewal and personalized-license plate website with an interactive-voice-response phone system that is still in place today. The results were dramatic.

Our cost per transaction for registration renewal went from about $9 to less than a dollar. Lines at DMV locations across the state thinned out. Staff time was devoted to working with citizens on more complicated transactions and problems. The DMV office became the place people went only if they could not get their business done online.

Alaska's mantra became "Get online, not in line," and we looked for similar opportunities elsewhere. Today, you can go online to Alaska's WebMart to access directly a variety of state services: to get a state business license or a hunting and fishing license, or to check on state-park cabin availability, child-support payments, or the status of your student loan. All of these services and more are just a mouse click away.

ROADMAP

Before Alaska could design and implement all of those subsequent services, we needed a roadmap. Alaska began crafting a telecommunications and information technology plan in March 1996.

Our goal was to keep it simple, but we also brought in as many people as we could. The final plan was the result of the work of nine internal multidisciplinary task forces of the best technical and policy people in state government. We held public hearings across the state. The final plan—the roadmap we needed—included 121 guidelines and recommendations for the future of information technology in Alaska.

Many of those recommendations profoundly changed the way we do business. As a guiding principle, the plan foresaw a fundamental shift in customer service, where citizens can directly access information without having to go though a specific agency. In many cases, those are available today; through our Webmart transaction portal, citizens can access services without having to know which division or department provides them. This is a step beyond each individual agency's offering its licensing and information online; it makes state government more accessible and more responsive to the needs of the public.

There were also specific recommendations, such as having everyone in state government reachable through e-mail. Striving to achieve that goal brought us to an aggressive stance in implementing an enterprise e-mail system.

YOU'VE GOT MAIL

The TIC plan mandated e-mail for all employees, and the TIC determined that there were no unique needs for agencies when it came to e-mail. Some basic principles apply to all users, such as the need for e-mail delivery, attachment capabilities, and an address that makes sense and adheres to a standard. The TIC assigned a committee to the task of designing an e-mail system that would meet these common needs and could be easily and efficiently managed with a relatively small staff. Today, a three-person staff administers the entire system.

Not only has a state e-mail system enhanced communications between and within agencies, but it has become an invaluable tool for communicating directly with citizens. From the top to the bottom of state government, citizens can now communicate with state policymakers and employees in a very personal, direct, and immediate way.

We believe that all state employees work for the people of Alaska, and members of the public should be able to reach their employees whenever they need to. The e-mail address and phone number of every state employee are listed in a statewide directory published on our state website under a "Whitepages" section. You can even try "Tony Knowles" and "Fran Ulmer," and rest assured, we will get the e-mail and your message will get through.

The foundation of democracy is access, and in the digital age, that means access through the digital medium. This is digital democracy in a very real sense, and Alaskans are not shy about using it.

GET A JOB

Another major project was to move the entire state personnel system online. Called "Workplace Alaska," it is another example of the best of what the digital world can bring to government business. It allows the public to work from home or a public library to search for a job, look up pay scales and job requirements, and submit an application. Our system allows you to store a resume and apply for multiple jobs by referring to the same resume, in addition to providing any other function you would normally be able to get by visiting a personnel office.

It is faster and more convenient than any in-person service ever could be. And it helps us do our jobs more efficiently. The system that Workplace

Alaska replaced was antiquated beyond description. We get many compliments from the people who use this system. They say it makes getting a job with Alaska easier—and we like that.

TAKE NOTICE

Another key example of how we are striving to connect citizens to state government is a service called "Online Public Notice." The idea was to take all of the state information that ends up buried in the newspaper legal notices and put it online—in a searchable, highly accessible database that people can use in the way that is most useful to them. Those notices include procurements, agency meetings, proposed and adopted regulations, grants, boards and commissions announcements, and other public notices.

These notices had been published in a weekly *Administrative Journal* printed by the lieutenant governor's office. This task was time-consuming, costly, and reached a limited audience. Our goal was to have enough online access and use to justify ending the printing of the *Administrative Journal*. The response has been impressive. From a journal that had just over 100 subscribers, we now have a website that gets thousands of users a week. In just over two years, we have gotten close to 200,000 unique users, and those numbers continue to grow. As a result, we stopped printing the *Administrative Journal* and haven't heard any complaints.

This is another clear example of how the state used technology to bring Alaskans into the decision-making process of government. We now reach citizens who might not have otherwise known about state government activities that could have a direct impact on their lives. With this system, people can look up projects all over the state or zero in on their community or region. They can see where state road construction is planned, where a new school is going to be built, or where and when a public meeting will be held in their area.

The system also has an automatic archive feature that locks the document after an assigned expiration date. After that date, the document is archived for historical use and can never be changed.

We think it is pretty slick. It is using technology to make democracy more effective. That is exciting.

And when it comes to democracy, what is more important than voting? Perhaps one thing: accurate voting, and here, too, technology has helped Alaska maintain one of the most efficient and accurate voting systems in the nation.

OPTICAL-SCAN BALLOTS: THE ANTICHAD

When it comes to election night, compiling the results from Alaska's 451 far-flung precincts can produce nail-biters that last days or weeks. There are election-night legends about election returns ending up at a remote bush airstrip for days or weeks or disappearing altogether under a snowdrift, only to be found during the spring thaw. These are perhaps somewhat apocryphal stories, but long election-night delays were the reality, with final results for many races dragging out for days as ballots were counted and recounted in Alaska's notoriously frequent close races.

Accurate and timely elections are a basic principle of modern democracies, and we saw a technological solution to Alaska's problem. We adopted an optical-scanning ballot-tabulation technology that combines the best of old and new technology: a combination of a bubble-sheet ballot with an optical scanner and a basic telephone modem.

The ballot looks like the standardized test answer sheets we have all used in school. You fill in circles with a pen or pencil next to your ballot choice. The optical-scanning machine, which looks much like a small copier, draws the ballot into its slot and instantly tallies the results. If there is an overvote or some other mistake, then the ballot is rejected instantly, and the voter gets a new ballot. This avoids many of the problems that plagued several other states during the 2000 national election. At the end of the night, all of the machines call a central computer, which tallies the statewide totals.

In the 1998 election, the first in which this system was used in Alaska, the wait for election night results—which previously took four to five hours or lasted into the next day—lasted only about 20 minutes. All but a very few results from outlying communities were counted. Not only is the system fast, but it is extremely accurate. This straightforward use of technology strengthens public confidence in the elections system.

FUTURESPEAK

We are now on the threshold of a whole new host of services. We are working to improve our enterprisewide directory structure so that our online delivery will be more seamless. We are working on an enterprise portal that will allow for secure transactions across agency boundaries, coordinated digital signatures, and secure logins.

Streaming video of Gavel to Gavel is continuing this year, with a full slate of committee meetings and floor sessions. This year, when we announced our proposed budget, all of the information was immediately available to the public on our website so that people could quickly find detailed information on proposed capital projects in their community. We even stream the annual Holiday Open House—an event at which we welcome thousands of citizens to the Governor's House to share holiday treats and entertainment. This year another 1,000 Alaskans joined the festivities through our website.

We are updating our information technology plan and have recently negotiated a partnering plan to deliver telecommunications in a more robust environment for state government. Furthermore, we are looking to expand Online Public Notices to include statewide press releases, and we are always looking to provide new services that can put people online instead of in line.

While we recognize that this is just the beginning of online technology, the possibilities for its use are seemingly endless, and the opportunities ahead are full of potential. We are proud of what we have accomplished and of the recognition that Alaska received in 2001 as the state that provides its citizens with the best service in digital democracy. But we know that we can always do better and that digital access is not equally available or affordable throughout the state.

We have worked hard to bring affordable Internet access to rural Alaska. In 2001, we asked for and were granted a waiver by the FCC to allow Alaskans in communities with no local dial-up or toll-free Internet access the right to use, during nonschool hours, telecommunications services currently provided to schools and libraries through the federal E-Rate program. This will allow rural Alaskans access to the Internet without paying hundreds of dollars each month for that access.

DIGITAL DEMOCRACY IN ALASKA

We have discussed some of the projects and strategies that have made Alaska one of the top states in bringing democracy to citizens by using the latest technologies. Our success in this area is a result of our rich history of using technology, our ability to adapt to quickly changing environments, and Alaskans' innovative and independent spirit.

The challenge of reaching across Alaska's tremendous distances to serve a relatively small and dispersed population means that we have the most to gain from technology and the most to lose by neglecting it. It is our continuing goal to use technology to erase distance as a barrier in our state.

We do not believe that there is ever only one specific technological solution to any given issue. The most important concept is having a solid commitment to use whatever means are most appropriate to connect citizens to their government.

Democracy is not guaranteed. If we are not diligent stewards of democracy, it can slip away bit by bit. The use of innovative technology is just one more way we can assure that citizens get the information they need to participate actively in our democracy. This is what will strengthen their connection and commitment to the principles of democracy. And it is just one more way that we, as elected officials, can strive to uphold our promise to our citizens that their government will be of the people, by the people, and for the people.

15

The Evolution of E-Government in Pennsylvania

Ed Rendell, Governor of Pennsylvania

We live in a period of tremendous change. While 20 years are but a blink in the history of our planet, the last 20 years have ushered in an unprecedented era of information availability—a period often referred to as the information age. Today, information is available to us on almost any topic imaginable via the Internet. Events that occur in Spain, Thailand, and Brazil are known across the globe almost instantaneously.

This information age is also changing the manner in which humans learn. Students in a rural school district in Pennsylvania can register for college-level courses at hundreds of universities online. This advancement in technology over the past 20 years is altering the way we learn, the way we act, and the way we communicate. In fact, this information explosion is ushering in a "borderless society." The recent explosion of service-sector jobs moving off shore to other nations also exemplifies this. Almost any service job that relies mainly on information can be done at any location.

Our society has yet to truly understand or embrace the capabilities of this technology. Businesses often still require employees to be present physically at an office location, when their job really could be done from home, thus saving overhead costs for the business. Employers often measure performance in terms of hours worked, instead of work products completed. School districts and local and state governments often work "within their borders" to solve problems, instead of letting technology work to enable resources, solutions, and ideas to be shared with other entities that may already have addressed this issue. The sharing of resources is not always natural to human behavior, unlike the behaviors of territorialism and turf; it is a natural human tendency to protect what is ours, and often, we do not care to share.

That is perhaps the biggest challenge of this new information age: the battle of the borderless information culture versus the traditional behaviors and values that have guided us since man's beginning. The businesses, individuals, and governments that understand this challenge and embrace its opportunities will thrive. Those that do not will continue to be involved in a conflicted struggle between control and cooperation. We must use the advances in the information age to use this borderless technology to improve our schools, our businesses, our government—our lives. We cannot turn back the hands of time. We cannot ignore this change; our future depends on embracing it to our fullest advantage.

The remainder of this chapter discusses Pennsylvania's history with the Internet and plans for Pennsylvania to continue to embrace this change. The brief history of e-government in Pennsylvania can be thought of in four specific stages:

- 1994–1996: birth of e-government
- 1996–2000: infrastructure and information period
- 2000–2004: application period
- 2004 and beyond: period of true interactive government

THE COMMONWEALTH OF PENNSYLVANIA'S PATH TO THE WEB

Pennsylvania has a rich history of leadership. From the signing of the Declaration of Independence in Philadelphia to the birth of America's steel industry in Pittsburgh, Pennsylvania has been an integral player in change.

Recognizing and responding to the signs of significant social change are not simple in the public domain. A modern day case in point . . . How does state government harness the power of computer or information technology (IT) to make government operations more efficient, deliver quality services to its citizens, and verify and protect the information collected?

In 1994, few Pennsylvania state government employees had access to desktop computers. Those who had networked computers were connected only to others in the same building or agency. Interagency e-mail was virtually nonexistent. The most effective way of transferring a document to someone in another state agency or building was to print it and ship it via interoffice mail or to deliver a floppy disk by hand. Even then, one had to hope that the person at the other end would be able to open the file since most agencies used incompatible word-processing software packages.

The commonwealth also lagged behind other state governments in its deployment of Internet technology. In 1995, Pennsylvania had the distinction of being only one of three states that did not have an Internet presence. Then, in late 1995, the commonwealth launched the first Pennsylvania state homepage (www.state.pa.us), which hosted "static" pages containing electronic versions of hard-copy documents simply transferred to the Web. The page essentially served as a table of contents by providing a listing of agency Web pages and the sites of major state programs available to citizens.

Having established an e-government foothold, the commonwealth also recognized the value of the Internet as a communications tool that is accessible to citizens 24 hours a day, 7 days a week, 365 days a year. Additionally, a new perspective emerged that saw technology not as an expense but as an investment and business enabler. Thus, it could be used to get the business of the commonwealth done more efficiently and effectively.

As part of its fundamental organizational commitment to this endeavor, in 1996, the commonwealth appointed its first chief information officer (CIO) to provide enterprisewide IT leadership. The state CIO, located in the newly created Governor's Office of Administration/Office for Information Technology (OA/OIT), was responsible for setting enterprise policy and standards and seeking out ways to use technology better within state government.

The creation of the OIT was a significant first step. Through public–private partnerships, OIT began to establish a technology foundation that would become the basis of e-government activity over the next ten years. Additionally, OA/OIT began to take a more critical look at commonwealth applications with a view toward leveraging them for "common solutions across the more than 43 distinct agencies."

This approach, coupled with several other factors, would prove critical to the level of success to be achieved in the area of IT. These factors include

- Executive sponsorship of enterprise initiatives
- A commitment to positive change
- An enterprise approach recognizing the value of leveraging resources and solutions
- Developing private-sector partnerships and perspectives
- Designing customercentric projects that benefit Pennsylvania communities and local entities whenever possible

These guiding principles continued to facilitate the ongoing transformation and evolution in technology and led to Pennsylvania's being named winner of the Center for Digital Government's "Best of the Web" award in 1998—just two years after the site was established. Hence, Pennsylvania was no longer at the bottom of the pack.

PAPOWERPORT—PENNSYLVANIA'S WEB PORTAL

With a Web presence now established, the challenge was to continue to improve homepage design, targeted toward development of a portal. This was similar to online tools provided by private-sector Internet pioneers such as Yahoo!, Excite, and Microsoft. The goal was to present information from the customer's perspective with minimal mouse clicks. This was facilitated by employing simpler, more intuitive, website-navigation visitor-interest categories, such as "Business in PA," "Learning in PA," and "Living in PA."

By clicking on these categories, visitors could directly access requested information, download forms, click links to other relevant sites, and obtain the e-mail addresses of offices or officials. This enabled the public to access customized information online and receive forms that may have previously required a visit to a government office.

In February 2000, plans were underway to launch PAPowerPort, the commonwealth's portal. A beta version was on the Internet for users to explore and offer comments on. The OIT also held town meetings across the state to elicit comments from business and technology leaders. In addition, a 12-member PAPowerPort Steering Committee was established to review and advise on policy decisions related to the Pennsylvania website. Following review of this collective feedback, the PAPowerPort was completed, and in October of that year became the official Pennsylvania website.

Through an ongoing focus on customer service, the PAPowerPort has been able to achieve ever-increasing usage and a continuous stream of positive testimonials from satisfied users. The PAPowerPort has freed state employees to provide more value-added services to citizens. By handling public requests for many routine government services, such as copies of birth certificates or tax forms, the PAPowerPort is allowing agency employees to devote more time to special customer needs or to offer additional levels of personal assistance. However, as late as 2000, the e-government experience was based almost exclusively on citizens and businesses accessing static information available through the site. Nonetheless, the infrastructure had been established to allow agencies to begin to receive information from its citizens. The race to the Web was truly underway!

RACE TO THE WEB

With the portal at the epicenter, the commonwealth began to leverage its success and flexibility as agencies launched their efforts to begin the electronic process of receiving information from their customers—citizens, businesses, and all levels of government. A key driver of this period of e-government was the goal to make services currently provided by the agency available online to the citizen. We refer to this period as the race to the Web because the agencies raced against each other, as well as sister agencies in other states, to provide services via the Internet. Pennsylvania has quite an impressive list of online services. The following are examples of this expansion of service offerings:

- Electronic tax-return filing
- Motor-vehicle registration
- New-business applications
- Integrated justice sharing
- Online human-services applications
- Integrated general government operations

Government to Citizen: Filing Tax Returns Electronically

The Pennsylvania Department of Revenue's (DOR) website is an example of the e-government transformation. The site was launched in 1995 as a marketing tool to support a specific tax initiative. In the beginning of 1996, the site was used primarily to support individuals during the tax season. It was later expanded to provide support for all customers throughout that year. Since then, the site has expanded into an all-purpose reference tool, as well as a primary instrument in the marketing of the department's electronic services.

The most popular feature is the library of downloadable forms. More than seven million forms have been downloaded in each of the last two years. Virtually every detail an individual, business, or practitioner could need is available online. The site also is the fastest way for the department to alert the public to news and changes in tax law.

In 1997, the department joined the U.S. Internal Revenue Service's e-file program, enabling taxpayers to file their federal and state tax returns electronically, together or separately. This service benefits the taxpayers by enabling the processing refunds in half the time compared to a paper return. It also benefits the department as the forms no longer require data entry. In 2000, the department added its pa.direct.file system to file returns, free of charge, over the Internet. Electronic filing is the most cost-effective method of processing a tax return. Approximately two million taxpayers used an electronic service to file their 2002 PA Personal Income Tax return—a 34 percent increase over the previous year. With an estimated saving of $1.40 per return that is filed electronically, the department estimates that it avoided costs of about $2.8 million. To file using pa.direct.file, a taxpayer needs to provide his or her Social Security number and an additional approved form of identification. As an additional service to businesses, DOR partnered with the Department of Labor and Industry to create the Electronic Tax Information and Data Exchange System (e-TIDES). Most business taxes and services can be filed through e-TIDES.

Citizens Driving the Web: Motor-Vehicle Registration Goes Online

The advent of true online transactions between citizens and Pennsylvania state government occurred in May 2001 with the launch of the Pennsylvania Department of Transportation (PennDOT) Driver and Vehicle Services Online Vehicle Registration website (www.dmv.state.pa.us). PennDOT's products and services impact almost all Pennsylvanians. This is particularly evident in the driver and vehicle services arena. PennDOT's services are used by the commonwealth's 10.2 million registered vehicle owners and 8.3 million licensed drivers. Directed by a commonwealthwide initiative in February 2000, PennDOT launched its site to make driver's licenses and vehicle registrations renewable online in May 2001. The site, www.dmv.state.pa.us, is available 24 hours a day, 7 days a week.

The first services to debut were online renewals of driver's licenses, photo IDs, and vehicle registrations. To complete an online renewal, customers must have Internet access and a major credit card. Some online transactions also require a personal identification number (PIN) as an added security measure. Consequently, an entire process was built to issue PINs. This included modifying the renewal application to include a PIN, developing a PIN-request process, and creating a service that allows customers to personalize their PINs.

To ensure the successful implementation of the new online services, several key activities were completed prior to the debut. First, a temporary Internet credential was developed for online driver's license, photo ID, and motor-vehicle renewals. The credential allows customers to stay mobile even if they do not renew online until that last minute before expiration. This involved close coordination with law enforcement, including the execution of several regional training sessions held across the commonwealth to inform law enforcement about the new credentials. Feedback from the training was incorporated into the final design of the online credential.

The commonwealth believes that e-government begins and ends with the customer. Thus, the use of customer focus groups was a key activity that led to the successful implementation of the online services. Customers such as driver's education teachers, students, and friends and family of agency employees were made part of the team. Providing customers with the ability to renew online was only the beginning. PennDOT undertook an extensive customer- and market-research study to determine what other Internet services customers wanted in the future.

In December 2001, Phase II of PennDOT's online services program began. Several new online services were added to the menu of driver and vehicle online services by the end of 2002. They included the purchase of driver history records for individuals and businesses, change of address for licensed drivers and registered vehicles, and driver's exam scheduling.

Since implementation of the Driver and Vehicle Services website in May 2001, more than 2.5 million transactions have been completed online. In 2003, an estimated 1.3 million transactions were completed online rather than using one of the other service channels, which include the mail, our full-service Driver and Vehicle Service Centers, private messengers, or any one of more than 200 online messenger locations. Customer surveys clearly indicate that the online services program is a success. On a scale of 1 to 5, Customer Survey Index (CSI) scores reflect a 4.72 in "ease of use" and a 4.71 score overall.

Government to Business Citizens: Pennsylvania Open for Business—All Day, Every Day

Providing entrepreneurs in Pennsylvania with a full-service business application was the thrust behind Pennsylvania Open for Business. More specifically, how could the commonwealth transform a time-consuming, paper-based business-registration process into one that would position the Commonwealth of Pennsylvania as one of the easiest places in the world to start, sustain, and expand a business through the use of Web-based resources? With this and a host of other questions confronting them, representatives from Pennsylvania's three main business regulatory and registration agencies were directed to identify opportunities for streamlining business processes and move them online with the aim of reducing operational costs and providing customers with daily, round-the-clock access to business registration services.

The Pennsylvania Open for Business site enables users to register an enterprise electronically with the commonwealth in two ways: conducting an online interactive interview or submitting an online version of the PA-100 Enterprise Registration form. The online interview is a step-by-step wizard that guides users through the process of registering an enterprise with the Departments of Labor and Industry, Revenue, and State. The three participating agencies electronically receive only the information they need to satisfy their business requirements. Prior to this service, business owners were required to complete multiple paper forms, each containing nearly duplicate information.

Since the live release of the site, www.paopen4business.state.pa.us, on September 10, 2001, the site has compiled an impressive list of achievements. With 214,000 unique visitors, more than 25,000 business registrations have been logged through the online interview tool. The statistics also show that a shift in usage from off-peak hours to working hours is occurring. These numbers demonstrate that more business-professional users are accessing the site during the day. With over 43 million total hits in the first year alone, usage indicators for the site demonstrate a significant amount of traffic for both transactions and questions. Today, between both Open for Business options, Pennsylvania receives an incredible 60 percent of its new business registrations electronically.

Government to Government—The Pennsylvania Justice Network, October 1998

This example of cooperation at the local, state, and federal levels in electronic government enables Pennsylvania to protect its citizenry better. Initiated in May 1997, the Pennsylvania Justice Network (JNET) demonstrates the benefits that technology can provide in the fight against crime by enabling authorized users to access offender records and other justice information across the different agencies, branches, and levels of government.

JNET is a collaborative effort of municipal, county, state, and federal justice agencies to build a browser-based, secure, multiagency, integrated justice system that provides continuous daily access to offender records and other justice information from participating agencies. JNET is accessed through desktop PCs and in the field by laptops in patrol cars.

The direct benefit of JNET to the citizens of the Commonwealth of Pennsylvania is safer communities because JNET provides law-enforcement officers with immediate access to critical criminal-justice information that helps them to perform their jobs more effectively. The availability of this information has enabled officers in the field to identify and apprehend suspected individuals, solve cases more quickly, and keep criminals off the street.

In addition, an integrated single system for justice information brings the cost of government down, and a single point of entry for information reduces errors. Benefits also include reduced costs associated with defendant and offender processing, faster processing of criminal cases, and minimized risk of releasing offenders who could pose a public threat. JNET has improved prosecution efforts and reduced delays through timely access to case information. The availability of photos through JNET has also prevented the arrest of innocent people due to misidentification.

The following examples illustrate how criminal-justice practitioners in the field have used JNET to identify and apprehend criminals, solve cases, and enhance public safety:

- The Pennsylvania Department of Corrections staff is alerted to a warrant issued in New York for a suspected 9/11 terrorist.
- A driver's license search application enables the Federal Bureau of Investigation (FBI) to search PennDOT database to reveal hijacking suspects.
- The Philadelphia Police Department uses JNET to solve a 21-year-old homicide case.

- A state police trooper accesses PennDOT photos to identify a rape suspect.
- JNET arms state police and FBI officers with photos of a school-bus driver during the kidnapping of the children on board.
- A county collections office uses JNET to locate individuals and collect previously uncollected court costs, fines, and fees.
- County officials use JNET to identify adults harassing minors on the Internet.
- JNET contributes to the arrest of a robbery suspect less than two hours after the crime.
- The Pennsylvania Department of State uses PennDOT photos to identify professionals operating with suspended licenses.

Prior to JNET, each agency had its own computer systems and databases. This resulted in a fragmented justice environment in which information sometimes took days or weeks to get to the appropriate agencies. JNET has helped to solve this problem and represents an unprecedented leap forward in information sharing and cooperation.

Solving the Human-Services Application Maze

Making essential human services accessible to citizens outside of normal business hours is possible through the Commonwealth of Pennsylvania Application for Social Services (COMPASS; www.compass.state.pa.us). COMPASS was first launched in October 2001 with applications for Medicaid for Pregnant Women and Children and the State Children's Health Insurance Program (SCHIP), which are administered through the insurance department. The application process for these programs is more streamlined than other programs; they have minimal eligibility rules and do not require a face-to-face interview. In subsequent iterations, COMPASS has been expanded to include a larger set of public benefits programs and other features. COMPASS applications were modeled on simplified paper applications for Medicaid, food stamps, and SCHIP. All online materials have also been tested for their literacy level.

COMPASS offers screening and application for all Medicaid programs, SCHIP, adultBasic, cash assistance, food stamps, long-term care, and home- and community-based services. COMPASS also provides screening for School Breakfast and Lunch programs. Assistance for online applicants is provided with help screens for each page, an e-mail contact, and a toll-free general help line. Since November 2001, all COMPASS screening and application materials have been available in English and Spanish.

As of June 2003, there are two versions of COMPASS: a public website and the Community Partner View for registered application agents who assist members of the public. Service organizations apply to become a registered application agent and sign agreements pertaining to confidentiality and the Health Insurance Portability and Accountability Act. Clients also sign a release of information form so that they can work with the agent.

Approximately 1,900 COMPASS applications were received in July 2003, making up about 2 percent of total applications received. COMPASS applications are increasing by about 100 per month. More than half of applications submitted on COMPASS are sent during normal business hours (9:00 a.m. to 5:00 p.m., Monday through Friday); 46 percent are sent during nonbusiness hours.

Accessing COMPASS is a more efficient way to apply for support programs than visiting a county office, with families becoming eligible faster online than with paper applications. Furthermore, the ability to apply for benefits at home or with an agent offers privacy for people concerned with the stigma of going to the county office. COMPASS was recognized for these contributions by earning a "Best of the Web" award from the Center for Digital Government in 2003.

Streamlining Government Operations: Helping Employees Work Smarter

Making internal government operations more efficient is the thrust behind Imagine PA, a business-transformation project launched in 2001. This extensive enterprise-systems project has streamlined accounting, budgeting, payroll, human-resources, procurement, travel-planning, and management functions across 53 commonwealth agencies.

In the late 1990s, state-agency business managers approached the OIT requesting upgrades to legacy business-software systems that had supported government operations since the early 1980s. Rather than take a patchwork approach to updating these various computer systems, which would have been more costly and less effective, the OIT recommended implementing enterprise resource planning (ERP) software used by the private sector to streamline their businesses and make them more competitive. ERP is a comprehensive, integrated software solution used to produce major finance and administration business for an organization. These streamlined processes are making state government more efficient and improving service delivery to the citizens and vendors of the Commonwealth of Pennsylvania.

Implemented in January 2004, a component of ERP, Employee Self-Service (ESS), went online for internal use. ESS shifts the ownership of each employee's personal information from the Human Resources Office to the employee, enabling employees to control their own data and leave requests directly from their desktops. With a one-time input of information, employees can now perform functions such as submitting time sheets, requesting leave, and changing an address—processes that may have once involved up to five people. Giving employees ownership of their information reduces the time, resources, and money that would traditionally go into performing these functions. The functionality for finance, budget, procurement, and travel planning were implemented in July 2002, with the functionality for payroll, human resources, and travel management also operational in January 2004.

Summary

The race to the Web was quite a tremendous success in Pennsylvania. Commonwealth citizens can apply for human services, renew their driver's licenses, open new businesses, pay their taxes, and apply for environmental permits—all online. These applications have been tremendously successful with a high degree of acceptance. However, have these applications truly transformed government? Clearly, the transformation has begun, but we are in the infancy period. Each agency has participated in the race as an individual participant. But, our citizens do not view government as 43 silos. They view the government as one entity. To truly transform government, agencies must embrace the information age by viewing government as the citizens view government. We must create a truly interactive experience for our citizens—this is our next great challenge.

PREDICTING THE FUTURE

As stated, the race to the Web created significantly improved services for our citizens, but it was done in governmental silos. It has not truly transformed government. The process of e-government is constantly evolving, and the commonwealth continues to remain attuned to how technology can enhance its ability to transfer information more interactively with its citizen customers.

Where Is E-Government in Pennsylvania Headed?

Our vision for the future is to create a much more interactive experience for our citizens. Citizens should be able to see the status of tax accounts, check child-support balances, and track human-service payments. Most likely, the future also holds a more democratic approach to government by allowing online voting, online discussion of critical issues facing our commonwealth, and virtual classrooms. Government must provide information to citizens as they see it, not as we provide it. A transition to a more customer-focused government has begun with the state's child-support program.

With changes emanating from the federal government in recent years, the nation's child-support program has evolved tremendously, and with it comes increasing responsibilities for the states. The Commonwealth of Pennsylvania Child Support Enforcement program recognized this growing need for enhanced customer service and developed a comprehensive child-support Web application to be the single source for child-support services.

Launched in June 2002, the Pennsylvania Automated Child Support Enforcement System (PACSES; www.childsupport.state.pa.us) is a highly secure website that serves as the portal for child-support customer self-service and information delivery to all customers and stakeholders of the program. This website is available for the various stakeholders of the child-support program. It provides the following benefits:

- Child-support payers and payees can view their payments online, check the amount of child support owed, review order details, check for any scheduled hearings or activities, make corrections to their mailing and e-mail addresses online, and subscribe to e-mail reminders for scheduled events. They can also access online direct-deposit forms.
- Employers can view and manage their list of employee-wage withholdings. They can also record their Federal Employer Identification number (FEIN) and make changes to their addresses, phone and fax numbers, e-mail addresses, and the names of their contact persons. The employers also have access to FAQs, a glossary, and site search functions.
- Lien processors, realtors, credit-bureau and lending-institution representatives, and others can search for liens online after they complete a secure registration form.
- Docket searchers like attorneys, journalists, child-support personnel, and others can search for PACSES dockets and obtain summary docket information without needing to go physically to the prothonotary's office.
- The general public can view information about the Pennsylvania child-support program, FAQs, the glossary, and contact information.

PACSES enables these stakeholders to access needed information instantaneously. For instance, if a defendant needs to view payments that he or she has made over two years to his or her various cases, he or she is able to obtain that information immediately via the portal. Child-support self-service through PASCES empowers users by giving them access to relevant case and member data and allows them to perform a variety of functions that previously required caseworker involvement. This promotes data ownership, which may potentially result in increased accountability in child support. In reality, this site allows citizens to be part of government operations—a first step in truly transforming government!

Revolutionizing Customer Service in Pennsylvania

The child-support portal is a beginning step toward our goal of creating this type of interactive experience for all citizens for all services—to be able to review all of a citizen's interaction with government. Each day in Pennsylvania, hundreds of thousands of citizens conduct business with the commonwealth or seek information on services provided by state agencies. Of these, tens of thousands will access the state website, PAPowerPort. In fact, during a one-month peak in the past three years, as many as 12 million user sessions were recorded.

Those not searching online may call any of the commonwealth's more than 600 distinct toll-free numbers, while others can walk into a state office or facility. It is evident that as the delivery of services and information becomes more prevalent and sophisticated, it is increasingly important for the commonwealth to further develop a solution to streamline its customer-service delivery functions.

With an increased number of customers, agencies have continued to make more information available online, but there may be unintended consequences of this success. Countless visitors do not use many of the services available, perhaps because they are simply not aware that these options exist. Research shows that it is taking visitors longer to access the information they need because it is buried within a link to a department or agency, and is therefore harder to find. Because online visitors view state government as one entity, a "one-stop shop" experience using an e-account would be ideal.

Customer Relationship Management (CRM) is a customercentric business strategy aimed at improving customer service with increased efficiency and effectiveness. It is essentially an enterprise tool to improve the relationship between a business and its customers. Over the past three years, leading-edge financial services and telecommunications firms have set the pace with CRM, and many have greatly benefited from the resulting customer satisfaction. The most evident examples of successful CRM strategies are found in banking and financial services firms. Many users can access their personal accounts via the Internet, conduct transactions, and print receipts, and should they need further assistance, they can call a toll-free number. The relationship between business and customer is therefore greatly improved, even personalized, while efficiencies and cost savings can be realized.

These services are evident across the Internet with any number of retail outlets where customized accounts are developed for the end user. With the advent of personalized, online e-accounts, it is becoming standard for a person to bank, shop, and make travel arrangements via secure websites. Citizens now expect government to expand its online services as well.

Citizen E-Accounts with the Commonwealth of Pennsylvania

The successful implementation of CRM will allow users to visit the PA-PowerPort and sign in as they would to their online bank or shopping service. Once their identity is verified, they will have access to their own personalized e-account, which will allow them to conduct online transactions with the commonwealth.

Whether citizens are seeking information about their car registration or tax returns, they will no longer have to point and click to move from agency to agency. Instead, a single view will allow them to use the site based on services and functions, not agencies, bureaus, and bureaucracy.

Consider that a typical Pennsylvania family may want to register its vehicle, submit tax returns, obtain fishing or hunting licenses, or schedule a vacation, all on the Pennsylvania Internet site. With sufficient background information, they could potentially have an online account with the state government. With the proper focus on this customer relationship, in terms of technology and operations, Pennsylvania is well positioned to make this a reality.

The development of a successful implementation plan would support all points of contact that a constituent has with state government, including phone, fax, and walk-in appointments. This assessment of services and a streamlining of processes across agencies in a centralized and coordinated fashion is a key part of CRM.

For those Pennsylvanians who are not yet comfortable with online transactions or do not have Internet capabilities, the CRM approach would include the streamlining and coordination of customer-service functions by telephone. Take, for example, the 311 system developed by New York City. By simply dialing that three-digit number, constituents can better navigate across departments and agencies. This 24/7 service allows for centralized customer service and ongoing performance measurement, given the tracking nature of the incoming calls. Centralization of the call centers allows them to serve not as mere go-betweens but as true providers of customer service that complements the online presence.

Pennsylvania is well positioned to take the next step by implementing a CRM strategy. Creating a streamlined delivery of customer-service functions with a "single view" of state government will help ensure citizen satisfaction as well as cost savings to citizens as taxpayers.

CONCLUSION

E-government is in its infancy. The possibilities of e-government allow us to pursue an interactive environment, where citizens have access to their information, can transact their business, and in the future, perhaps, participate in the process of governance. The evolution of technology allows us to pursue a borderless society of information exchange. We must continue to evolve our processes and behaviors to take advantage of this unique period in our history.

16

Streamlining in Arkansas

Mike Huckabee, Governor of Arkansas

For years, one of the most dreaded days for Arkansans was the day they had to renew their automobile license tags. State government had developed a convoluted system that required a vehicle owner to go to the county courthouse to obtain proof of personal property tax assessment and proof of personal property tax payment before going to a state revenue office, where a wait in a long line was the norm. Proof of liability insurance also was required. And the vehicle owner had to find a licensed vehicle-inspection station, have the vehicle inspected, and bring to the state office an inspection certificate.

If any of the necessary documents were missing, frustrated citizens were unable to register their vehicles. The process forced Arkansans to lose as much as a day of work, resulting in millions of dollars of lost productivity annually. This was one of the few direct interactions many Arkansas taxpayers had with their state government. And it often left a bad taste in their mouths. The complaints I heard across the state about the car-tag-renewal process easily outnumbered the complaints about other areas of state government. From such a broken system, we put together one of the most successful systems of its kind in the country. The credit is due to a public–private partnership that grew out of our desire to offer better services and the necessity of having those services available in a short period.

The Arkansas Department of Finance and Administration (DFA) harnessed the technology resources of almost 20 private-sector entities, including large corporations such as IBM to one-person computer shops, to accomplish the streamlining of the car-tag-renewal process. The goal could not have been achieved without these private-sector partnerships. What occurred in Arkansas is a testament to what can be accomplished by government when it is willing to cast aside its traditional role, roll up its sleeves, and design a process that puts the customer first.

Arkansas' vehicle-registration program is delivered to taxpayers from 115 full-time and 25 part-time state revenue offices. Prior to December 22, 1997, every application for registration and title had to be typed manually, and the assessed fees had to be calculated manually. Daily cash register balances and fee reports were also prepared manually. Access to the state's vehicle-registration system by state employees was limited to performing record inquiries and processing annual car-tag renewals. All other transactions were typewritten, bundled, and mailed to DFA's Office of Motor Vehicles in Little Rock, where a central data-entry process entered the transactions into the computer system.

Using batch-processing methods, registration certificates and certificates of title were produced and mailed in separate envelopes from Little Rock. It was an archaic process that had changed little in 40 years. It was cumbersome and error prone. The use of computer technology was limited primarily to that of record storage. We had to do something, so I made the design of a new system one of my priorities when I became governor in July 1996.

Partnering with IBM provided the state with the flexibility to increase and decrease project manpower rapidly during various stages of the project. It also gave the state the ability to obtain the services of people with highly technical skills who could not be attracted to full-time government employment. We set out to achieve the following goals:

- All vehicle-registration transactions performed in state revenue offices would be online, real-time updates to the state's computerized vehicle-registration records.
- Taxpayers would receive over-the-counter issuance of their vehicle-registration certificates instead of a temporary certificate with the official registration coming later in the mail.
- Certificates of title would continue to be centrally issued, but the system would make it feasible to initiate overnight title issuance.
- All sales tax and registration-fee calculations and cash register functions at state revenue offices would be fully automated.
- All license plate and decal inventory functions at state revenue offices would be fully automated.
- The daily reporting functions in state revenue offices would be fully automated.

All of those changes could be achieved administratively, but legislation was required to achieve our other goals. Prior to the January 1997 session of the Arkansas legislature, a comprehensive package of further reforms was developed. The legislation would do the following:

- Repeal the vehicle-safety inspection program, which had been created in 1968 in response to a federal mandate. The threat of cutting off federal highway funds to states without inspection programs was never enforced, and the federal mandate was repealed. Arkansas' safety-inspection program was of questionable value because of the limited scope of the inspections performed. A vehicle inspection costs $3.50. Of that, $1.50 went to the state and $2 was retained by the inspection facility for the services performed. Few garages could afford to tie up their facilities and personnel for $2. As a result, the program was a burden on taxpayers in rural areas because they often had to drive long distances to find licensed inspection stations.
- Repeal the requirement to show proof of personal property assessment.
- Repeal the requirement to show proof of payment of personal property taxes.
- Repeal the requirement to show proof of automobile liability insurance, replacing it with a program requiring insurance companies to provide an automated monthly report of policies in effect.
- Allow the state to accept credit card payments for annual car-tag renewals without assessing a surcharge.

All of this made sense to us, but change is never easy, and this issue became one of the major battles of the 1997 legislative session. Every aspect of the program, except authorizing the use of credit cards to renew, encountered stiff opposition.

Elimination of the vehicle-safety inspection program raised questions of serious concern from bond attorneys at the Arkansas Development Finance Authority. They feared the program's repeal would place the state in default on bonded indebtedness for prison construction since proceeds from the state's $1.50 per decal charge were pledged to the retirement of those bonds. To account for this, we decided to charge a fee of $2.50 per registration (still $1 cheaper for the taxpayer) with $1.50 of that going toward retirement of the bonds.

Some legislators also feared that the elimination of Arkansas' inspection program would also result in unsafe vehicles being operated. However, its demise has not resulted in any increase in the number of unsafe vehicles on Arkansas highways. The majority of legislators came to realize that the inspection program had done very little to enhance vehicle safety.

Furthermore, county and school district officials opposed repealing the requirements to show proof of annual personal-property assessment and proof of payment of personal property taxes. They viewed it as a threat to counties' ability to obtain accurate assessments and collect personal property taxes, which would heavily impact public school funding. We had to find a way to retain the personal property tax enforcement capabilities of the existing process, or the whole plan would meet with defeat in the legislature.

The answer was to create a state-supported system in which county assessors and county collectors could electronically notify the state's vehicle-registration system that a vehicle owner had assessed a vehicle and had paid all personal property taxes that were due. The electronic notifications would be placed automatically on the vehicle-registration records and used by employees of state revenue offices to verify proof of assessment and payment of personal property taxes. We proposed that the state provide the necessary computer hardware, software, and telecommunications links to each county assessor and county collector free of charge. The funds to do this would come from the additional $1 of the $2.50 fee we were using to replace the $3.50 that previously had been charged for vehicle inspections. The statutory deadline for implementing these changes was set for January 1, 1999.

Finally, repealing the requirement for taxpayers to show proof of vehicle liability insurance and replacing it with an automated system met with mixed reaction from the insurance industry. Major insurance-company executives were opposed to the requirements of monthly reporting. Their concerns centered on the costs for programming and the absence of a national standard for automated reporting of insurance coverage. They feared that they might have to develop separate programs for each state adopting similar legislation. However, that opposition was concentrated at the corporate level. Local insurance agents tended to support the concept, believing the monthly reporting of the policies in effect would reduce the number of people buying insurance solely to renew their car tags, then canceling those policies.

Through numerous meetings with insurance-industry representatives to educate them on the proposed program, the opposition was overcome. We enacted legislation that requires each insurance company providing coverage in Arkansas to report electronically to the state by the seventh day of each month. The report must include a record of each auto liability policy in effect the previous month. Companies failing to report in a timely fashion can be assessed a penalty of $250 per day. The state had to establish a vehicle-insurance database that could be accessed by state revenue office employees, state law-enforcement agencies, and local law-enforcement agencies. The legislation required that the database be operational by January 1, 1998.

Legislation authorizing the use of credit cards as a form of payment for annual car-tag renewals by phone or over the Internet was not opposed. An important aspect of this legislation was a provision authorizing the state to pay credit card company fees as an operational expense, which allowed us to avoid placing a surcharge on customers. Such a surcharge would have been counterproductive to one of the primary goals we were trying to achieve, namely, promoting the use of phone and Internet renewals to reduce traffic in state revenue offices.

As soon as the necessary legislation was passed in the spring of 1997, a steering committee was established to implement the changes. The committee consisted of a governor's office representative, representatives from the DFA, representatives from the state Department of Information Systems (DIS), and representatives of county assessors and county collectors. Committee members quickly determined that due to the short time frame for implementation, heavy private-sector involvement would be necessary.

A contract was issued to IBM to assist in the project, and an IBM representative was added to the steering committee in an advisory capacity. IBM deployed a team of experts statewide to assess the hardware and software being used in each of the state's 75 counties. Those assessments, which were necessary before additional steps could be taken, were completed in a matter of weeks. The steering committee then broke the project down into three areas—the insurance verification process, the personal property tax verification process, and the phone and Internet renewal process.

Automated insurance verification processes already had been installed in other states, and commercially developed software and systems support were available from the private sector. After studying the requirements for the insurance database, however, the decision was made to develop and maintain the database in-house rather than to contract with a commercial software vendor to provide the service. State officials began meeting with insurance-industry representatives to formulate a plan. It didn't take long until actual systems development was under way. The insurance database would contain the information necessary for the state to verify automatically that each vehicle was insured at the time of annual tag renewal. All insurance companies writing auto liability insurance coverage in the state were required to report information for all policies in effect. Each company then was required to provide monthly reports of cancellations and new policies issued. The verification process was developed and implemented within six months. At the time of implementation, there were more than 300 insurance companies reporting coverage on almost 1.6 million vehicles, reflecting a compliance rate of about 85 percent of the registrations in effect.

Automating the personal property tax verification process was a bigger undertaking. Under the Arkansas constitution, assessing and collecting personal property taxes are functions reserved for county government. Those duties cannot be assumed by the state. We had to develop a way to permit county assessors and collectors to notify the state automatically each time a vehicle was assessed or a taxpayer paid personal property taxes. This would require a statewide telecommunications network to transfer personal-property assessment and payment updates between the 75 counties and the state. Other complicating factors were as follows:

- The county assessments conducted by IBM found a diversity of hardware and software systems being used. Some county assessors and collectors

had mainframe computers, while others were using personal computers. There was no requirement that an assessor and collector in a county have compatible software.
- Most counties maintained their assessment records by assigning each taxpayer a personal-property account number. A few smaller counties, however, relied on nothing more than a taxpayer's name and address.
- Some assessors and collectors created new account numbers each year for each taxpayer.
- Some assessors and collectors in the same counties did not even share common account numbers for the same taxpayers.
- The vehicle information included in each taxpayer's assessment records was limited to the year, make, and model data on vehicles. These records did not include vehicle identification numbers (VIN) to identify each vehicle assessed. The state's vehicle-registration system, however, was structured by VIN and did not use a common owner identification number that linked all vehicles owned by an individual.
- Owner names were not always consistent between county records and state vehicle-registration records. It was not unusual for vehicles to be titled in the names of minors or college students but assessed on parents' personal-property assessments.

Because of these complexities, the steering committee took a phased approach to developing the personal property tax verification process, dividing it into a collector phase and an assessor phase. It was clear that much of the development of these two phases would have to be performed by the private sector. In addition to the contract with IBM, 27 contracts were issued to 16 private vendors and two county information-system departments for developing the county-based portions of the plan. The private vendors were already providing software to the counties, and their assistance was essential. In many cases, they had developed the county systems, and modifications by outside parties would void the vendor warranties.

The steering committee determined that the collector phase should be developed and implemented first since the payment verification process did not require collectors to identify specific vehicles. This would be less complicated than the development effort for the assessor phase. The telecommunications infrastructure used for transmitting collector and assessor updates to the state was developed as part of the collector phase. The technology used for transmitting and receiving data between counties and the state is state-of-the-art guaranteed-messaging software developed by IBM. Since collection and assessment data is transmitted to the state from more than 150 collector and assessor sites, the probability of network outages is a risk, requiring a messaging system that ensures delivery of transmitted information in instances where connectivity is lost and then reestablished. Not only did we need to guarantee message delivery, but the system had to be versatile enough to accept and process messages accurately from the various operating systems in the counties.

Developing the telecommunications infrastructure was just one aspect of the collector phase. A collectors' database was developed on the state system that would accept tax-payment status updates from county collectors. Using the combined technical resources of IBM and state agencies was critical in the development of this database. In addition to creating the state database, each of the 75 county collector systems had to be replaced or modified to ensure that taxpayer account information was consistent with the county's assessor system. The private vendors who provided the systems, which are supported for each county, performed these modifications and replacements. As the vendors completed their modifications to each county collector system, a testing process incorporating 182 test procedures was conducted. The testing process was developed and coordinated by IBM technical personnel. Each collector's system had to pass certification testing successfully to begin transmitting data to the state's database. The target of March 31, 1998, for completion of the collector phase was met.

The next phase of the personal property tax verification process—automating the tax-assessment verification procedure—was more complicated than automating the tax-payment verification process. In addition to being able to identify the taxpayer, we also had to be able to identify the specific vehicle being assessed. And we only had 18 months to complete this. As with the collectors' systems, each of the 75 county assessor systems had to be either replaced or significantly modified. Having assessors and collectors on the steering committee who were officers in their respective associations was vital to the success of the project. Not only were they experts in the personal property tax field, but they also had the respect of their peers. As a result of their participation, the counties agreed on the following:

- All assessor and collector records would have personal-property account numbers.
- The account numbers would have to be consistent between assessor systems and collector systems.
- A taxpayer's personal-property account number would be permanently assigned and carried forward from year to year.
- All assessment records would include the VIN for each vehicle assessed.

These changes had to be incorporated into the assessors' systems, in addition to the modifications required for their systems to transmit assessment notifications to the state system automatically. These tasks fell to the private-sector partners. Meanwhile, an assessor database had to be developed on the state system. Assessment notification from the assessors' systems to the state database would be transmitted using the same telecommunications interface that was developed as part of the collector phase. The scheduled completion deadline for the county modifications was November 30, 1998. As private vendors completed their modifications on county assessor systems, those systems went through the same extensive testing certification process as the collector systems. IBM technical personnel again coordinated the process. All county systems but one were operational by January 1, 1999, and that one was operational shortly thereafter.

Successfully developing and implementing an automated personal property tax verification process was at the heart of streamlining the car-tag-renewal process in Arkansas. It meant going from an environment that allowed no electronic communication between the state network and county systems to an environment with an extensive data-communications network that ensures statewide connectivity and the transmission of data. The extensive use of private-sector resources was critical to the success of this phase of the project. While requiring a great deal of coordination, it also allowed rapid deployment of technical resources to every county so that we would not jeopardize the warranty status of county assessor and collector systems.

The final process required for meeting our streamlining objectives was creating the ability to accept and process renewals by phone and the Internet with payment by credit card. Again, the steering committee chose to partner with private enterprise. The process would be developed by the private sector, and the contractor would also conduct a significant portion of the operation after implementation. A request for proposals was issued on April 15, 1998. Responses were due May 22, 1998, with the contract to be awarded on June 10, 1998. The vendor was required to have the system running by January 1, 1999.

Proposals were received from five vendors. Five members of an evaluation team each awarded points in the following manner:

- Up to 100 points for proposed system architecture
- Up to 50 points for vendor hardware support
- Up to 100 points for vendor software support
- Up to 100 points for vendor past performance
- Up to 200 points for system performance
- Up to 150 points for cost

The cumulative score for each bidder was tallied and then averaged to determine the successful bidder. IBM averaged 511 points out of a possible 700 points and was awarded the contract. We dubbed this the Streamlined Auto Renewal (STAR) system. IBM had to design a system that would do the following:

- Accept customer phone calls or Internet access 24 hours a day, 7 days a week.
- Use numeric information entered by the customer to retrieve vehicle-registration information. Using only numbers on the phone was necessary to avoid the errors that frequently occur when people are asked to use letters. Customers are required to enter a numeric renewal-identification number followed by a numeric verification code that is printed on the renewal reminder.
- Verify that the customer has assessed the vehicle being renewed, paid all personal property taxes due, and insured the vehicle.
- Require that customer verifies that the record retrieved is the one he or she intends to renew.
- Include the ability on the Internet for the taxpayer to enter a change of address.
- Require entry of a credit card number and, on the Internet, provide for printing a receipt. The telephone system would provide the customer with a confirmation number.
- Update the vehicle-registration system to reflect the record as renewed, including assigning the control number of the new license plate validation decal from an inventory list.
- Create a daily report at midnight.

The daily renewals are transmitted automatically from IBM to the state revenue division, where registration certificates are printed. At 8 a.m. each day, registration certificates from the previous day's phone and Internet renewals are delivered to the Office of Motor Vehicles. The assigned decals are attached, and the renewals are placed in the mail. A customer who used the STAR process at 11 p.m. can still be assured that decals are in the mail the next workday.

IBM deposits all renewal fees collected by credit card into a state account. IBM then pays all credit card company service charges, providing the state with a monthly bill for the transaction costs incurred. The state then pays the bill as an operational expense.

The streamlined registration-renewal process was fully implemented by January 1, 1999. Arkansas residents no longer had to carry a folder filled with papers to a state office and stand in line just to renew their car tags. In fact, they no longer had to leave home at all. It was as simple as picking up the phone or logging onto the Internet. Looking back at what we accomplished, I realize our major challenges had been as follows:

- Meeting time constraints. Experts in the information technology industry estimated a project of this magnitude would typically take at least four years to complete; we had 18 months.

- Dealing with numerous software providers. These private vendors and county agencies had varied levels of technical expertise. Some served one county. Some served a number of counties.
- Establishing a stable environment between the state and counties for data communication.
- Merging state, county, and insurance-company information.

The keys to our success were

- *The level of priority established.* I made this project one of the major goals of my administration and was personally committed to its success. I knew that if we could accomplish this, then we would show taxpayers that state government could be customer friendly, and this would set the stage for improvements in other areas. My commitment included ensuring that all state resources required were allocated and that we had the full commitment of every state agency involved. This created an atmosphere that did not include failure as an option.
- *The level of cooperation received from the counties.* Even though some county officials had opposed changes during the 1997 legislative session, the opposition disappeared after passage of the program. The attitude was, Now that it is the law, let's work together and get it done. The cooperation of county assessors and collectors was essential to resolving technical and operational issues.
- *A world-class technical team.* By partnering with IBM and other private-sector companies, we were able to obtain experts not only from the United States but also from Canada, England, France, Germany, India, Israel, and Mexico. Some were assigned to the project for extended periods, while others were only needed for a few days. All brought technical skills that were essential to the completion of the projects.
- *State-of-the-art technology.* We had to design a communications network capable of interacting with virtually any system. It also had to be capable of withstanding service interruptions without a risk of losing any data that was being transmitted when an interruption occurred.

The renewal process has been a resounding success. In 1998, 94 percent of Arkansas motorists went to a state office and stood in line to renew their car tags. Only 6 percent used the mail-in procedure. Ten months into the new program, 15 percent of Arkansans were already renewing by phone, Internet, or mail. That is more than double the rate of the previous year and is expected to double again. Even those who still come into state offices are happy because they no longer are required to present burdensome documentation. The process runs smoothly and quickly. Most are in and out in less than five minutes.

The streamlined renewal process also set the stage for streamlining other state and local government functions. By connecting counties to a statewide telecommunications network, we have opened the door for the electronic transfer of information in other areas. We could use the network to transmit listings of tax-delinquent land parcels from county collectors to the state land commissioner or even transmit personal-property assessment values from the state to each county assessor. The possibilities are limited only by the capability of the network to handle the traffic volume.

This project clearly demonstrates that government can successfully partner with private enterprise to overcome seemingly insurmountable challenges. I am proud of our accomplishment, and most importantly, the taxpayers are happy. They now point to this as a shining example of a government reform that worked.

17

Providing Digital Government Services around the Clock through the Louisiana Services Directory

Mike Foster, Governor of Louisiana, and Joan McGee, Louisiana Office of Electronic Services

In January 2000, at the beginning of his second term, Gov. Mike Foster announced a new plan for fostering the integration and effective use of technology for a better Louisiana. The plan, "LA Connections: Louisiana's Blueprint for a Digital State Government" (www.doa.state.la.us/oit/docs/LaConnectionsBluePrint.pdf), was a direct response to his call for leveraging technology to defeat poverty, build wealth, and create opportunity in Louisiana. It also reflected the state's commitment to finding new and creative ways to serve all of the state government's customers—residents, visitors, existing and potential businesses, government employees, and other governments. LA Connections was envisioned as the means through which the state's digital government strategy would be implemented.

A major component of LA Connections is the Louisiana Services Directory, a multiagency project that gives citizens the opportunity to access state government more efficiently. Launched in 2001, the Louisiana Services Directory makes an online catalog of detailed information about services offered by state agencies readily available. It is a comprehensive electronic compendium of information about the services offered by state agencies, both directly and indirectly. It is accessible to citizens 24 hours a day, 7 days a week via the Internet.

In order for the online directory to be as comprehensive as possible, the term "service" is defined broadly, including licenses and permits, registrations, filings, certifications, databases, publications, online transactions, and publications. The Office of Database Commission (ODBC) offered some guidance in determining the services to be included in the directory. It determined that the directory should include the most frequently requested information, be general in nature, assist citizens and businesses in conducting their business with the state, and improve communication with the public.

The ODBC (later renamed the Office of Electronic Services), the project leader of this initiative, put the implementation plan in place by November 2000. To test the directory, a scaled-down version of the services directory was piloted on the Internet in June 2001, with an initial count of 44 records from five pilot agencies. The governor formally launched the Louisiana Services Directory, which consisted of 600 records from 11 agencies, at a press conference on July 2, 2001. By March 2003, over 20 agencies maintained over 1,000 records in the Louisiana Services Directory.

WORKING GROUP

The groundwork for the directory was laid in July 1999. The ODBC formed a working group, with participants from the Departments of Economic Development, Labor, Social Services, and the Louisiana Library Network (LOUIS) at Louisiana State University. Based on a preliminary study of similar applications available online at that time, the working group focused on three service-directory projects initiated by other states and analyzed their strengths: Texas and Washington maintain directories of health and human services while Connecticut provides information on business and consumer licenses.

The Texas directory, "Finding Help in Texas,"[1] focuses on health and human services delivery (www.hhsc.state.tx.us/tirn/tirnhome.htm). Two excellent features of this directory were integrated into the Louisiana project. The first is a geographical search of the database by city or by county; the second is a search by target group (e.g., seniors, children, visual impairments, terminal illness). The Access Washington Directory is a collection of resource listings that provides information on health and human services online in Washington State (www.awrd.org). This directory can also be searched geographically by region (eastern or western half of the state) and by more targeted areas (zip code, city, or county). Finally, the Connecticut Licensing Center provides business and consumer licenses in one convenient place (www.ct-clic.com). License types (initial, renewal, duplicate) are bundled together at the initial search so that users can easily determine the logical parts of each license or permit. This feature has been adopted in the Louisiana Services Directory.

AGENCY PARTNERS

Mindful of the wide ranging differences in the level of technology expertise across state agencies, five entities were chosen as initial partners for the pilot: three large departments with extensive computer capabilities and two small agencies with minimal computer support. Early on, everyone associated with the project realized that its success depended largely on the ability of agencies and their staff to implement the project with a minimum of technology expertise.

Based on user statistics garnered from Internet hits, phone calls, walk-ins, and correspondence records, the agencies inventoried and prioritized their most highly requested services and information resources. The goal of the agencies was always to identify what people want from state government and give it to them.

The ODBC set the record-creation policy and provided both a secure interface for agencies to register and maintain their information in the online directory and management guidance for the project.

DATABASE STRUCTURE

With assistance from the programming staff of the state's Office of Information Services, the database design was structured to be responsive to varying agency needs and to be compatible with the state's information technology infrastructure. Careful multiagency planning was undertaken to make the records of the database as trouble free and intuitive as possible. After consultations with agency partners, the database layout was finalized to conform loosely with the Dublin Core data requirements. Each record provides detailed description of the services; prerequisites and appropriate documents needed; links to downloadable forms, manuals, and brochures; e-commerce links when agencies offer these transactions; direct links to relevant websites; and instructions on ways to contact the agency—e-mail, telephone (toll-free when available), fax, and mailing and physical addresses. To ensure consistency, every record from each of the agencies is displayed in one identical format, making it easy for users to predict the information that every record provides.

The Louisiana Services Directory is written in Active Server Pages and uses a Sybase database. The database is accessed through Structured Query Language (SQL) searches. SQL statements are used to update data in a database or to retrieve data from a database. Use of a shared database management system significantly reduced the infrastructure cost. The most significant cost was personnel resources expended on the project by database designers, programmers, and testers. Extensive testing over a three-month period of the administrative, agency, and user sections by the ODBC and agency partners ensured system stability and integrity.

TRAINING OF AGENCY PARTNERS

In the summer of 2001, the governor sent a letter to all agencies soliciting their support for the project and instructing them to appoint an agency coordinator to facilitate the inventory of services and information resources, approve project assignments, and schedule staff training. An enterprisewide implementation team was formed as the result of enthusiastic buy-in from administrators and staff, who realized early on that they could answer the same question that they receive many times during the day by directing people to the one accurate and current record that would now be available on the Internet.

Agency coordinators are responsible for populating the database with agency-specific information on services and resources and for establishing a maintenance program, which ensures that the information is always current and accurate. Agencies have total control over their own records—selection of services, record information, review and approval, and update and maintenance. The ODBC also designed and implemented a training module for agency partners consisting of a how-to manual, thesaurus, and keyword index to facilitate searching, online help instructions, and a user-evaluation form. It also provides the server where the database of the directory resides.

Over a period of nine months, the ODBC staff conducted 48 demonstrations and training sessions for over 500 personnel in 28 organizations.

It was necessary to provide several training sessions in large departments to accommodate the large number of people designated to populate the directory. Agency partners were resourceful in implementing the push to populate records: departments were divided into small units, with each unit responsible for compiling, deciding on the content of, and maintaining its records. Administrative controls to ensure accuracy and correct spelling and grammar were managed by a central working group, which approved the records before they were released on the Internet.

LAUNCHING THE DIRECTORY

The initial agency partners, the Louisiana Departments of Labor, Revenue, and Culture, Recreation, and Tourism, as well as the Governor's Office of Disability Affairs, provided the first 50 records. Within months, three large agencies—the Departments of Environmental Quality, Health and Hospitals, and Public Safety—released their records and added more than 400 records to the database. By November 2001, the Louisiana Services Directory contained more than 600 records from 11 agencies. The INFO Louisiana template was adopted for the user screen to leverage the familiarity of the state portal. To enhance visibility, the Louisiana Services Directory icon is prominently displayed on the main screen of the state portal at www.louisiana.gov.

At this time, the Verity search engine was adopted to allow simple or advanced searches, depending on the skill of directory users. Furthermore, to ensure that users get the results they want, the directory format supports four different types of searches: alphabetical, by department, by keyword, and by category or subcategory.

The search facilitates access to detailed information about these services through a single entry point. To maximize access to the directory, the assistance of the public library system was solicited through the Louisiana State Library since no Louisiana resident is more than 14 miles from a public library. Louisiana is fortunate that there are 2,018 public Internet workstations in the 65 main libraries and 264 library branches in Louisiana. Public libraries were requested to alert patrons to the information contained in the directory.

BENEFITS

The Louisiana Services Directory provides a gateway where citizens can access and locate information about services from state departments and agencies; thus, it provides the following benefits to the state's residents:

- It is a more convenient way for citizens to access state services information.
- The robust search capability eliminates the need for users to understand state government organization. For example, not many citizens know that the State Library of Louisiana is under the Department of Culture, Recreation, and Tourism.
- Category and subcategory lists allow for searching across agencies; for example, "Children and Youth" bundles all of the services from all agencies with records in the directory: the Departments of Education, Social Services, Labor, and Culture, Recreation, and Tourism.
- Information is easy to understand because records are presented in a uniform format, even when various agencies populate the database.
- A single entry point through the state portal ensures citizens comprehensive access to all services information.
- It is easy for agencies to ensure that current information is available.

USER STATISTICS

From June to December 2001, a total of 26,849 records in the Louisiana Services Directory were accessed, with an average monthly total of 3,835. In 2002, 99,865 records were accessed with an average monthly total of 8,322. For the first three months of 2003, 11,508 records were accessed every month, an increase of 333 percent from 2001.

Records with the highest user access in 2002 revealed the wide use of the directory by diverse populations: Vital Records (birth and death certificates, marriage licenses), Driver's Licenses, Medicaid Information, License Plates,

Unemployment Insurance Benefits, Support Enforcement Services for Child Support, Licensing Program for Health Care Providers, Counseling Services, Food Stamp Program, and Vendor Registration and Bids.

The agencies whose records had the highest user access in 2002 were the Departments of Health and Hospitals, Public Safety, Social Services, Environmental Quality, Labor, Transportation and Development, Revenue, Economic Development, and Natural Resources and the Division of Administration.

PROJECT COST

Industry estimates based on data from Forrester Research contend that Web self-service is the most cost-effective method of customer service. The average cost of a phone-based service is over $32 per transaction; the average cost per visit to a Web self-service is approximately $1. Based on these cost data, the Louisiana Services Directory has not only enhanced the service capability of the offices with records in the database but has also realized considerable cost savings. For minimum cost, agencies have realized that directing citizens and businesses—who used to call, write, fax, or visit for information—to the Louisiana Services Directory, provides them with the online records which answers their questions

RECOGNITION: BEST PRACTICE

The Center for Digital Government and the Progress and Freedom Foundation recognized the Louisiana Services Directory as a "Best Practice"[2] in its 2001 survey, which was based on a comprehensive poll of chief information officers in the 50 states. The survey examined digital technologies in several categories: e-commerce and business regulation, taxation and revenue, social services, law enforcement and the courts, digital democracy, management and administration, and education and transportation.

The Louisiana Services Directory also received a "Best Practice" citation in the management and administration category of leading applications of digital technologies. The citation reads, "The Louisiana online services directory can provide information on all manner of services, databases, forms, records and other relevant information, because a search of the system reaches across the state government agencies to find the right information for the customer."

THE NEXT STEP: ASK LOUISE

The Office of Electronic Services periodically analyzes the feedback and e-mail questions received by the Louisiana Services Directory and INFO

Louisiana. Based on the questions and feedback responses, the staff compiled a list of the 50 most frequently asked questions over the previous two years. This enabled it to initiate another information resource, ASK Louise, in June of 2002, which provides citizens and businesses with the answers to these questions more quickly. There are 50 question-and-answer records in the database. Each record provides comprehensive information: description of service or information resource, directory contact (phone, fax, e-mail address, mailing and physical address), access to downloadable forms, e-commerce links when available, and active links to relevant websites. Users can ask their questions through e-mail if answers to their questions are not found on this knowledge base, and answers are e-mailed back, usually within two business days.

Based on user access data, ASK Louise has satisfied a definite need. In less than a year, the number of users consulting the database and viewing the answers more than doubled from 4,062 sessions in June 2002 to 10,620 in March 2003. The responses to questions are categorized, and the following ranked categories had the highest user access in 2002: licenses, permits, and certifications; government; general information; public services; tourism, recreation, and travel; business; health care and social services; education; and employment resources.

The ASK Louise application is a very efficient and affordable information tool, with a total annual cost of approximately $24,000.

LOUISIANA'S ELECTRONIC GOVERNMENT

The Louisiana Services Directory and ASK Louise both allow citizens to find the information they need without having to know the structure of state government. Both have become important information resources for citizens and businesses, enabling them to access the information they need on the Internet 24 hours a day. Through the Louisiana Services Directory and ASK Louise, Louisiana's electronic government never closes.

ENDNOTES

1. It is now called the Texas Information and Referral Network.

2. Louisiana was one of only eight states singled out for the "Best Practices" citation in the annual report on the technology profile of the states, *Digital State 2001* (p. 15), published by the foundation (www.pff.org/publications/digitalstate2001.pdf).

18

Georgia on My Mind: Providing Services to the People

Sonny Perdue, Governor of Georgia

In January 2003, Gov. Sonny Perdue became the first Republican governor in Georgia since reconstruction. Perdue campaigned for governor on a platform of restoring public trust in state government and empowering all Georgians by eliminating undue interference by government bureaucracies. He brought a vision of government for the people that included providing services at a time and place convenient to his constituents. He challenged the state agencies' leadership to step away from their traditional methods of doing business and to improve services and citizens' access to them.

The challenge to the Georgia Department of Human Resources[1] (DHR) was to improve efficiencies, institute accountability, and provide services to a growing population. Agencies began examining the status quo and stepping into the twenty-first century. This chapter outlines the effects of this forward-thinking concept and the leadership of DHR's Office of Child Support Enforcement (OCSE), which accepted Governor Perdue's challenge and transformed this agency.

GEORGIA'S OFFICE OF CHILD SUPPORT ENFORCEMENT

The disintegration of the family in America has a profound effect on society as a whole. Newspapers and television newscasts touch on many components of this problem each and every day, but rarely is the problem of child-support collection addressed. In federal fiscal year (FY) 2003, $21 billion in child-support payments were collected by state agencies nationwide. The child-support issue is a volatile subject because it is surrounded by two of the most emotionally charged subjects: money and children. This chapter outlines Georgia's efforts to address issues facing governments all across America.

The Georgia OCSE handles more than 500,000 active child-support cases. These cases involve 1.5 million men, women, and children. In state FY 2004, the OCSE collected $549 million in child support. The majority of the funds collected are disbursed directly to families. The agency's mission is to improve the lives of children and families by providing services through the location of noncustodial parents (NCPs); establishment of paternity, support, and medical orders; and the enforcement of those orders. State staffing has not increased for the past ten years, although the program continues to grow more complex.

An NCP is the parent not in the home full time with the child. The custodial parent (CP) is the full-time caretaker of the child and can be the mother, father, grandmother, aunt, or some other party who has the child living in the home full time.

The increase in divorce, separation, and out-of-wedlock births has caused the child-support caseloads to soar. Also, federal laws now require child-support payments to be deducted directly from the NCP's paycheck and submitted to a government payment-processing center.

In order to keep up with increasing caseloads and the demands of the people he serves, the governor challenged DHR to develop innovative strategies to provide the services people were demanding at the time and place convenient for them. At the same time, the strategies needed to provide OCSE professionals with improved efficiencies so that more could be done with less. The following two e-government innovations were developed to address constituent satisfaction and limited resources.

CONSTITUENT SERVICES PORTAL PROJECT

OCSE constituents only had two avenues to obtain specific information about their cases. They had to call either the OCSE hotline for payment information or the OCSE case manager handling their case. Both of these avenues were restricted to constituents and employees. Busy telephone lines frustrated constituents, as did the limited time frames in which case managers were available to respond to telephone calls. The case managers were frustrated because valuable time was spent answering telephone calls instead of taking action to collect child support. The Constituent Services Portal Project (CSPP) allows constituents to access case information at a time and place convenient for them. The case manager's time can then be used to take action to collect more child support.

The resource savings identified from this project include reduced time spent by case managers on lower-level data entry. This time is now spent on

Table 18.1. CSPP Metrics

Activity	*OCSE Metric (minutes)*
Update custodial parent's demographic information based on telephone call or visit to the OCSE office	5.0
Provide payment information to custodial parents	4.25
Mail direct-deposit application requested by telephone	7.75
Provide direct-deposit application requested by office visit	5.0
Update direct-deposit information from application	2.0
Stop payment requests	9.25
Update noncustodial parent's demographic information	5.5
Provide paper application for child-support services upon request	5.5
Create a case by registering the application in $TARS and posting the application fee (discussed in later section)	13.0

higher-level activities that will increase the child support collected and sent to families. Table 18.1 outlines the time saved by OCSE when a constituent makes updates directly into the CSPP. This time can now be spent on activities to obtain more child-support orders and to take enforcement actions to collect more support. For example, the average time it takes to petition the court to establish an order is 29 minutes. Therefore, for every six constituents who update their own demographic information, OCSE can prepare one additional case for court.

DEBIT CARD

The debit card was developed to reduce the cost of sending child-support payments to families. The tangible savings are $2 million per year for printing, postage, and handling. The intangible benefits include no stolen or lost checks, no need for stop payments, and the money reaching the family more quickly.

CONSTITUENT SERVICES PORTAL PROJECT

Citizens increasingly expect convenience and immediacy in their relationships with businesses and governments. These expectations pressure government to provide convenient, immediate, and secure interactive information services and business processes via the Internet. The CSPP is DHR's first attempt to meet the citizens changing expectations. This initiative not only makes child-support payment information available 24 hours a day, 7 days per week, but also moves the agency into e-governance by allowing constituents to become actively involved in activities relating to their cases. The CSPP provides child-support services and case information via the Internet to child-support clients at home, work, or any Internet-connected PC. In addition to providing timely information in a more convenient fashion, the CSPP enables OCSE to concentrate its limited staff resources on the productive tasks of collecting support rather than the important but unproductive tasks of data entry.

The CSPP was a collaborative effort between government agencies and a private company. The project was designed, developed, and deployed with employees of the OCSE's Office of Information Technology (OIT),[2] the Georgia Technology Authority (GTA),[3] and Accenture.[4] This e-governance project is similar to an online banking or cell phone "My Account" feature. Registered users can view information about their accounts, or what we call "cases," and they can provide transactions such as payments or new addresses.

CSPP RELEASES

The project was developed and deployed in five releases. Each release built upon the strength of the former release.

Release One

In release one, the functionality included basic e-government-type information. The public pages were displayed, and administrative functions required to register with the site, as well as manage password resets, were implemented. Additionally, CPs could make direct updates to their address and employment information and view child-support payment information. They could also request check images and stop payments on outstanding checks. The check-image and stop-payment functions are similar to what can be found on most banks' online resources.

Child-support recipients are anxious to learn if a child-support payment has been made. The number-one question asked by CPs is, Do I have a payment? In Georgia they call the automated voice-response system 1.8 million times per month. Through the CSPP, OCSE now sends constituents an e-mail each time a payment is made, advising them to check the CSPP for payment updates. If no payments have been made or the payments are not in the amount expected, the question becomes, What is the status of my case? The CSPP also provides this information to constituents. Case activities are displayed to both CPs and NCPs, showing the recent actions that have been taken on their cases. OCSE case managers can include messages and additional information within the case activity to provide constituents with detailed and up-to-date information about the status of their cases.

Release Two

In release two, NCPs were given access to payment and case information. They were also given the ability to provide new address and employer information to OCSE. CPs could now update direct-deposit information from the CSPP. The direct-deposit function is an immediate update, and any child-support check processed after the information is entered will be deposited directly into the bank account number specified by the CP.

Since the advent of the debit card, which will be discussed later in this chapter, the direct-deposit functionality has been a popular item with CPs. The traditional method of obtaining direct deposit of child-support payments required the CP either to download the application from the OCSE website or to call an OCSE office to request that an application be put in the mail. Upon completion of the application, the CP had to mail it back to the OCSE office or travel to the office. The child-support worker would enter the information into $TARS (child-support DB2 database) in the order in which it was received. The direct-deposit application is now fully automated, allowing the CP to enter the required data. All payments received from that point forward are deposited directly into the CPs bank account.

Release Three

In release three, the clients could search for a child-support office by city or county. They could also submit e-mail directly to the office handling their cases. To close a child-support case, a CP was previously required to submit the request in writing. A feature in this release allows the CP to submit the request for closure online if his or her case status and type allows it. When the CP tries to close the case, a database search insures that he or she is not receiving welfare or Medicaid or does not owe money to the state. If the CP passes these criteria, then the case is automatically closed with an alert to the child-support worker. This release also included the ability for either party to provide location information about the NCP. One reason child support cannot be collected is that the worker doesn't know where the NCP lives or works. The information provided must be displayed in the child-support system for the child-support worker to view and verify.

Release Four

In release four, people needing child-support services can apply for the services online and can pay the application fee via credit or debit card. The NCP or his family and friends can also make child-support payments online with a credit or debit card.

The CSPP enables citizens to apply for child-support services online. The application process is driven by the responses received from the applicant. As the applicant completes the application, only relevant information is displayed based on the applicant's response to the previous question. For example, applicants who already have a child-support order will not be required to complete lengthy paternity affidavits.

The traditional method of applying for child-support services involved mailing the application or visiting the office. The paper application is 15 pages long due to the many possible circumstances. The application costs $0.78 to mail, which is costly for citizens and agency alike.

Applicants can save the online application if they need to locate pertinent information or do not have time to complete it. When they do submit the application, it is electronically sent to the OCSE office that handles the county where they live. The child-support worker receives an alert that a new application is available. He or she can view the information provided and, if the data are reliable, can accept the application, which then creates a new case in $TARS. This saves the child-support worker an average of 20 minutes per application. The time saved is used to proceed to the next step in the life cycle of the case, which speeds up services and the receipt of child support.

Release Five

In release five, the site became bilingual, with the option to view it in English or Spanish. The site will have the ability to host other languages as well. A child-support guidelines calculator was included, which allows interested parties to input income and family information to determine what their child-support payments could be. A frequency calculator was also made available, which converts weekly payments to monthly amounts, or monthly amounts to weekly amounts. Additionally, NCPs are able to refer themselves to the OCSE Fatherhood program, which provides life skills and job training to improve employment opportunities for the NCP. Another important feature of release five is the CSPP demo, which allows nonregistered users to view the functionality of the CSPP.

The functionality of the CSPP allows child-support clients to participate actively in their cases. They can provide the information at a convenient time without the need to telephone or write the appropriate child-support worker. Once the data are submitted, it automatically updates the child-support DB2 database. This is the same database, known as $TARS, used by the OCSE case-management system.[5] Therefore, any information the client updates is immediately available to child-support workers, and any updates made by OCSE case managers are immediately available to the clients.

The OCSE's goal is to become more proactive in the process of collecting support. Traditionally, a reactive methodology has been used, meaning that huge amounts of child-support arrears accumulate because actions are not taken early enough in the process. The CSPP prevents this by providing reminders to CPs and NCPs of appointments, court dates, and scheduled actions.

SECURITY

Security is of utmost importance to the GTA, OIT, and OCSE. The CSPP incorporates the following leading security practices:

- Authentication, authorization, and secure communications
- Version-controlled releases
- Restricted access to source and runtime code
- Trusted code
- Peer-to-peer certificates
- Encryption/SSL (128 bit)
- Role-base security model (application roles and Web Services roles)
- Credentials to DB2 using RACF
- Application-level security

Only authorized constituents can access information pertinent to their cases within the CSPP. Requirements include

- Authentication of all users accessing the website
- Storage of the authentication token in the user's session
- Expiration of the user's session after a predetermined time of nonactivity

Registration with the CSPP can only be successful if the person is a participant on an OCSE case. The person must have an active Social Security number in the $TARS database and must obtain a unique client identifier to register. Additional security measures are in place for sensitive cases involving family violence, providing additional protection against unauthorized access. The GTA Portal Call Center (PCC) assists users with navigation through the site, registration issues, and the resetting of passwords.

ARCHITECTURE

The CSPP is a pure Web Services application on the Georgia.gov Sun portal and has been designed as an *n*-tiered solution that partitions application

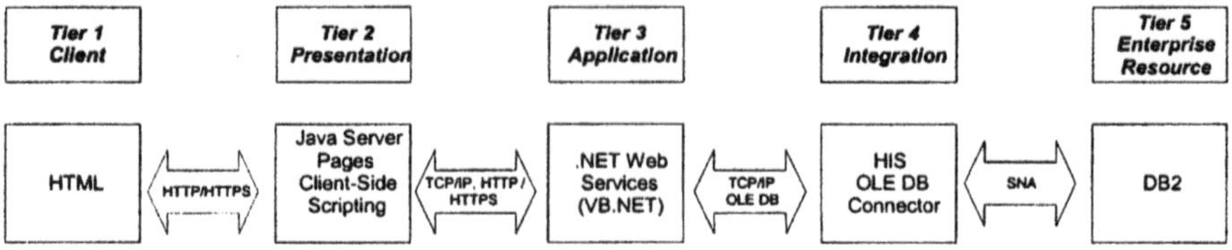

Figure 18.1. Application Architecture.

functionality into five independent tiers, enabling integration with core business systems and other e-business applications:

- *Tier 1:* Client-browser-based access is provided via the Georgia.gov portal. Browser requirements are current and include two previous Internet Explorer and Netscape releases.
- *Tier 2:* Presentation logic—Using Java Server Pages, JavaScript client-side processing, and Java server-side processing, the presentation tier leverages the Georgia.gov portal controls to deliver content.
- *Tier 3:* Application logic—.NET Web Services built using VB.NET are accessible via SOAP calls from the presentation layer and make calls to the existing DB2 database via an OLE DB connection.
- *Tier 4:* Integration—Host integration server (HIS) provides an SNA connection between the application and enterprise resource tiers.
- *Tier 5:* Database management—The existing $TARS DB2 database is used as a real-time data source. The DB2 database will also be used as the application database to store saved transactions and usernames and passwords.

Figure 18.1 illustrates the five-tier application architecture.

The full benefits of *n*-tier architecture are realized by establishing standardized hardware and software designs for each tier. This process enables the creation of a menu of shared services for use in planning, designing, and deploying new applications.

CLIENT REACTION

The response to the CSPP has been overwhelmingly positive. Without any formal marketing, the portal site had registered 42,084 users as of August 15, 2004. There have been 5,820 applications for service submitted online. Users updated 11,153 addresses, 13,347 phone numbers, 6,726 employers, 6,984 applications for direct deposit, and 936 stop-payment requests, as well as information on 6,622 insurance providers. Without the CSPP each of these actions

Category	Hits per Category
Administrative Tasks	1,100
Apply Now	4,720
My Case Information	20,026
Our Services	85,625
View Payments	35,785
Provide Information	154,383
Total	**301,639**

Figure 18.2. CSPP Hits to the Site for the Month of April 2005.

would have required staff time. The new way to provide and update data has been embraced by the child-support community, as indicated in figure 18.2.

APPROACH

How did DHR decide on this approach? OCSE knew that it needed to change its approach to providing information, services, and business processes substantially to give its stakeholders the quality and quantity of information, services, and business processes desired in a timely, efficient, and low-cost manner. Therefore, OCSE began first by outlining its business and technical objectives:

- Business objectives
  —Increase citizen's access to OCSE information based on participation
  —Increase citizen's satisfaction and knowledge of OCSE's services
  —Reduce redundancy and improve productivity in the delivery of services
  —Increase OCSE employee satisfaction and retention in OCSE
- Technical objectives
  —Create a flexible, interactive, secure environment to disseminate and obtain information
  —Integrate of $TARS with the CSPP

OCSE also wanted to know what information and functionality CPs and NCPs preferred. A survey was completed, and 350 responses were received from both CPs and NCPs outlining the functionality they preferred. The survey also discovered that almost 50 percent of our constituents have access to the Internet at least once per week. Most have access through their employers, but many of them visit their local library to gain access.

The CSPP has stayed within the planned time frame and budget. This can be attributed to the project-management skills of Shelly Metschan[6] and George Chaplin.[7]

The CSPP is the completed version of what once was known as "Where's My Child's Check?" (WMCC). When others said "can't," three people persevered and made WMCC happen. Terry Patterson[8] and Cindy Moss,[9] at the direction of Robert Riddle, worked nights and weekends to put the first iteration of WMCC into production. WMCC simply displayed the last six checks sent to the CP, but it was hugely successful and set the tone for the development of the CSPP. The CSPP is on its way to being the very essence of what e-governance is all about: providing needed services to the citizens of Georgia in a timely and efficient manner.

DHR E-DISBURSEMENT FOR CHILD SUPPORT AND PAYROLL

This section discusses the nationally acclaimed debit card project. In reviewing current business practices, DHR determined that producing and administering the paper checks needed for child support and payroll was using large amounts of resources. DHR also determined that citizens and employees were experiencing problems receiving the paper checks. A task force was convened to determine a better way of administering these payments. The DHR "e-disbursement" electronic debit card was born.

The criterion for the debit card was supported by DHR's strategic plan, OCSE program objectives, and Office of Financial Services (OFS)[10] requirements.

The final product had to provide an efficient and cost-effective solution to administer child-support payments, as well as payroll for "unbanked" employees. DHR's goal was to significantly decrease the number of paper checks generated. Implementation of the DHR debit card has already generated operational and productivity improvements and will reduce the administrative burdens associated with paper checks.

The e-disbursement project is a collaboration of the state of Georgia, Affiliated Computer Services (ACS), and the MasterCard® corporation, designed to streamline the way funds are disbursed to CPs. This is achieved by providing clients a MasterCard debit account.[11]

Payments due to clients are deposited in the MasterCard accounts, and the clients are given MasterCard debit cards for use with their accounts. The debit cards can be used like any other debit card to purchase goods or services. The cards are not credit cards—the clients are not charged interest on any transactions involving these cards, and they cannot borrow money on these cards.

The e-disbursement project is administered through the ACS program Electronic Payment Processing Information Control (EPPIC™). This program is used to add certain types of client records and to administer to all clients. The user works in the EPPIC system through a Web-based application called the Administrative Terminal (AT). The AT is the interface that gives the user an interactive means of setting up and maintaining client accounts.

The e-disbursement project includes programs for two types of clients:

- OCSE clients who receive child-support payments
- Payroll clients, that is, state employees whose banks do not support, or who have decided not to use, direct paycheck deposits

The AT can be used for certain administrative functions by OCSE office personnel and by payroll office personnel. Almost all actions concerning OCSE clients are completed through automatic processing of batch files sent between DHR and EPPIC and are not handled through the AT. For this reason, OCSE office personnel have more limited AT access.

The debit cards are issued through batch-file processing. New cards for payroll accounts and replacement cards for both OCSE and payroll clients can be issued through the AT. New cards are issued through the AT as the last step of setting up a new account. Child-support accounts are automatically submitted for card setup when the case meets the selection criteria. Determining the appropriate criteria was a challenge; however, a group of OCSE and OIT staff developed a sound plan.

Each card has a unique 16-digit personal account number (PAN) embossed on its front. That number is also encoded in the magnetic strip on the back of the card. Cards are associated with e-disbursement cases and are linked in both the DHR system and the ACS system by a unique nine-digit program number. Replacement of a card generates a new PAN, and the client must select a new personal identification number (PIN) for the card. Robert Riddle chose the state flower of Georgia, the Cherokee Rose, for the design of the debit card.

CPs and DHR employees have a choice between receiving their payments via direct deposit or via the debit card. Prior to the beginning of this project, 80 percent of child-support payments were made via paper checks. The remaining 20 percent were issued via direct deposit or electrontic funds transfer (EFT) to other states. The goal of the e-disbursement project is to reduce paper checks to 5 percent of the total disbursements.

The project began as a pilot in May 2004, with 17,000 child-support recipients receiving a debit card. The first phase of implementation was carried out over a four-month time span, with 178,000 CPs receiving a card. As part of the selection criteria, CPs selected for debit cards were those who received a child-support payment within the last 12 months.

DHR has made great progress in meeting the goal of only 5 percent paper-check disbursements. Payroll is either administered via direct deposit or the debit card. Child-support payments are administered as follows: EFT, 2 percent; paper checks, 8 percent; direct deposit, 10 percent; and debit card, 70 percent.

The benefits of the program to CPs, employees, and the DHR are numerous. There is no worry about checks being lost or delayed in the mail, returned due to a bad address, or stolen, and the cost of cashing a check is saved. "An unexpected but important side effect of the debit card has been the boost of self-esteem it has afforded clients who are otherwise unable to obtain a bank account or credit card through any other means. Possession of the Debit Card provides them with a sense of prestige," said Gail Bowen.[12] DHR staff no longer needs to spend time processing stop payments or canceling checks.

The project has been a huge success. CPs have overwhelmingly accepted the debit card. In fact, clients who do not meet the criteria for receipt of a card are demanding the issuance of one anyway. There is no cost of administering the debit cards for DHR; however, DHR has been able to reduce administrative costs such as check printing and postage. The debit card project is an exceptional example of how e-government can work for the people and simultaneously reduce the cost of doing business.

CONCLUSION

Governor Perdue sums up his commitment to the citizens of Georgia in this statement:

> My administration is committed to changing the culture of state government to be principle-centered, people-focused, and customer-friendly. By working every day to restore the bonds of trust between the people of Georgia and their state government, we can create an open and responsive government that truly represents all of our citizens.
>
> The greatness of Georgia is, and will always be, our people—our optimism, our enterprise, and our compassion for one another. Together, we can build a new Georgia—the educated, healthy, safe, and growing Georgia that we all desire.

It is this commitment that has allowed the OCSE agency to provide e-governance to its constituency. It is not often that a government agency can provide better service for less money, but that is exactly what Georgia has succeeded in doing!

ENDNOTES

1. DHR administers social services programs for the state of Georgia, including welfare, child-protective services, public health, aging, and child support.
2. OIT is DHR's technology arm for all DHR agencies.
3. GTA is the state of Georgia's technology-governance agency.
4. Accenture is the vendor obtained through competitive procurement process to develop the CSPP.
5. $TARS—the Support, Tracking, Accounting, Reporting, System—has received full certification by the U.S. Department of Health and Human Services, and OCSE processes are fully automated.
6. Shelly Metschan is DHR's director of portal projects.
7. George Chaplin is the Accenture project manager for the CSPP.
8. Terry Patterson is the chief technology officer of Patcon Inc. and was working as a DHR contractor during the development of WMCC and CSPP.
9. Cindy Moss is the director of operations for OCSE.
10. OFS is the DHR entity responsible for payroll.
11. This information is from the *AT User Guide* developed by ACS as a requirement of the DHR contract.
12. Gail Bowen is mail administrator in the Governor's office.

19

The Development of South Dakota's Service Direct Portal

M. Michael Rounds, Governor of South Dakota, and Otto Doll, Chief Information Officer of South Dakota

Today a South Dakota citizen or business can easily find any state government process (i.e., as represented by a form) by going to the South Dakota state government's Service Direct website. All state forms, now numbering over 1,300, are only three clicks away on the Internet. One can find information, download forms for printing, and fill out forms online for electronic submission to the state. Many state forms can be processed entirely online for immediate service.

Service Direct is a one-stop shop for state forms and services. Our goal is for customers to have a successful interaction with South Dakota state government. This chapter tells the story of how such a simple-sounding capability came to be. Many obstacles had to be overcome, and numerous lessons were learned along the way.

VISION CAME OUT OF NECESSITY

Citizens and businesses were often confused and unsure of which state agency to contact to get things done. People had to make several phone calls or visits to state agencies during regular office hours to find the right agency for help or to get one of their forms. In January 2001, some 35 percent of state forms were only available from a state government office in paper form.

We believe that citizens should be able to quickly access all South Dakota state government forms on the Internet, 24 hours a day, 7 days a week. There should be no need to know which agency to contact. The Internet portal concept (an electronic window for direct access to state services) was deemed the best vehicle to enhance citizen and business use of state government forms and to provide one-stop shopping for them. The portal needed to provide online access to state forms that generated over 8 million transactions annually with South Dakota's 762,000 citizens and 23,000 businesses.

The primary goal of the Service Direct project was for citizens and businesses to have a successful interaction with South Dakota state government. Service Direct makes government more efficient by freeing businesses and citizens to direct their energies to business and personal pursuits. The availability of online electronic transactions saves the state the costs of printed forms, public mailings, and the storage of completed paper forms. Furthermore, the public is able to interact with the state government in a timely fashion. Online transactions are edited as they are submitted, reducing the potential for missing or inaccurate data. The portal also enables state agencies to direct resources toward other areas of their missions. With the availability of electronic forms in one place, the state is providing the public with a more successful and satisfying interaction with state government.

EVERYONE HAS A PART TO PLAY

An e-government task force was formed as the conduit for ideas and project work between the agencies and the centralized information technology (IT) organization, the Bureau of Information and Telecommunications (BIT). Membership comprised agency representatives (to serve as e-government facilitators) and each agency's BIT point of contact (chief technology consultant).

The legislature did its part by authorizing $400,000 for the project. While seemingly a lot of money, traditional methods of deploying e-government across all agency forms were estimated to cost $12 million. We realized our shoestring budget would necessitate a creative approach to delivering on the e-government promise. The legislature also removed the requirements for notary and original ink signatures, allowing electronic signatures instead, and added new federal (or state) laws governing what constitutes a signature.

YOUR FORMS TELL A STORY

The process of developing South Dakota Service Direct started with an initiative to have all public forms available online to provide better service to the public. The first step was to develop an inventory of all public forms for each agency. Inventory information collected included form title; status of the form (currently online, downloadable, or only on paper); transaction volume; end user of the form; fee required; signature, notary, or additional documentation required; and existing agency application computing/network infrastructure.

Our key challenge was surveying the agencies with regard to what forms they had and their characteristics. We were faced with the challenge of establishing where we were so that we could tell where we were headed and what exactly we were facing. Little did we know that the results of the survey would ultimately provide the metric by which the agencies' progress would be monitored. As we went along, we encountered some problems because the survey needed to be refined, and we had to go back to the agencies with secondary questions about their forms. We accomplished this by using our BIT agency Point of Contacts to collect the additional information. We were able to refine our inventory findings without asking the agencies to perform a lot of extra work. This inventory revealed the state-agency transaction dynamics. Note, we use the term "transaction" to mean the use of a form.

First, we learned that a few agencies do the most work. A half dozen agencies (Departments of Commerce and Regulation, Social Services, Labor, Revenue, Agriculture, and Environment and Natural Resources) have three-fourths of the forms, while a dozen forms (such as motor-vehicle titles and fishing/hunting licenses) generate more than half of the transactions. Some 50 percent of the forms were involved in fewer than 100 transactions per year, and 80 percent of the forms were used fewer than 1,000 times a year.

While the numbers may be small, the dynamics discussed throughout this chapter should apply across the states. South Dakota, like all states, does the following: tax, license, permit, inspect, grant money, protect, disseminate information, and develop resources. The difference is that South Dakota knows what it has—in January 2001, only one other state knew how many forms it had!

The second dynamic from the survey is that the agencies with the most forms did not generate the most transactions. This was evident in that the Department of Commerce and Regulation had 27 percent of the forms, while the Department of Revenue had 38 percent of the transactions.

The survey also pointed out a "spectrum of difficulty" relative to automating forms. This knowledge would allow all state work to be categorized and prioritized. The easiest forms only require editing the data that is entered. The next most difficult form requires additional documentation—anything from training certificates to photos to identity papers. Matching up the information to the electronic transaction is difficult at best. The next level of difficulty is the signature requirement. Electronic signatures add complexity and cost to online transactions. Another notch up in difficulty is the notary-public signature. Since, to some degree, an electronic process cannot ensure the state of mind of the person signing (i.e., is the person signing under duress) without a human present, electronic signatures can never fully replicate a notarization. Finally, many state processes require either a visit by a state official (e.g., inspectors, case workers) or a visit to a state office (e.g., driver's eye exam, trophy-fish measurement).

Many agencies require signatures for the majority of their forms, but in total, only 69 percent of all forms require a signature. We found many signature requirements to be dubious at best. Consider the staffer who, when asked why a form had a signature, replied, "There was room at the bottom of the page, so we stuck in a signature block. Don't all forms have a signature?" Luckily, only 21 percent of the forms require notarization. Two agencies, the Governor's Office of Economic Development and Lottery, required both signatures and notarization for all forms. Some 39 percent of the forms require additional documentation, and 10 percent required personal contact.

Another dynamic relates to how ingrained the difficulties are within agency processes. We found that the signature, notarization, additional-documentation, and personal-contact requirements could be invoked through statute, administrative rule, agency policy, or some other guideline (such as federal statute) outside the control of state government. Luckily, personal contact and notarization are mostly required at the discretion of the agencies. Only a third of the signatures were at agency discretion.

A fifth dynamic centers on whether a fee is required by the transaction. We found that the majority of forms have no fee. The significance is that a credit card transaction can serve as a signature—this is what most Internet commerce does today. Back in 2000, the South Dakota legislature passed the Uniform Electronic Transactions Act allowing this. As a result, some agencies (such as the secretary of state and the Department of Commerce and Regulation) can significantly reduce the electronic signature requirements of their electronic forms.

Finally, we learned that three-quarters of our forms were intended for businesses.

KNOWING THE DYNAMICS HELPED US DEFINE A SOLUTION

Identification of these dynamics and discussions with agency program managers led us to include the following functionality in the portal:

- Ability to download state forms
- Access to information about all state forms
- Access to all state online forms and applications
- Access to many state publications
- Search for forms by category, agency, or keyword
- Search for forms by "Life Events" timeline (e.g., forms arranged from birth through senior age groups)

- Search for forms by business cycle (e.g., start, grow, or run a business)
- Search for forms by stand-alone events (e.g., find a job)

Service Direct had to embody the following benefits:

- One-stop shopping for forms
- Quicker, easier access to state forms
- Consolidation of all information about state forms so that users are only three mouse clicks away from any form's information, download, and online execution, eliminating the need to go through an agency's website. The citizen or business does not have to know the structure of state government agencies to find and use a form
- Faster, cheaper, and more accurate interaction with the state
- More effective delivery of state government service to South Dakota's citizens and businesses. As transactions are submitted electronically, processing forms requires less staff time. Legible, edited, and complete data are submitted, and less paper storage space is needed to store the transactions. By having forms in electronic format, it is much easier for agencies to share forms with, or pass them on to, other agencies.

KEEP THE SOLUTION STRAIGHTFORWARD AND SIMPLE

After the inventory was complete, the next step was to work with the agencies to provide all forms in a downloadable format. We used IT programmers, college students, high school students, and agency program staff to put all forms online.

The next step was to develop a portal for all agency forms and their Web pages. Hot links are provided for some of the most popular forms citizens use. Businesses will use the many links provided in the "Business Cycle" section related to starting, growing, and running a business. This takes the user to a page from which to select the desired form. The user can also select categories of forms or all of the forms for an agency, as well as find a form by keyword search. The portal uses the pop-up window design so that the user can have the information page and the download or online page available at the same time.

The "Most Frequently Used" button is at the top of the page. The "Access All State Forms/Pubs" is the fastest path to a given form. Here all state forms are listed by service category and by agency. One can also search by keyword.

All forms have an information icon that the user can click to go directly to the information page. This page describes the form, who would fill it out, when, and why, and how to fill it out, as well as providing contact information if there are questions about completing the form. The user may choose the download icon or the online icon to complete and submit the form.

Searching for the right form is made easy via a "Life Events" timeline for locating services used by a specific age group. The life cycle timeline captures events average citizens will encounter or participate in during their lifetime. The citizen can also use the stand-alone event buttons for specific actions related to recurring lifetime activities, such as finding a job or dealing with one's health. Also, hot links are provided for some of the most popular forms citizens use—these tend to be seasonal in nature.

The site points businesses to services for starting, growing, and running a business.

Service Direct requires users to register on their first visit to the site and to enter a login user name and password on subsequent visits. The user is in a secure transaction mode during this process. The profile information is voluntary and is different for a business than it is for a citizen. Profile information is used to authenticate the type of user and will be used to prepopulate form fields for the user. The user can update this profile information at any time.

As the agencies continue to develop Web pages, they are more aware of how their Web pages fit into the larger picture. To make it easier for the user to get around each agency's Web pages, the agencies are developing Web pages with a common navigation, look, and feel.

Having all of the links in one place enables the state to check for and respond to broken links immediately since agencies continually maintain their websites and often provide links to other related agency sites. The portal also enables the state to capture statistics on the Web pages and to perform analysis on forms that experience heavy transaction volume, as well as to point out the forms that are not being completed online.

The form titles and links are stored in a Structured Query Language database that is easily updated and maintained by agency staff. Agency staffs maintain their agency forms and links through a password-protected administrative function.

Reports, which are run at weekly and daily intervals, provide statistics indicating the effectiveness of this service. We review, grade, and report to the agencies on the status of priority 1 and 2 W3C accessibility. Bobby is used along with manual and WatchFire review of pages. Items that are tracked include click through paths (pages viewed), duration of visit, hits (site-usage totals), page of departure, referring page, time of arrival, type of browser, unique users, and user comments and feedback.

AGENCIES NEED TO TAKE CONTROL

Once the forms were identified, inventoried, and provided as downloads on the portal, we were faced with the challenge of how to get the agencies to also move to online forms. We needed to find a way to provide online forms without taking the systems through a potential IT bottleneck of developing requirements and sending all of the systems through a traditional development process. Often, the forms involve a very limited number of transactions.

BIT, the central IT organization, developed the eForms system around the Adobe Acrobat product. We developed templates and processing rules for agency staffs to make their forms executable online—this also created a statewide consistent look and feel. An eForm can be created in which citizens fill in the blanks, editing occurs, calculations are made (such as totaling columns or calculating percentages or fees), and the form is e-mailed to the state agency for processing. As the eForms process was developed, agency personnel were trained to take the forms into this interactive experience.

We categorized the forms according to "first-do," "do-next," and "not-do."

The first-do category included forms with higher transaction volumes and no restrictions preventing them from being truly online forms. The user could sit down at his or her PC, bring up the form, complete it, click submit, get a response, and then get up and walk away—submitting the form was done!

The do-next category included forms with low transaction volumes and those that still had some restriction that prevented them from being easily put online, such as additional documentation or notarization requirements.

Finally, the not-do category included forms that should not be available online, for instance, forms that include a drawing, such as livestock brands, trademarks, and surveyor's plats, and forms that require a personal interaction between the state and the user, such as the inspection forms jointly completed by the state and the public for health inspection and gas pump and scale inspection and verification, as well as applications that have to be made in person by a citizen.

USERS LIKE THE EXPERIENCE

The South Dakota Service Direct portal has been in operation since August 1, 2002. The Service Direct portal is available at www.sd.gov or via a link from the state's home website at www.state.sd.us. Since its launch, 8,000 households and 1,500 businesses have registered on the portal. This may not seem like a large number, but remember that South Dakota has only 400,000 households and 23,000 businesses. Hence, we have 2 percent of the households and 6.6 percent of the businesses online after nine months.

As of April 2003, the portal contained information links on all state forms, downloadable copies of all state forms, and two-thirds of all state forms either doable online or requiring a visit by a state official. Of 23 agencies, 14 have all of their forms doable online.

Our formal satisfaction survey, reachable when the user logs out of the portal, showed a 2.0 average experience on a scale of 1 to 4, with 1 being excellent. Unfortunately, we only had 96 survey responses over eight months. We went to a "smiley face" satisfaction survey and have received 367 responses in the first month. Again the users rated the site a 2.0 out of 4, with 1 being excellent.

OUR EXPERIENCES POINT THE WAY TO THE FUTURE

There are a number of directions we would like to pursue based on our experiences with Service Direct:

- *Advertise, advertise, and advertise.* We feel that 40 to 50 percent of an agency's workload needs to be done online before major efficiencies can be realized.
- *Improve access to federal forms from our portal.* Right now, we do a little to align state government forms with federal government forms. We currently point an individual to the corresponding federal site. Eventually, we want to provide direct access to the corresponding federal form, not just to the home page of the federal agency. Ultimately, we wish to do the same with local government forms.
- *Improve upon our logical grouping of forms.* For example, we would like to provide a logical set of forms to the public based on the type of business individuals may be considering starting (e.g., there would be a different set of forms to complete if one were starting a gas station versus a health club).
- *Fill in forms as much as possible for the user.* For instance, name, address, and telephone numbers would be prefilled.
- *Support digital signatures.* This is not a technical, but strictly a cost, issue.
- *Conduct all transactions in real time.* The ultimate user experience comes from instant closure on a transaction.

20

Delivering the Promise of E-Government

Vera Katz, Mayor of Portland, Oregon

When I was first elected mayor of the city of Portland in 1992, E-Government was more a distant vision than a promise an elected official could deliver upon. Government was only just emerging as a presence on the Internet here in Portland, and we had only recently begun discussions with the community about public access to online information and communication. That, in 2002, we were able to say with confidence that our city would soon boast a 24-hour city hall accessible to all is testimony to the power and force of technology. The journey from the fledgling and disparate attempts of our city bureaus to navigate the digital world to today, where we are just months away from truly being one online city anywhere, anytime, has been arduous and is literally changing the way we do business.

Portland's first steps toward capitalizing on the potential of information technology (IT) included the introduction of internal e-mail and employee Internet access, development of individual bureau websites, and internal use of mapping tools. The use of different browsers and software programs created problems that became apparent only when bureaus needed to share information. Public demand for easily accessed information at a citywide level drove the development of a geographical information systems (GIS) hub that could coordinate mapping information from multiple sources and the creation of a corporate Web presence. These advances, although significant, still did not qualify as E-Government. The case studies in this chapter show the evolution of our technology practices toward a true Portland E-Government system and the lessons learned along the way.

FRAMEWORK FOR THE TRANSITION TO E-GOVERNMENT

Today most bureaus of the city of Portland recognize the opportunities presented by the innovative use of IT, and some individual bureaus have already taken steps to provide new information and service-delivery options to citizens. Almost all city bureaus have an Internet presence, and many have an intranet presence. All bureaus can receive communications and electronic documents via e-mail. There are a few examples of e-commerce at varying levels of maturity and several examples of citizens being able provide input or initiate processes via online forms. Some bureaus even require digital document submission or have migrated their polices and procedures to the Internet. Others are working on online tracking systems for the public.

Bureaus also periodically revisit their business processes, pursuing savings and efficiencies. For instance, the Bureau of Development Services, in conjunction with other public works bureaus, recently overhauled its permit-issuing system and streamlined its multibureau process to increase speed, effectiveness, and access for contractors and home owners.

Data-sharing relationships exist with Multnomah County and Metro, our regional government, as part of online mapping services. As a result, Portland's Corporate GIS program has worked closely with several bureaus to produce leading-edge, map-based online applications for the public.

The Bureau of Information Technology, the Police Bureau, the Office of Neighborhood Involvement, and one of the city's recognized neighborhood associations are collaborating on a project—eVolvement—to provide citizens new technology tools for interacting with government. This project is putting computers in the homes of low-income families to test an online, portal-oriented approach to improving citizen involvement in community policing in the Portsmouth neighborhood.

These are some of the many valuable, but often unconnected, bits and pieces of a twenty-first-century digital government throughout the citywide organization. Therein lies the challenge—to create an E-Government whole greater than the sum of its parts. We believe the answer will be to use corporate policymaking to bring citywide coherence and cohesion to data management, resource management, internal operations and processes, and service and information delivery—true E-Government.

THE EARLY JOURNEY AND THE ENTERPRISE GIS HUB

In 1996, several city of Portland bureaus had mapping systems for internal use. These systems used different software that the bureaus felt best met their business needs. However, public interest was growing for access to everything from zoning maps to demographics to being able to see what capital-improvement projects would be coming to their neighborhoods. Bureaus also found themselves either needing access to data from other bureaus or needing to share data directly across bureaus. With disparate software and hardware in place, data were also being duplicated on different systems, a redundant and inefficient use of resources.

After considerable study and planning, the concept for an Enterprise[1] GIS hub that would provide shared data storage through a standardized approach was developed and piloted. Portland's data engineering and technological design focused on Web-based technology and a component-based approach, establishing an environment that has supported many subsequent innovations and allowed design components to be developed once but used repeatedly.

Today, the GIS hub, based on ESRI products, provides a centralized data warehouse to which various bureaus contribute the data sets they maintain. These data sets comprise 200 layers stored in geodatabase and shapfile formats and include cadastre, transportation, water and sewer delivery networks, zoning and land use, natural resources, and digital imagery. In the past few years, integration with the city budget has begun, with a standardized approach to collecting geographic, narrative, and financial data on capital projects, which are now available online.

The common format for viewing and using these data sets is the Internet, thus making information accessible across all bureaus and to the public. From the casual user's perspective, the Enterprise GIS hub is a website that accesses all enterprise data for the city and the surrounding metro area. Users are able to browse and query the data online.

The GIS hub makes the diversity of underlying systems transparent to the user and provides scalable, e-enabled, casual, and expert user access. The GIS hub is a unique solution that provides an alternative for jurisdictions that require a structure that meets multiple participants' needs without their having to share a single system. The hub approach is especially appealing to jurisdictions that want enterprise capability but have historic investments in disparate systems, training, and data.

In Portland, the hub is used to leverage these historic investments and provide the most cost-effective solution to making business improvements and meeting goals for enterprise capability. The business-case evaluation of the hub project indicated substantial net savings based on the elimination of redundancy, improved processes, and one-time savings. The hub is helping Portland maintain its goal of 70 percent reusability of its corporate-technology infrastructure and is estimated to have saved about $9 million in redundant and disconnected resource commitments over a five-year period.

The city of Portland has worked arduously since 1998, through strategic planning for all its IT services, to evolve from an eclectic collection of relatively independent IT organizations into a consolidated enterprise or corporate IT resource-management and service organization. Along the way, the organization collaboratively set some initial corporate standards, developed key corporate technology tools, improved the city's network infrastructure, and centralized administration of all IT staff. The city has achieved many, but not all, of its original goals.

The E-Government initiative is the next logical step in Portland's IT evolution. The first steps toward E-Government have focused on the robust capabilities of the GIS hub. To date, Portland's Corporate GIS program has worked with several bureaus to produce the leading-edge, map-based online features for citizens outlined in the following case studies.

Online Mapping at www.portlandmaps.com

The city of Portland launched a new map-based information service, PortlandMaps.com, in 2001. PortlandMaps uses Web-based mapping technology to provide detailed and quality information about city neighborhoods. The information provided on the site has always been available to the public but has not necessarily been easy either to access or view spatially.

The city's Corporate GIS team worked with multiple city bureaus to compile and map information frequently requested by citizens, using the Enterprise GIS hub for data access. Using an address or an intersection, users can create maps showing a variety of information, including detailed property-assessment information, aerial photographs, crime statistics, environmental hazards, nearby schools and parks, zoning designations, water and sewer lines, and upcoming capital-improvement projects. Developing PortlandMaps required data sharing among city bureaus, Multnomah County, and Metro.[2]

PortlandMaps receives over one million hits every month from employees, the business community, and the general public and has proven to be a valuable public-access tool. As one citizen wrote, "I just discovered this site last night. I wanted to let you know that I am very impressed with the quality and quantity of information presented. Your site is easy to navigate through and very user friendly. We spent literally hours looking at various pages and learned a lot about our neighborhood."[3]

Online Crime Maps at www.portlandpolicebureau.com/crimemapper.html

Launched in February 2001, CrimeMapper is a publicly available Web-based tool that identifies and tracks neighborhood crime. CrimeMapper helps the community and police boost Portland's community-policing and crime-prevention efforts. The goal of CrimeMapper is to employ these existing strategies, while using the information on the website to target problems before they develop into serious situations requiring additional police services.

Since the 1970s, the Police Bureau has used maps to display crime patterns and illustrate crime profiles. These handmade maps were able to display patterns but not detect them. The bureau moved to its first automated mapping system in 1988, and for the first time, static data (such as streets, boundaries, and patrol districts) and transient data (such as reported crimes, stolen autos, and calls for service) were mapped together. This provided the ability to detect patterns and "hot spots." It was not until 1998 that mapping stations at each police precinct could provide more timely data through a Crime Analysis Mapping Information Network system, developed using federal grant funds.

As a community-policing agency, the Portland Police Bureau still needed to be able to share crime-mapping capabilities with community public-safety partners, such as crime-prevention specialists in the neighborhoods and the public. An Internet-based tool was essential that would provide timely data in an accessible format that would not require specialized software or hardware.

CrimeMapper creates maps using a database of Part 1 crimes from the Portland Police Data System. In addition, CrimeMapper can also create detailed graphs and reports. This GIS-based system makes information about reported crimes widely accessible to the public and service providers. By providing complementary links to service providers, the site encourages active involvement in crime prevention and problem-solving activities. The application also provides an ongoing history of crime incidents so that public-safety partners such as the Police Bureau, the County Parole Office, the neighborhood Crime Prevention Program, and neighborhood and business associations can evaluate community-based initiatives against their impact on reported crime.

The Police Bureau obtained Bureau of Justice Assistance Block Grant funding for the Internet project in 1999. The city's Corporate GIS team employed its experience developing other Web-mapping applications to develop and implement the CrimeMapper application quickly and cost-effectively. Project staff solicited input from the Office of Neighborhood Involvement crime-prevention staff and the Chief's Forum as well as Police Bureau managers. The result was a user-friendly tool that provides detailed crime information while maintaining confidentiality.

The application leveraged the city's GIS hub technology investment to complete the project. Corporate GIS built CrimeMapper in just a few months to the bureau's specifications, including the necessity to perform well at typical household Internet-connection speeds.

CrimeMapper turned out to be even more than the project managers originally envisioned. Corporate GIS and the Portland Police Bureau realized early on that comprehensive "spatial reports" could be generated automatically by the system based on a simple address or point entered by a user. What was initially conceived from the perspective of traditional mapping applications with advanced user-interface options was reengineered into a spatial-report approach that simplified displaying and querying the information. This way, the complexity is handled by the application, and users are presented with the information and maps specific to the location of their choice.

With a valid street address, intersection, or address number, the application provides a map of Part 1 crimes surrounding a specific location within Portland. Viewers can look at type of crime, reported date, or date range and also use the application to display information in graph form. Graphing and reporting features display crime data by month, day of week, and time of day. Users can also view crimes by point of occurrence and by crime density.

The Police Bureau is committed to maintaining the confidentiality of sensitive information. CrimeMapper does not retrieve or display victim or suspect information or details about specific crimes. Nor does it provide point locations of sexual-assault crimes, which are displayed only on a density grid. The CrimeMapper database is updated monthly, provides one full year of data on Part 1 crimes, and includes an online help file with crime definitions.

CrimeMapper also provides links to Police Bureau resources and programs, as well as to other problem-solving, law-enforcement, and neighborhood-resource links. CrimeMapper tracks crime incidents and reduction success, providing accountability and reinforcing police problem-solving partnerships with the community. In addition, the report and graphing features encourage greater distribution of statistical information to the public and foster more detailed crime analysis.

Online Carpool Matching at www.carpoolmatchnw.org

Portland is well known for its progressive transportation and land-use policies and programs. The Transportation Options Division of the city of Portland provides programs and activities designed to encourage people to walk, bike, carpool, or ride public transit as their first choice for transportation and to remove barriers that prevent them from doing so.

CarpoolMatchNW, launched in April 2002, was created to reduce barriers to carpooling in the Portland area, including eliminating jurisdictional boundaries and a lack of coordination between three existing regional rideshare programs.

The Transportation Options Division formed and coordinated a multiorganizational committee, including representatives from transit agencies, other jurisdictions, employers, and transportation management associations

(TMAs) to break down the barriers to carpooling in the region. These agencies worked closely to develop an online tool offering a seamless carpool and vanpool matching service to 15 counties in Oregon and southwest Washington. The committee was intimately involved in developing the site and planning the promotional campaign.

When Corporate GIS learned about the transportation division's project, the team was eager to share the tools it had developed for CrimeMapper and PortlandMaps with CarpoolMatchNW. A series of negotiations proved that using CGIS's in-house tools was the best solution for the mapping component of CarpoolMatchNW, and they joined the development team.

The Climate Trust, a Portland-based nonprofit organization dedicated to reducing greenhouse-gas emissions, provided funding for the project. The primary objective of the CarpoolMatchNW website is to reduce carbon dioxide emissions by providing an easy-to-use regional database for Rideshare matching. The site won the Environmental Protection Agency's 2002 Climate Protection Award for reducing local emissions of greenhouse gases.

Because the project sought to remove barriers to carpooling, it was essential that technology did not itself create a new barrier. Changing travel behavior is difficult, and if users do not have a good website experience, the region loses opportunities to reduce car trips. Therefore, it was essential that the site be reliable and accessible and perform well.

The application was designed so that internal technical and authorized rideshare staff alike can maintain the application. The technology is also easily adaptable for future modification, and the site was designed with scalability functions so that it can be applied on a statewide basis in the future. Users with slower modems were considered during graphic design, and the site also meets all required state accessibility requirements.

CarpoolMatchNW is customized to unique user-transportation needs and preferences and includes several key features. The website gives the user control in finding a rideshare match. Applicants can instantly see whether a match exists for them and are able to find the match that suits them best. Users can immediately send an e-mail to any of the names on their search list. By allowing people to establish a relationship through the anonymity of e-mail before more personal contact is needed, the website provides a greater sense of security and control. CarpoolMatchNW combines the region's three rideshare databases, providing more opportunity for matches.

Customer-service representatives remain available by phone to help people who do not have access to the Internet or who are having trouble. Frontline staff also has access to CarpoolMatchNW and can use it to assist their work. The site is currently being translated into Spanish and Russian to better serve Portland's regional population.

During the first eight months, most marketing of CarpoolMatchNW has been to businesses through low-budget, one-on-one outreach. This resulted in 1,060 user registrations, which was a tremendous increase over the few hundred names in the region's pre-CarpoolMatchNW rideshare databases. Thirty-day and six-month surveys were sent to each participant with a 30 percent response rate to date. So far, 20 people, or 2 percent of survey responders, have reported finding a carpool partner.

Reporting carbon dioxide reduction, the number of users, and their travel behavior are key components of this application. The success of CarpoolMatchNW is dependent upon robust reporting capability. The division is projecting a reduction in car traffic from use of this website. The target is to reduce vehicle miles by an estimated 160 million, save 8.5 million gallons of gas, and reduce carbon dioxide by 70,000 metric tons over the project's ten-year period. Personal follow-up with users who have found a carpool is used to verify carbon dioxide reduction.

The Transportation Options Division learned several key lessons as it developed CarpoolMatchNW. By performing beta tests to ensure that the mapping components functioned for people who typify the ultimate user and to verify the accuracy and robustness of the GIS data, the division was able to launch the site with confidence that it would provide good results for its users. The division also delayed some features of the site that were not essential for public use. They are still working on the administrative reporting aspects and translation of the site into Spanish and Russian. Another key consideration is replicability or expansion. By ensuring that these types of applications conform to practices and procedures common to other similar agencies at as many levels of government as feasible, the originating agency can ensure easy adaptation of related data and programs to the Internet.

Online Housing Resources at www.housingconnections.org

The mission of the Bureau of Housing and Community Development is to work in partnership with the community as the professional steward of the city of Portland's community-development resources, serving as a catalyst to stabilize and improve neighborhoods. With the 2002 launch of Housing Connections, the bureau expanded its services to the Internet, offering the most comprehensive and integrated resource for affordable, accessible, and special-needs housing in the region.

With today's greater access to computers at home and work as well as through libraries and friends, an increasingly diverse pool of people is using the Internet. In fact, 70 percent of households in the Greater Portland-Vancouver Metro Area are on the Internet, and Nielsen NetRating has rated Portland as the "most wired" city in the country.[4] While there remains a digital divide, particularly among income and education levels, Portland's online population is steadily looking more like the general population. In fact,

38 percent of those in Portland households earning less than $30,000 now have Internet access.[5]

The concept for Housing Connections arose from public involvement in the joint consolidated plan of the city of Portland, Multnomah County, and the city of Gresham for 2000 to 2005. The consolidated plan is a collaborative plan for local housing and community development. As the Bureau of Housing and Community Development worked with multiple public stakeholders, difficulty finding affordable housing and housing services emerged as a critical issue.

Several related problems were also identified. There was no centralized source to search for affordable housing or services in the Portland, Oregon, region. Only one-third of survey respondents during the planning process knew which agency to turn to for help with specific housing issues. Frontline housing-agency staff also reported that 80 percent of public calls had been referred to them by another housing agency, even though they were about issues the referred agency did not handle. Due to the large and complex service-delivery system, frontline staff often did not have the necessary knowledge for appropriate referrals, gave inappropriate referrals, or were too late to avert a crisis. Staff turnover, a complex network of constantly changing programs, and the short time frames of most housing cases required a widely accessible, easily updated source of information.

As they examined these issues, stakeholders and housing planners determined that an online system could consolidate current information on affordable, accessible, and special-needs units and also provide easy links with housing services. In September 2000, the Bureau of Housing and Community Development received a Department of Commerce Technical Opportunities Grant to develop Housing Connections.

The goal for Housing Connections was to provide up-to-date housing information online with user-friendly tools customized to the needs of three major user groups—renters, landlords and property managers, and housing-agency staff. The bureau sought to direct users to the appropriate resources, streamline access to services, and improve collection and analysis of housing data.

A core team of staff from Housing and Community Development and from Corporate GIS planned and developed Housing Connections. In addition, a design team of representatives from nonprofit housing providers, property-management companies, and regional governmental partners including Multnomah, Clackamas, Washington, and Clark Counties in Washington helped with the project. Key partners in the project included the Federal Technical Opportunities Program and Housing and Urban Development, as well as the Mt. Hood Cable Regulatory Commission through additional grant funds.

To address the project's challenges—lack of centralized information, disparate business processes, and diverse user communities—the technological infrastructure of the site needed to bridge existing limitations. The Housing Connections solution includes both Web applications and services to meet several business needs.

A "Housing Locator" feature allows landlords to list and renters to search for affordable, accessible, or special-needs housing. The Housing Locator includes a database searchable by address, area, and school district. Available data includes detailed property descriptions, photos and floor plans, and interactive GIS maps of surrounding amenities, including parks, grocery stores, transportation, and more. Using the Housing Calculator, renters can determine their median family income (sometimes required for eligibility), as well as an affordable monthly rent payment based on their income.

Three additional features are scheduled for launch in 2003. Through the Housing Services Locator, users will be able to search for services provided by local agencies addressing a variety of housing barriers and issues. A Waitlist Management tool will allow renters to apply for multiple property waitlists online and keep their contact information up to date. This same tool will allow property managers to manage waitlists electronically. An online rental application will allow renters to apply to multiple properties with one electronic application.

By creating a central location for housing information, Housing Connections has streamlined housing processes for low-income renters and the agencies that assist them. Users can currently search through over 28,000 units listed on Housing Connections. Over 85,000 housing searches have been completed on the system since its launch in May 2002.

Summary

All three of the preceding case studies demonstrate some basic keys to implementing successful E-Government components. First, in all cases, the relationship between the city bureau and the Corporate GIS team was distinguished by complementary, but distinct, roles. The bureau exhibited a thorough understanding of its business need and the issues or problems it was looking to technology to solve. Likewise, Corporate GIS demonstrated a proficient grasp of those business needs and was thus able to explore and provide effective technical solutions.

Other elements of these projects contributed to their success. Each provides direct and easy access to information empowering for citizens. They are the result of partnerships where key users worked closely in planning and testing the technological tools. This aided in guaranteeing user friendliness, and thus future use of the sites. They all use reliable, high-quality data and provide information in accessible formats.

WHAT IS E-GOVERNMENT TRANSFORMATION?

E-Government transformation is the evolution from a basic Web presence to a fully connected and integrated digital environment where citizens, businesses, other governments, and employees can seamlessly interact with government 24 hours a day, 7 days a week. With E-Government, a true 24-hour city hall becomes a reality.

E-Government transformation is the fourth phase of the Gartner Group's "Four Phases of E-Government" model.[6] Phase 1 is "Presence," a stage of E-Government development characterized by the land rush simply to have a cyberspace placeholder, a website, on the Internet. In the United States to date, federal, state, and local governments have implemented more than 10,000 websites to inform the public about government agencies.

The next phase, "Interaction," features websites that provide basic search capabilities, forms to download, and links to other relevant sites, as well as the e-mail addresses of offices or officials, enabling the public to access customized information online and receive forms that may have previously required a visit to a government office. Many governments also put requests for proposals and bidding regulations online as a precursor to e-procurement.

The evolution to the "Transaction" phase is characterized by applications that allow constituents to conduct and complete entire tasks online. During this stage, governments build online self-service applications for the public and use the Web to complement other service-delivery channels. Typical services migrated at this stage include paying utility bills, fines, and permit and license fees. Some governments are making their bid-submittal processes available over the Internet to allow bidders to submit electronically. Others are allowing the filing of court documents. This is the current stage for many agencies and the most immediate target for many E-Government initiatives worldwide. It provides not only the benefits of 24/7 availability but also opportunities to develop cross-agency, common, shared services.

The "Transformation" phase is the long-term goal of almost all national and local E-Government initiatives. It is characterized by reengineering government service delivery to provide constituents a single point of contact that makes government organization totally transparent to the public. This phase relies on robust customer-relationship management tools and new, alternative service-delivery capabilities that reshape relationships between citizens, businesses, and government.

Transformation enhances the ability of constituents to participate directly in government activities. Examples of transformation include highly tailored websites, or "virtual agencies," where government information is geared toward the public, and citizens can perform transactions all in one place, with seamless interfaces back to the agencies involved in the transactions and opportunities for citizens to give electronic feedback to decision makers on policy issues. This phase also includes the development of state-of-the-art intranets that can link government employees who work in different agencies. Governmental transformation will also include the design of extranets that allow the seamless flow of information and collaborative decision making among federal, state, and local government agencies; private and not-for-profit sector partners; and the public.

In the Gartner model, while it is unlikely that any bureaucracy will jump right to transformation, it is not necessary that every bureau or agency go through all four phases. It is sometimes feasible to skip to interaction or even transaction without going through the other phases. A government, bureau, or agency can also run its sites in different phases of development. For example, a city's building-permit department might be well into the "Transaction" phase and accepting credit card payments over the Internet, while its utility department has a website that only gives office locations and hours.

WHY E-GOVERNMENT?

Over the last decade, the Internet has revolutionized the way people and businesses communicate, share information, and conduct transactions. The power and convenience of e-mail alone has revolutionized the way we communicate. As people and businesses turn more to the Internet as the medium of choice for commerce and communications, the public can reasonably expect these valuable experiences to be available from their government as well.

The Internet has enabled consumers to shop, obtain information, and conduct business 24 hours a day at their convenience. These experiences have led citizens to expect the same convenience and cost-effective delivery of government services. For the government willing to embrace the digital economy, the results can be very beneficial. Research has shown that, "Depending upon the service, early studies indicate governments are saving up to 70 percent by moving services online compared to the costs of providing the same services over the counter."[7]

Today, more than ever, government is faced with the challenge of engaging its citizens in democracy. E-Government embraces new technology as a tool for building communities, enabling democracy, enhancing service delivery, and streamlining internal operations.

The city of Portland's internal stakeholder group includes those who deliver services, those who provide the infrastructure, and those who authorize how government services get delivered. Together, they share responsibility for guiding the transformation to E-Government.

Bureaus share a common goal of providing a better public experience through more efficient service delivery. The effectiveness, efficiency, and integrity of the citizen experience rely on agencies coming together around common infrastructures, protocols, and interfaces. E-Government, done well, creates a mutual, interdependent environment across the family of agencies.

It is our vision that the city of Portland will be an international model of innovative, inclusive, responsive, effective, and sustainable E-Government, providing information and services to meet the present and future economic, social, and environmental needs of our community. To realize that vision, we are moving toward an enterprise portal approach to provide all Internet and intranet users convenient, secure, reliable, responsive, and cost-effective access to services, information, and opportunities for interaction and participation. One early example of the power of interactive, user-oriented, online service delivery is the Police Bureau's online Public Information Office.

Police Online at www.cgis.ci.portland.or.us/PBWebNotify.cfm

In June 2002, the Portland Police Bureau launched an online Public Information Office news site to serve as the primary distribution method for police press releases and CrimeStopper alerts and as the primary source for releases, photos, and news-related information.

This online public information "officer" offers 24/7 access to breaking news and automatically distributes information to the press. This approach eliminates the cost, time, and waste associated with faxing and mailing information on paper and the staff time involved with maintaining mailing lists.

Media and other users can sign up for a 24/7 e-mail notification service. Subscribers automatically receive the type and frequency of news they have requested when it is added or updated, conserving resources and reducing distribution problems. Subscribing to releases and alerts is easy, and users can update their custom subscriptions to vary the type and frequency of information they want to view or receive.

Visitors, including the public, can view, sort, and search news releases and alerts without having to subscribe to the service. Because the site may include photos, graphics, detailed contact information, and other related information (including case numbers), in-depth information is readily accessible to the media and public 24 hours a day. Icons in news articles alert users to any available information, with camera icons for photographs and paperclips for other attachments.

All news information remains online so the media can access archives and retrieve past information at any time. By augmenting the site with photos and background information, the Police Bureau makes it easy to develop, present, and track stories while allowing officers and support staff to remain focused on crime prevention and response.

The Portland Police Bureau's Planning and Support Division and Portland's Corporate GIS program developed the site and its subscription service jointly. Launch of the site included notice to media contacts that current fax and e-mail distribution of news information would be discontinued following a subscription period.

Notably, the new application allows authorized staff to post and augment information directly on the Web, eliminating the need for technical translation into HTML. This speeds direct access to information from bureau rather than technical staff, ensuring immediate release of the most up-to-date information from the officers and support staff who are in the field.

DISCUSSION

Electronic government provides the unique opportunity to unite all bureaus or departments in a jurisdiction to serve constituents 24/7. An enterprisewide view can help government leverage the public's investment in technology to provide services built around user needs, allowing users to complete all related tasks in one place.

A founding principal for the successful transformation to E-Government is looking at information and information services as a centralized resource. E-Government requires information sharing, joint development and use of technology, participation in enterprise contracts, shared portals, and other means to leverage technical resources. It includes analyzing the benefits of internal development versus outsourcing to achieve a secure, service-rich infrastructure as quickly as possible. At the citywide level, all new technology systems should be developed so that they can be easily incorporated into the E-Government Web-enabled architecture using open standards.

One of the promises of E-Government is to provide a single face of government to constituents. A comprehensive view of government and its mission must take priority over that of any individual bureau or division. This comprehensive view must be defined, communicated, and implemented through internal policies, standards, and guidelines that unify electronic service delivery. Portland's leadership is providing guidance and direction based on the following principles and beliefs.

E-Government is already fundamentally changing the way people interact with government in Portland. Legal groundwork for E-Government is still being laid. The federal government is taking an active role in establishing standards, including the Paperwork Elimination Act, the Electronic Signatures in Global and National Commerce (E-Sign) Act, the Uniform Electronic Transactions Act (UETA), and many more. Local government can be proactive in the development of new legislation that will ensure the success of E-Government services and information.

While E-Government should eventually realize cost savings through increased efficiency, often significant initial investment is required to develop the technical infrastructure, applications, and operational support required to implement electronic service delivery. Removing legislative and administrative barriers to innovative, nontraditional funding sources such as technology funds, subscription and convenience fees, joint funding between multiple bureaus, agencies or third parties, and advertising would provide needed incentives.

Ensuring that private information and confidential communications will remain secure and private is critical. The city is working to establish a thorough and binding privacy policy regulating the collection and storage of personal data, including sharing of data among government entities and the public. Data harvesting, while a potential funding strategy, must be carefully crafted to respect the need for privacy. In addition to privacy issues, public trust in E-Government is contingent upon the security and reliability of the online services and infrastructure. We are currently evaluating options and developing plans to strengthen physical, network, and data security.

Digital government must also be accessible to as many citizens as possible. Accessibility requires addressing the resistance of reluctant and inexperienced users, including those with special needs, in addition to tackling the implications of geography, economics, education, culture, and physical disabilities.

One of the barriers to efficient implementation and operation of online services is that applications are typically funded and developed as standalone entities. With the evolution from a mainframe environment to server-based computing, fragmentation is even more common. Since two of the main expectations of E-Government are to provide a seamless interface to government services and concurrently reduce the cost of service delivery, there is a need to provide a common, flexible technical architecture and infrastructure to support new services. This infrastructure must be based on open standards that ensure a high degree of interoperability among different hardware and software platforms from multiple vendors.

E-Government success is dependent on high-level sponsorship and leadership support. Because it requires a change in the way government agencies conduct business and a paradigm shift in how bureaus or departments view their services and service delivery, lack of high-level leadership can lead to breakdowns in the corporate approach necessary to make the transformation to true E-Government.

With E-Government, especially through the portal approach underway in Portland, an agency's services become defined as part and parcel of the service of the government as a whole. Services are categorized not by the function of a single bureau but from a user perspective. Thus, the commonalities among services become more important than their individuality. At the same time, the system must remain responsive to each agency's business approach and business needs.

THE FUTURE OF E-GOVERNMENT

In Portland, we are discovering that with strong leadership sponsorship and support and a collaborative, business-needs-oriented approach by centralized technology service providers, the promise of E-Government is becoming a foreseeable reality. The new tools of PortlandOnline will keep content management in the hands of bureau and agency professionals, while IT professionals can focus on technical solutions to the business needs of the public, city bureaus, and the city organization as a whole.

The E-Government initiative will be centered on a Web portal called PortlandOnline. This branding is critical as it defines what we are and how people can remember where we are. We are Portland, and we are online. Branding is one of the most important aspects of any new service. The new portal will be available using .com, .net, and .org.

PortlandOnline will focus on moving the city of Portland through the Gartner Group's third and fourth phases of E-Government—"Transaction" and "Transformation." PortlandOnline, the Web portal, will change the focus from multiple points of contact with multiple government agencies to a single point of contact organized around the needs and life events of citizens and businesses.

This realignment of access will emulate the successful models for online access to services. It transcends the traditional presentation of services that is based on a jurisdiction's formal organization structure. PortlandOnline will integrate and organize services and information based both on models of successful citizen-oriented portals, which organize information by the citizen's need or intent, and on the input from local stakeholders. Multiple city agencies and even other regional organizations may be combined online to deliver services to citizens from a single online location 24/7.

The city of Portland will create an environment that makes sense to the citizen and be intuitively understandable, with a uniform look and feel, again providing the seamless integration of government services. PortlandOnline will provide a single portal to reach all existing Web services provided by bureaus today, as well as transforming to new services. These features will be supported at the corporate and bureau levels through reuse of standardized components, consistent applications, standardized enterprisewide infrastructure, and revised business processes.

While most of Portland's current websites provide static content that must be published and maintained by skilled technical staff, a new content-management service is becoming available for new and transforming websites. Currently, a handful of webmasters throughout the city maintain websites and are responsible for publishing content; this leads to valuable technical resources being spent on routine maintenance and updates rather than developing new e-solutions. The answer is to develop an enterprise content-management system so that the few will no longer have to publish content for the many. Anyone who is given permission will be able to publish content easily to the enterprise portal.

A simple Web-based publishing tool will enable anyone to submit content from sources such as Microsoft Word documents, Excel spread sheets, charts, PDF documents, Web links, and images. The service will also be configured to allow a review-and-approval process for Web content where desired.

E-commerce functionality is being developed to include the ability to process payments by credit card, electronic check, and automatic debit and to create purchase orders with proper accounting to cost centers. The system will directly interface with the city's financial and banking systems to provide complete audit and cost-accounting functions. Also, the service will allow client access to the record of any transaction performed with the city.

The E-Calendar will be another central service that will allow posting of any event, meeting, class, or other function that can be accessed by anyone through the PortlandOnline portal. The E-Calendar will interact with other components, such as E-Registration, E-Payment, and E-Notification services to allow a person to search the calendar for an event, register for it, pay any associated fees, and receive confirmations of registration and payment, as well as a reminder on the event day.

Service management is the centralized management for any service or action request. With the envisioned E-Service request, any issue, concern, or request can be logged into the system. Where the request is "e-enabled," the system will present the appropriate service. Otherwise, the system will then route the request to the appropriate individual or business unit. All requests for services can be viewed and tracked across the enterprise for true one-stop resolution. No longer will the customer have to locate the entity in charge to get something done.

Internal as well as external requests will be handled in the system. Examples include getting a new phone, moving furniture, or reporting a pothole, graffiti, or fallen stop sign. Any service that requires the gathering of information and routing to a specific business unit can be automated. However, as one of the most important functions of the service will be the ability to track the progress of any request, the system must integrate with the business processes and systems that are used to record that progress. The person submitting the request will be able to monitor progress using a tracking number or code.

Online forums offer a unique and convenient way for citizens to communicate with each other and their government. The E-Democracy Forums available through PortlandOnline will allow posting of comments and questions into topical categories, where other individuals using the forums can respond and create an online discussion of important issues and events. An internal version of these forums would provide city employees a new way of collaborating on projects. Online forums are available 24 hours a day for the user's convenience, can be used either anonymously or nonanonymously, and may be moderated or not, depending on user preference and city policy.

Polling services are often used to assess public sentiment on a given issue. By adding polling services to an online portal, the city of Portland will have an automated way of soliciting citizen input on key policy decisions. Polling services can be created to interface with mapping to allow for geographic analysis of results. For example, poll results can be reported to see how residents in various neighborhoods responded to the poll.

Notification services play an integral part in any city. Using the Internet for E-Notification can streamline and automate the distribution of press releases, memos, or other content for public consumption. Using notification services can assist with managing contact lists, creating subscription lists for content, and enable distributions to multiple organizations in an efficient manner.

Based on planning to date, users will be able to configure and personalize PortlandOnline to deliver information and services based on their preferences. User preferences will be maintained so that whenever and wherever the user accesses the site, that user will be presented with his or her own customized view, once it is assured that the privacy of the user's preferences can be protected.

For example, a developer may wish to see only information related to permits, zoning, and capital-improvement projects. A neighborhood user may not be interested in commercial building permits but interested in community activities, city council hearings, budget meetings, or community events. By customizing their preferences through PortlandOnline, users will be able to receive automatic notification of policy decisions of interest in their neighborhood or of events that fit a predefined profile.

Streaming video enhances the availability of important public discourse, including council meetings, hearings, and other communications. By using streaming video services, citizens will have 24-hour access to a library of anything the city wishes to offer in video format. Video streaming and archives are already online for Portland City Council meetings. Expanding this service to include other public meetings, internal training, and other applications will add a new dimension to public and employee interaction with the city. Coordination of other resources through PortlandOnline, such as the documents being discussed at a city council meeting, will enhance the ability of the citizen to participate.

Wireless communications technology is opening new opportunities for E-Government. Cell phones have become the norm and are indispensable communication tools. The ability to send and receive information while not physically connected to a network will open up a plethora of productive enhancements. Public-safety organizations have been using wireless technology to send critical information to police, fire, and medical units for some time. The widespread availability of wireless functionality will enable services to be accessed not only through traditional means but using devices such as personal digital assistants and other Internet-enabled devices.

CONCLUSION

The promise of E-Government, a light on the horizon a mere ten years ago, is now becoming a reality around the country. Some jurisdictions are further ahead in one area, some in others. For Portland, the tools of E-Government are providing meaningful ways for the public to understand and connect to the work we perform as the stewards of a safe, healthy, livable city. Early indicators show that new online tools available through the GIS hub are effective for the public and our workforce as well. Our early trial runs with the PortlandOnline portal are already resulting in streamlined service delivery, on-demand service for the public, and retention of content control by professionals in our city bureaus. As an elected official, I believe the ability of these systems to track and report real-time outcomes and performance is a substantial and welcome gain that increases our city's accountability and credibility in the eyes of the public we serve.

ENDNOTES

1. Corporate or citywide.
2. The Portland metropolitan area's regional government.
3. City of Portland, Corporate GIS.
4. City of Portland, Bureau of Housing and Community Development.
5. City of Portland, Bureau of Housing and Community Development.
6. "Gartner's Four Phases of E-Government Model," Gartner Group Inc, 2000.
7. "The Quest for Electronic Government: A Defining Vision," Institute for Electronic Government, 1999.

21

City of Edmonton E-Business Program

Bill Smith, Mayor of Edmonton, Canada

In the city of Edmonton, we are proud of our initiatives for developing better ways to serve our citizens and stakeholders. The city's e-business program is an excellent example of a pragmatic and productive approach to improving services, while holding the line on costs by ensuring that our investments in e-government practices and technology deliver real value.

The city of Edmonton is a single-tier municipality governed by a mayor and 12 councilors from six wards. By geographic area, it is a large city of 700 square kilometers (about 270 square miles)—larger than Toronto, Chicago, Detroit, or Philadelphia. The city employs about 10,000 staff, who deliver a full range of municipal services, including police, fire, ambulance, and transit services.

Edmonton has a population of 687,000 people, but our stakeholders also include residents of 21 other municipalities in the Edmonton region. With a regional population of 967,000, Edmonton is the sixth largest metropolitan area in Canada. We expect the regional population will reach one million people by 2005.

Edmonton is the capital city of the province of Alberta, Canada. It is also the principal and central municipality in Alberta's most productive industrial region, the supply and service center for the vast resource-rich area of the Canadian northwest, and an educational, cultural, and entertainment center. Our thriving and diverse economy grew by 4.2 percent in 2002. The forecast is for continued robust growth.

Supporting rapid growth and maintaining Edmonton's existing service levels and infrastructure, while keeping property taxes competitive, are ongoing challenges for the Edmonton City Council. In late 2002, in response to these challenges, the city administration proposed an e-business program to the city council. The proposal incorporated expanded website services to improve convenience for the citizens and businesses of Edmonton and to help the city sustain existing levels of service.

The e-business program is driven by three primary factors. Our citizens are demonstrating increased use of the Internet and the city's website; our population is growing, which increases the projected need for services; and citizens and other stakeholders are demanding new and more extensive self-service access to government.

Use of the city's Internet and intranet sites has grown rapidly over the past three years. In 2000, the city's website had approximately 730,000 visits. In 2002, this number increased 280 percent to over two million visits, and we are expecting three million visits to our website by the end of 2003. Clearly, citizens are starting to rely on the website as a source of information and services, which is the city's intent. For the benefit of both citizens and businesses, the city needs to offer expanded website services.

Edmonton is also facing increased demands on its current services. Our population is growing at a rate of approximately 1.5 percent per year, so in the next five years we should have 50,000 more residents. E-business initiatives support the need for increased services at reduced costs by shifting routine services and transactions from more expensive service-delivery methods, such as in person and by telephone, to lower-cost service delivery on the Internet.

Internet use continues to increase in both the private and public sectors, including all levels of government. Citizens and stakeholders want self-service access to governments. Moreover, all levels of government are providing and expanding online services, and citizens and businesses also expect their local governments to provide this service. An expanded e-business program does not replace existing ways of doing business with the city, such as using the telephone and over-the-counter service; it offers an option that is available from homes and businesses outside traditional office hours.

City council recognizes that urban sustainability calls for innovative ways of delivering services. In an environment of tight budgets and increasing demands, initiatives must demonstrate the capacity to contribute to the long-term sustainability of the city. After careful consideration, city council determined that a well-planned and well-executed e-business program would meet this objective. During its 2003 budget deliberations, the council approved an e-business program.

The mandate given to the city administration was clear—develop e-business initiatives that will improve service, increase customer satisfaction, and reduce or limit the cost of providing services.

DEVELOPING AN E-BUSINESS PROGRAM

The city of Edmonton began by reviewing its current website and developing a comprehensive e-business strategy. To ensure accountability and commitment among the stakeholders and to promote a corporatewide focus, the city established an E-Business Steering Committee and an E-Business Office. This governance structure allows key stakeholders to have direct involvement in setting priorities, identifying needs, and guiding the strategic-planning process.

The steering committee is composed of senior administration staff from each city department and is chaired by one of the department heads. The committee reviews, approves, and updates the e-business strategy to ensure the program remains aligned with the city's corporate objectives.

The E-Business Office conducts the planning and management roles required to implement the program. It manages the projects, develops the annual e-business plan, measures performance, and manages the more technical aspects of the program, such as standards development and Web-application management.

The e-business strategy is the foundation for the e-business program. It describes the vision and principles that guide the selection and development of all e-business initiatives.

The principles state that e-business solutions must do the following:

- Be determined by customer needs and developed to ensure an integrated user experience across all city of Edmonton digital channels
- Further enable the city of Edmonton's corporate vision
- Be accessible to all, including citizens, customers, suppliers, partners, and employees
- Ensure that the city of Edmonton's websites (Internet and intranet) are the official source for current and accurate information
- Have resources and funding in place to ensure the impact to the organization is net positive
- Provide seamless integration to back-office systems and encompass an integrated view of people, process, and technology
- Value employee and customer needs
- Provide confidence and trust through security

DESIGNING A CUSTOMER-FOCUSED WEB INFRASTRUCTURE

During spring 2003, the E-Business Office commissioned a survey of 1,200 residents and over 100 businesses and conducted nine focus-group sessions with residents, businesses, and city staff. With this research, the office determined how residents and businesses were accessing the city's website and what city services they wanted to use through the Internet.

The results revealed that approximately 77 percent of residents have access to the Internet from home, work, school, or public libraries. The survey also showed that the telephone is the preferred and most common method of contacting the city; the Internet is second. Citizens want to use the city's website to access transit schedules, to obtain information on recreation events, and to register and pay for recreation programs.

Businesses want choices in how they work with local government. Many of our businesses are placing their products or services online, and they expect to be able to do business in this way. Over 95 percent of the businesses surveyed had Internet access, and more than two-thirds of those businesses used the Internet to conduct their daily business activities. They have incorporated the Internet into their business routines and processes. Just as banks are offering various ways to access their service, the city needs to offer similar options to the business community. Businesses want to use the city's website to access land information such as zoning, assessment and taxation, and building permits and licenses.

In response to feedback from both citizens and businesses, the city redesigned its website. With more information on the home page, the new portal website allows citizens and businesses to gain rapid, single-door access to information and services, regardless of the users' location, the location of the information, or the format in which the information is stored. All information, services, and applications that the city offers online are integrated into this portal.

The new website is customer focused to ensure that users can navigate intuitively around the site. It is organized into topic areas that were extensively tested with citizens and businesses through focus-group sessions and include such categories as arts, culture and attractions, roads and traffic, and recreation.

The new website (www.edmonton.ca) is also tailored to specific communities of interest, such as pet owners, families, and seniors. The seniors' link, for example, includes information that may be of interest to seniors, such as bus passes, community-service programs for seniors, and assistance with snow removal.

The home page is changed daily to reflect the most current city news and to feature specific topics of interest, such as proposed bylaws before city council. Users can also customize a copy of the city's home page by moving the information that is most important to them up front. For example, local plumbing and gas contractors can move the e-permit and license application to their customized city of Edmonton home page so that they can quickly access city permit and license services.

Accuracy and consistency are key qualities of the new website. The site uses software and revised business processes to keep information current and to ensure that the website remains the official source of information. The website also incorporates a standardized look and feel, which is based on desired website attributes identified by survey respondents and focus groups. These attributes are supported through the use of customized templates, appropriate visuals, and a consistent writing style.

The e-infrastructure of the new website also supports future changes. Additional online services will adapt to the portal framework and previously developed functions. With this in place, the city can leverage its investment in existing technology to implement new applications and services rapidly and economically.

SELECTING POTENTIAL E-BUSINESS INITIATIVES

The public, businesses, civic administration, and politicians have been submitting an increasing number of suggestions and requests for online information, services, and applications. These suggestions and requests have prompted many potential e-business initiatives.

The E-Business Steering Committee approved and implemented a formal process for evaluating these initiatives against three criteria: alignment to corporate goals, contribution to financial and other performance measures, and potential of achieving benefits. Initiatives that scored well were incorporated into the annual e-business program budget and forwarded to city council for their consideration and funding approval.

Alignment with Corporate Goals

Alignment with corporate goals measures how proposed e-business initiatives support the goals and objectives laid out in Plan Edmonton, the city's municipal-development plan. The plan describes a long-range vision for Edmonton, identifies the city's priorities, and provides strategies to address those priorities.

Each initiative is rated on how well it advances the vision and priorities of Plan Edmonton, which are to support Edmonton's vibrant economy, to sustain Edmonton's quality of life, and to achieve excellence in providing services to people and managing the city's resources. To meet these objectives, proposed initiatives need to make it easier for citizens and businesses to do business with the city.

Financial and Other Performance Measures

The proposed e-business initiatives are also evaluated using a cost-benefit analysis to determine if they will provide a positive net present value within a three-year window. Each initiative is assessed on the following: potential reduction in, or avoidance of, effort on an ongoing basis; savings such as reduction in printing costs; and increased revenue resulting from improved payment processes and increased sales.

In addition to fiscal performance measures, the proposed initiatives are evaluated on their contribution to our economic prosperity, social well-being, enhanced service for customers, and compliance with legislated requirements.

Probability of Benefits

The third evaluation category assesses the probability that the proposed initiatives will deliver the anticipated benefits. Potential benefits are also measured on the degree of impact they have on processes and procedures, the extent to which staff will be impacted by the change, and the receptiveness of internal and external customers.

Risk is evaluated in several categories, such as the extent to which commitment to and accountability for the benefits of each initiative is shared across the enterprise. If the benefits and accountability are shared across most or all departments, there is a higher potential of achieving the benefits.

2003 E-BUSINESS INITIATIVES

The e-business program for 2003 developed and implemented three initiatives: an automated transit trip planner for transit users, an online registration and payment option for recreational programs, and an expanded e-permit and license service for businesses and residents.

The automated transit trip planner allows transit users to plan trips in real time. Previously, transit users had two options to access information. They could contact the Transit Call Centre either by phone for an immediate response or by e-mail for a response within 48 hours.

Last year, the Transit Call Centre received over 500,000 requests for trip-planning information. Shifting even 10 to 20 percent of these requests to the website for self-service information will help the call-center staff manage the growing call volumes resulting from increasing transit use. To compete with private vehicle use, transit services must make information as accessible and easy as possible.

With the automated transit trip planner, transit users can enter pertinent information and get an immediate response on which bus to take at what time. In the future, people will be able access this service at any location or time via a mobile Internet device such as a Web-enabled cell phone.

An online registration and payment option for recreational programs enables residents to access information and registration services for all city-run programs. Previously, customers could register only over the phone or in person at specific facilities. This can be inconvenient, frustrating, and time-consuming for both customers and staff.

With a single program directory and registration process in place, residents can select programs, locations, and schedules that best meet their needs. This will improve customer satisfaction and increase participation in city-run programs.

An expanded e-permit and license service enables businesses and residents to apply and pay for additional city permits and licenses online. This expansion is being done in phases. This service began with two permits, one for heating and ventilation and another for plumbing and gas. Currently, companies can apply and pay for certain construction permits and book their building safety inspections online.

As online services expand, developers will be able to apply for subdivision applications and submit their applications and development plans online. Citizens will be able to apply and pay for pet licenses online. The goal is to provide citizens and businesses an opportunity to apply and pay for all city permits and licenses online.

IMPLEMENTING THE INITIATIVES

To implement these initiatives, the city had to change how it did business. The online transit trip planner was integrated with work processes, and Transit Call Centre agents tested the online application for several months. The online process is a significant change from their practice of creating a trip plan using paper-schedule binders. Although it is faster for an experienced call-center agent to create a trip plan manually, the online transit trip planner will improve the efficiency of this service and allow more citizens to access it.

For online program registration to be successful, registration and payment processes needed to be standardized. Edmonton has 52 recreational facilities. Each facility had its own registration and payment process. Many had different refund and cancellation policies. The staff at each facility was often unaware of availability in other programs and was, therefore, unable to help customers if their facility's programs were full

A team of staff in the Community Services Department developed new rules and procedures for online program registration and payment. The changed business processes were rolled out to 300 front-counter staff in over 52 facilities. A Web application was then developed to support this standardized and simplified registration and payment process.

Expanded e-permit and license services were implemented, along with significant business-process changes. This initiative began in 2001, and expanded over the next two years. The multiphase approach allowed administrative staff to incorporate the necessary changes into their business practices and allowed technical staff to leverage investments in technology for use with other permit components.

Customer input is an important component in developing e-permit and license functions. For example, rapid data entry is critical to our building-contractor customers. The e-permit and license application was developed so that when customers log on and validate their identities, the system produces a series of permit screens with all of the necessary data inserted except the change of address. Contractors can now process a row of condominiums in one quick session.

Customer feedback is a critical component of all proposed online services. If it is difficult to identify specific customers, focus groups are used to ensure that the online services meet website usability standards.

MEASURING RESULTS

For each proposed e-business initiative, benefits are defined and captured in a benefits register that documents details (e.g., measurement criteria), expected results (e.g., anticipated outcomes), and baseline and target values. The benefits register is a critical component of the e-business measurement program. It ensures that the program delivers the expected benefits. If the desired benefits fail to occur, then tolerances and adjustments are recorded, the party that is accountable is identified, and corrective actions are specified to get the initiative back on track.

An online transit trip planner also offers the potential for substantial benefits. This is in part because a large proportion of transit riders are young, and they are generally students. A recent study showed that 99 percent of Edmonton's high school students use the Internet.

In the first year, we expect to move approximately 10 percent, or 55,000, of the existing callers from the call center to the online, self-serve option. This movement to self-service is expected to reach 20 percent by the third year. This will allow the city to manage the growth in transit riders. Ultimately, all customers will benefit because as some move to online service, existing call-center staff will be able to keep pace with the demands resulting from our increasing population. Customer satisfaction with the Transit Call Centre is expected to remain at the current level of 95 percent, as fewer callers will wait in a telephone queue or hang up without completing their requests.

Online program registration will help the city achieve its goal of increasing participation in programs. While city-owned and city-operated facilities (e.g., ice arenas, swimming pools) are almost completely booked, the programs are seldom filled to capacity. In 2002, the fill rate in programs was 74.5 percent. We anticipate that this will increase to 82.5 percent over the next three years, resulting in additional revenue from programs by an estimated $75,000 per year.

As citizens shift to online registration in programs, customer satisfaction will improve, and civic administration will save time and money. We anticipate that by the end of the first year, citizens will have completed 15 percent of program registrations online. Online registration is projected to rise to 35 percent by year three, resulting in a net saving of $90,000 per year. In 2002, customer satisfaction with the overall program registration process was at 86 percent. Our goal is to increase satisfaction to over 90 percent.

The e-permit and license application also offers significant benefits that will continue to increase as additional permits and licenses are placed online. As online business services expand, customer satisfaction is expected to increase due to the convenience of no telephones, no trips downtown, no parking, and no lineups. City staff will also benefit since offering more self-service options to contractors will better allow existing city staff to manage the demands of Edmonton's increased construction activity.

Currently, call-center staff input data for several types of permits. We initially estimated a 10 percent participation rate on the use of e-permit applications, rising to 20 percent by year three and resulting in a net saving of $54,000 per year. As will be discussed in the Monitoring Results section, the take-up rate was significantly higher. Also, the call center currently receives approximately 70,000 telephone requests for inspections per year. Providing contractors an opportunity to book their own inspections over the Web (assuming a 50 percent take-up rate) will save the city over $91,000 annually by year three.

Another benefit will be the additional revenue that is collected from increased permit and license applications. We anticipate that citizens who might not otherwise apply, due to the time and effort required to do so through offline channels, will access online permit and licensing services.

MONITORING RESULTS

As of fall 2003, portions of the e-permit and license application had been in use for approximately two years. An evaluation of the program results was revealing. We anticipated e-permit applications to have a participation rate of 10 percent for the first two years. It was significantly higher, averaging 28 percent. Figure 21.1 shows the monthly percentage of heating and ventilation permits and plumbing and gas permits issued online.

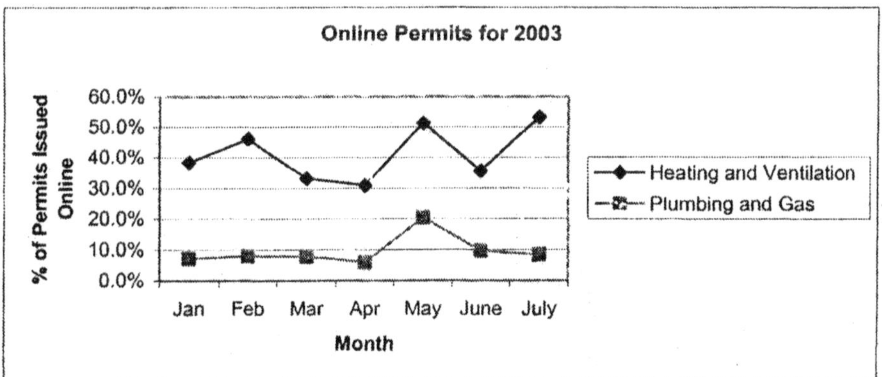

Figure 21.1. Online Permits for 2003.

Heating and ventilation contractors are clearly pleased with the online method of doing business. Although only 20 percent of this contractor market is using the online service, the larger firms readily adopted this new way of doing business with the city. On average, 42 percent of all heating and ventilation permits are issued online. The use of the online permits by plumbing and gas contractors yielded less dramatic results. Approximately 10 percent of this contractor market is using the online service. In total, 8 to 10 percent of plumbing and gas permits are issued online. This lower use of the online channel by plumbing and gas contractors has remained unchanged since the initial implementation.

The Planning and Development Department investigated the reasons for the difference in usage. On the surface, usages for heating and ventilation businesses and plumbing and gas businesses appears to be similar since both are involved in the construction industry. The investigation, however, revealed that heating and ventilation businesses are often larger, while plumbing and gas businesses are more diverse. They are generally smaller and have fewer office staff, who are less comfortable using the computer. An in-depth survey is currently underway to determine how to make e-permit services more attractive to plumbing and gas contractors.

Despite record numbers of permits being applied for and issued, service to the city's business customers has improved. Customers no longer have to wait in lengthy lines or telephone queues to conduct their business with the city. They can apply and pay for permits at their convenience. In 2003, approximately 15 percent of the online permits were applied for outside the traditional office hours of 8:00 a.m. to 5:00 p.m.

Our customers have also realized unexpected benefits from e-permit business. They are using the application to track and monitor their companies' performances. For example, they can track the number of inspections they have requested, the number of permits they have completed within a period of time, and the results of the inspections.

CONCLUSION

The success of Edmonton's e-business program is demonstrated by our ability to respond to increasing demands from citizens and businesses by providing easier and faster access to city services and information and, whenever possible, at reduced costs.

It is a customer-focused, enterprise approach that is grounded in solid strategy and principles. All e-business initiatives are using the portal framework and infrastructure developed to make it easier for customers to navigate through the site and find information and services.

Selection of potential e-business initiatives is based on a structured process. How well do the initiatives align with the city's strategic goals of improved access and better service? What do they contribute to the city's performance in terms of financial and measurable qualitative indicators? And what is the probability that the initiatives will deliver their anticipated benefits?

The application of technology in business has the potential to deliver measurable value. In the city of Edmonton, e-business is about business first—providing the services our citizens need and want at a justifiable cost. Technology is valued for its ability to improve service, contain costs, and increase the satisfaction of our citizens and businesses in their dealings with the city.

Results are measured to ensure that e-business initiatives deliver identified benefits. If results fall short of expectations, initiatives are reevaluated and redirected. All e-business initiatives are designed, measured, and, if necessary, modified to improve service to customers, resulting in increased customer satisfaction and reduced costs for the city.

Cities today are facing the increasing challenge of managing their infrastructures and maintaining their services within tight budgets. In this climate of fiscal restraint, Edmonton looks forward to meeting the challenge of remaining an economically and socially vibrant community. Through innovative management and initiatives such as the e-business program, we will maintain our quality of life while meeting the demands of our growing population.

22

Using Technology and Making E-Government Work

Patrick McCrory, Mayor of Charlotte, North Carolina

Charlotte is a Sun Belt, Southern city that has witnessed dramatic growth and worked to prepare its citizens for the twenty-first century. The city is currently the twenty-third largest city in the United States, with a population of 565,000 people within its city limits of 270 square miles. As the second largest banking center in the United States, Charlotte is home to the Bank of America and Wachovia Bank, which merged with First Union National Bank on September 4, 2002. The eight Fortune 500 companies headquartered in Charlotte lead the city's main employment base, in addition to US Airways' 7,000 employees. Because of the strong corporate community and efforts by the local school system, Charlotte is a technology-friendly city. According to the Progressive Policy Institute, 36.7 percent of Charlotteans have Internet access at home or work, and 77 percent of Charlotte-Mecklenburg school children use computers in the classroom. While growth and infrastructure issues have dominated the city agenda for the past 15 years, the city has also worked to prepare for the great challenges facing the community over the next 20 to 30 years, including the technology needs of the future.

INCREASING PRODUCTIVITY AND ENHANCING COMMUNICATION

Charlotte generally uses technology as a way to increase productivity in the workforce and enhance communication opportunities. However, it took a long-time to use technology in such a manner. In 1995, when I was first elected mayor of Charlotte, I was the first mayor in its history to put a computer on the mayor's desk. Admittedly, I had my 13-year-old nephew help me figure out how to use it, but before then, the city never had e-mail sent to the mayor's office. Things, like e-mail, that were once considered cutting-edge technology have now become basic components of conducting business. When I was first connected to e-mail, I only received and sent a limited number of e-mails.

Now, seven years later, the mayor's office receives about 70 to 80 e-mails a day from citizens. This increase in e-mail volume and the electronic-data storage space needed for the city's 5,000 employees continues to challenge the information technology department. E-mail, in particular, has completely changed the dynamics of communication between public officials and citizens. Many citizens enjoy the autonomy associated with e-mail when they have a complaint or want to offer feedback on a certain position or vote of their elected representative. They also enjoy the direct access of communicating with their public officials regarding the smallest of issues, such as making a garbage complaint, to stating their arguments for a zoning-issue vote.

The use of technology by both the young and old has been a fascinating evolution. The technology surge has been a challenge for people in their forties, who did not use computers growing up. The younger generation feels much more comfortable on the computer and is capitalizing on that technology for knowledge enhancement and resource access. Schools are promoting computer use in various ways, such as encouraging students to contact government officials over the Internet and doing presentations on PowerPoint. And this is from sixth graders. Without realizing that we grew up in a different era, many of our students and young adults expect the baby boom generation to understand modern technology. However, some of the most active people sending me e-mails today are senior citizens and retirees—and I know many grandparents use the Internet to keep in touch with families and share pictures among relatives.

COLLABORATION

One of Charlotte's successes as a city is that we engage in numerous partnerships and collaborations of technology, with our website being a highlight. A great technological achievement in Charlotte was creating a shared website between city government and county government (www.ci.charlotte.nc.us). Since 1997, the city of Charlotte and Mecklenburg County have been the only two local governments in the country to share a website. Charlotte is very proud of the website, which won the Digital Government Award in 1999. In addition to the Digital Government Award, Charlotte was recognized by TekInsight for progress in "adopting and utilizing digital technologies to improve the delivery of services to citizens."

The joint city-county website can be accessed in one of three ways: through a county Web address, a city Web address, or the joint Charlotte-Mecklenburg Web address. These three different tools enable entrance to the website, then allow a viewer to link to other websites throughout the city, county, and nation, including the local chamber of commerce (www.charlottechamber.org) and Convention and Visitors Bureau (www.visitcharlotte.org). There are frequent commonalities between the Charlotte and Mecklenburg County political bodies, as we share 19 consolidated services, so it made sense for the city and county to collaborate on the website to share costs, technology features, and service resources for this project. One benefit of a consolidated website for citizens is that they can look up information about their city and county elected officials on one website. The website also features a Board of Elections section that verifies voter registration and provides the location, with maps, of designated voting sites. The city and county work to ensure that the system is updated frequently and are currently working on a complete redesign of the website to add more online services and increase ease of customer/citizen use.

CLOSING THE DIGITAL DIVIDE—COMPUTER ACCESS TO NEIGHBORHOODS

In order to promote computer literacy and increase access to technology, the city of Charlotte has collaborated with the Charlotte-Mecklenburg School District, Volunteers, and Partnership Office to support a program entitled "Computer Access to Neighborhoods." These 38 sites located around the community—including YMCAs, churches, housing-authority sites, parks-and-recreation facilities, neighborhood service centers, and four schools—were developed to help break down the digital divide and provide access to technology to communities and families that do not currently have it. First Union/Wachovia Bank donated all of the computers, and Time-Warner Cable donated Internet access so that children and adults in certain geographic areas can use the technology for free GED instruction, summer youth programs, and resume development and job research. The goal is to expose children to computers and technology, with children getting first priority on the computers and adults using them when kids are in school.

E-GOVERNMENT

When people think of technology, their immediate thoughts are of e-mail and the Internet. The new dynamic in technology is to develop a technology structure to support e-government to promote transactions between businesses or citizens and government. E-government is defined by the city of Charlotte as the transformation of public-sector internal and external relationships through net-enabled operations, as well as information and communications technology to optimize government service delivery, constituency participation, and governance.

Most public officials in large cities are working with some type of e-government system. New York City, under Mayor Rudy Giuliani, used e-government for public-safety initiatives, even before the events of September 11, 2001. Charlotte and New York City have both been successful in using e-government as a means of conducting business and delivering information to citizens.

Charlotte is working to use this technology of e-government for a host of basic services like paying water and sewer bills, requesting new water service or cut-off and service repairs, submitting customer-service requests, and purchasing supplies and materials from vendors. Most city fees can now be paid online, such as those for licenses, citations, transit passes, pet licensing, and red light (SafeLight) violations. Our ability to offer payment transactions through a secure online network is possible as a result of a partnership with First Union/Wachovia Bank.

The city offers literally hundreds of e-government transactions, with some being better used than others. Presently, citizens wishing to pay their bills or purchase permits are benefiting most from Charlotte's online services. Such transactions as obtaining a business-privilege license, yard-sale license, and even parade permits can be applied for, granted, and paid for all through the Internet. One of our particular focuses is on speeding up the permitting process required by the city and county for a host of issues.

Providing one-stop shopping can be one of the biggest tools of technology for government services. When developers are constructing a building, they need literally hundreds of permits. As recently as three years ago, people had to pay separately for all of the permits required by the city and county. Now Charlotte requires only one payment for all of the different permits, and this process is saving a tremendous amount of time. Furthermore, that one payment can be made through a computer system, easing the process for developers and other citizens who, in the past, had to go to the county to write a check, then to the city to write a check. They might have had to write three or four different checks within our governmental organizations. The system was streamlined after realizing that numerous complicated steps in the process were inconveniencing all parties concerned.

While the technology is available and being offered, we still have much work to do to communicate to citizens that we use e-government. One area in particular that has yet to be embraced by Charlotteans is the ability to pay parking tickets online. Presently, we only average payment of 25 parking fines per month via the Internet. While the transaction level is not where we want it to be at this point in time, we believe the program has potential for increased usage.

Technology Objectives

The following driving forces are behind Charlotte's use of technology:

- Enhancing customer services
- Increasing city staff productivity
- Containing costs while offering more services

While we feel we are meeting the three most important objectives we are trying to achieve through technology, with enhancing citizen service as our primary focus, we are clearly realizing internal benefits. Charlotte's use of the Internet and all it has to offer is admittedly still in the infancy stage; yet, technology is clearly benefiting many of our internal processes.

We have a customer-service system that allows us to track citizen complaints or requests for service from the day the complaint or request is made to the day it is addressed and by whom. Human-resource functions and transactions are widely used on our Internet, including submitting resumes and job applications online and providing safety information and expense forms for employees.

Technology still clearly has a "wow" factor, from utilizing a personal data assistant that is also able to operate as a phone, to accessing old historical government documents in the comforts of one's home, often times outside "normal" business hours and without fees. Despite the excitement many of us share for technology, as a policymaker, I have to focus on policy issues and not get caught up in the glitz of technology. Enhancing government services at a cost savings to governmental agencies and the taxpayer is something that every politician can support. Managing technology and policy issues is not usually given much consideration, yet it is crucial to successful e-government. Charlotte has realized that updating policies is the first step to implementing e-government. Policies that were implemented 20 years ago may not be effective with the new electronic technology. As we further implement technology resources, it is actually causing review of the policies, such as contracting policies or application policies. We have duplicate forms for many different departments, and now, when putting them on the Internet, we have to review them to ensure they make sense and are applicable to e-government. This process of active learning has been very beneficial, if for no other reason than our having taken a step back and asked the following basic questions:

- What does the customer want?
- How many customers are actually going to use this service?

- Does the service lend itself to the overall city focus areas?
- How much would it cost to replace and keep up?
- Would the city save money by doing this?
- Do we outsource this service, or can it be provided by the private sector?

The last question raises some major issues due to the growing number of contract services offering technological services. The type of customer using this technology needs emphasis. We are finding out that it is not the retail customer who really needs e-government; it is the business customer. Charlotte receives its greatest complaints from the business customer, often times from the construction industry regarding the permitting process, but, generally, about most things related to city contracting and procurement.

Broadening E-Government

The next technology step is to find new ways to tie our services into not only the county government but also surrounding governments. Communication between governments is a key component as we incorporate technology. We try to share information or technology in a way that provides win-win situations. We have made a good start with Mecklenburg County and our joint website, but we still have a ways to go in such areas as a radio and signal system for all public-safety agencies in the county and region.

One success is the state of North Carolina's procurement procedure for purchasing equipment, which allows local governments to purchase from their contracts to buy bulk equipment, be it cars or other big-ticket items. Another procurement service offered by the state of North Carolina that the city's Business Support Services is using is the North Carolina Interactive Purchasing System (NCIPS). Both the city of Charlotte and Mecklenburg County post bid-proposal opportunities on the NCIPS, which then automatically sends an e-mail to each vendor that is registered on the state system and has indicated interest in receiving notification based on certain categories of services. Traditional bid-notification methods are still used, but this system has helped to reduce mailing and printing costs, while increasing the number of potential vendors.

Additionally, the city of Charlotte was the first city in North Carolina to implement a SafeLight program, where cameras are placed at intersections to photograph cars running red lights. This has been very successful for the city in reducing accidents at high-wreck intersections, but it is still very controversial since we are using technology for enforcement. Drivers receive a ticket in the mail when their license plate is photographed entering an intersection after the light has turned red. While this system has been helpful for the city and customers, lawyers are not pleased due to elimination of the court phase as this is only a civil infraction under North Carolina law. But, true to our technology-friendly operations, we can also collect red-light fines over the Internet. This use of technology for public safety has encouraged eight other North Carolina municipalities to implement the SafeLight program.

Effectively Engaging in E-Government

Use of this new technology necessitates some caveats. Costs, operations, training for employees and customers, and security must be considered to engage in e-government effectively. Charlotte budgeted more than $2.4 million in fiscal year 2002 to enhance our e-government capabilities.

Given the amount of money we spend on technology, cost control is a key issue. There are many ways that the cost can become much greater than was initially anticipated in a budget. When considering costs, the thought process must delve far beyond the initial purchase of equipment. Long-term upkeep costs and the purchase of contemporary equipment as the technology improves are important considerations. Computers now have countless gigabytes of memory, and the flat-screen monitors, CD burners, and DVD players that were not imaginable just five years ago are available to the public. In addition, the advantages and shortcomings of leasing versus purchasing equipment must be considered. Web designers command high fees, raising the need to decide between in-house staff and outsourcing the support of e-government services. These matters must be contemplated before technology is incorporated into your city, not after the process has started. A qualified individual has to be responsible for operations and for updating the system. The city of Charlotte has two staff members assigned to e-government, with a cross-section of departments represented on our e-government strategy group, which is chaired by a Budget and Evaluation staff member.

The use of new technology involves citywide training of employees, as well as training for customers. Employees must understand how to use the technology and feel comfortable using it for daily work activities. Training your customers to use technology is another matter. An evaluation is necessary to determine how many of your customers have access to computers. Sensitivity is key when considering the economic background of citizens who may not be able to access e-government; many in the community do not have computers, which is why we focus on access to technology through the Computer Access to Neighborhoods program and the public library system. Without a personal computer, is there any way for a citizen to access this type of service or information? Charlotte's answer is yes, but we want to encourage people to try e-government as we believe they will enjoy the experience.

Automated Meter Reading

One example of effective e-government is the city's implementation of new technology for water-meter readings. Automated Meter Reading (AMR) uses meters equipped with radio transmitters that obtain meter readings from a mobile van. The pilot project using this new technology has reduced costs, increased customer satisfaction through more accurate billing, and improved operations. To complete the more than 200,000 meter reads, the old system required 36 meter readers, and it took more than 30 days to complete the meter readings for a monthly billing cycle. However, with the introduction of AMR, the same number of reads now requires only one meter reader and takes ten days. The city has found cost savings in terms of personnel, equipment and maintenance, support staff, and call-center activities. Improved operations have yielded reduced water loss, faster and more accurate reads, and fewer estimation and billing errors. Not surprisingly, similar to implementing any new technology, AMR requires significant upfront capital investment. However, after careful consideration, the payback in three to four years and the improved customer service and operations are well worth the $3.7 million implementation cost.

CONCLUSION: LOOKING TO THE FUTURE

Through the implementation of such programs as Community Access Neighborhoods, SafeLight, and Automated Meter Reading, the city of Charlotte is realizing both the benefits and challenges of e-government. The city is actively working to anticipate customer requests and needs and is constantly responding by changing its service offerings. Our ultimate goal is for Charlotte's e-government to be a convenient, secure, and effective way of providing accurate and timely information and services, offering citizens an opportunity to participate in open government, and contributing towards a positive image of Charlotte to the world. I believe Charlotte is well on its way to achieving that goal, which will continue to allow Charlotte to be a technology-friendly city that is prepared for more growth and the issues it will face in the new millennium.

23

Technology as an Investment in Neighborhoods: Tampa's Neighborhood Information Page

Pam Iorio, Mayor of Tampa, Florida

Early in my administration, our city government committed itself to improving the delivery of services where our citizens live: at the neighborhood level. To that end, we asked each city department to develop creative and innovative ways to support the city's Investing in Neighborhoods initiative. In support of that new initiative, our Department of Strategic Planning and Technology, which oversees the city of Tampa's website operation, developed its Neighborhood Information page, providing a prototype for the kind of innovative electronic government upon which we will be working in earnest to expand.

Our Neighborhood Information page, part of the city's TampaGov.net website, serves as a virtual tour of every corner and aspect of the city of Tampa. If you are thinking about relocating your family or your business, or if you find that you have developed special needs that you suspect one neighborhood might address better than another, or if you desire to help improve a neighborhood in which you already work or reside and need to know how your neighborhood measures up to others throughout our city, then our Neighborhood Information page gives you access to the latest statistical information and physical descriptors.

Information presented there includes land-use percentages, population, ethnic diversity, resident income, housing type, resident education level, and council districts, all accessed by selecting a particular neighborhood on a map. The page also displays community indicators, helping to put the statistical information in perspective by providing a measure of a neighborhood's condition relative to other neighborhoods. Highlighted in *Planning Magazine's* September 2002 issue, and again in the February 2004 issue of *Government Technology*, Tampa's Neighborhood Information page is gaining recognition as an innovative approach to sharing the invaluable information provided by geographic information systems and ongoing efforts in community planning.

OVERVIEW OF THE NEIGHBORHOOD INFORMATION PAGE

Tampa's Neighborhood Information page is an effort to create a one-stop Web page for neighborhoods. It contains statistical profiles within the city, maps, links to neighborhood association Web pages, and photos of neighborhoods.

Here, users can easily navigate through Tampa's neighborhoods. The 116 square miles of the city of Tampa are divided into 16 subsectors measuring 3,000 to 5,000 acres. Each subsector represents two to seven neighborhoods. A census profile is provided for each of the subsectors, comparing each neighborhood to the citywide profile, thus enabling viewers to compare the neighborhood's demographic and social characteristics to those of the entire city. Each subsector also has space for photos of the geographical area, so viewers can get a visual tour of the community.

Additionally, land-use maps and graphs showing population growth are available. For selected subsectors, there are in-depth profiles. Links to a spectrum of neighborhood organizations and websites are also provided.

What distinguishes Tampa's Neighborhood Information Web page is the development and implementation of a unique research tool called the Neighborhood Indicator. Based on indicators measuring conditions within a specific neighborhood or combination of neighborhoods, selected neighborhood characteristics—like population, employment, park acreage, and water use—are compiled for each subsector. With a simple click of a button, 25 data elements can be accessed. The citywide average is also displayed, so viewers can immediately learn how a particular condition measures up to the rest of the city. Finally, a small color-coded bar enables viewers to understand instantly how the neighborhood subsector compares to the citywide average.

The Neighborhood Indicator search engine gives city of Tampa residents the status of conditions and services provided in their neighborhood. Furthermore, it helps to put this information into citywide perspective. The engine returns several indicators measuring city service-delivery performance and conditions related to land use, housing, employment, transportation, environment, economy, public safety, and recreation. It also features a color coded "EKG," providing a quick way to visually relate the value of each indicator to the city average, as well as the status of a neighborhood in relation to the citywide average. For example, a neighborhood indicator that is within 20 percent above the city average returns a light green bar. An indicator ranging between 20 and 50 percent above the city average returns a darker green bar. Conditions below the city average are reflected by colors in the red range.

The page has four views, helping users to access and search neighborhood indicators. First, residents are able to view all indicators for a specific neighborhood subsector. This view provides a comparison to a citywide average. Next, residents can also view selected indicators for a specific neighborhood. This option returns the same information as above but limits the output, providing a way to focus on a few indicators at a time. A third view allows for an inspection of indicators for two different neighborhoods, providing a side-by-side comparison of neighborhood subsectors, as well as comparison to the citywide average. Finally, the fourth option presents a view of rankings of neighborhood subsectors by indicators. This view also allows residents to see how their neighborhoods compare with all other neighborhoods for a specific indicator.

Therefore, neighborhoods that display a pattern of predominantly green bars indicate a neighborhood ranking above the citywide average. Where mostly red bars dominate, the neighborhood ranks below the citywide average. However, a green or red bar does not necessarily translate into a "good" or "bad" rating. For example, a subsector with a crime rate 50 percent below the city average would have a corresponding red bar for the crime-rate indicator. Obviously, however, a low crime rate would be considered a positive indicator.

The distribution of the bars can also assist in the identification of deficiencies within a neighborhood. A predominance of a certain color for one of the major indicator areas (e.g., transportation, housing, employment) might indicate a condition worthy of additional study. The indicators provide a meaningful way to understand where a neighborhood is in relation to other areas within the city. Accurate indicators can alert citizens to problem areas before they become too big to fix.

This dimension of TampaGov.net's Neighborhood Information page can empower residents to make better, more informed decisions that affect their neighborhoods. Telling residents that they have 32 acres of parkland is informative, but putting that information into perspective by telling them their neighborhood is served at 75 percent of the citywide standard or that their neighborhood falls in the bottom half of all areas in the city for available parkland empowers residents and city government to decide to take corrective action. Using Tampa's neighborhood EKGs, residents are able to identify neighborhood strengths and weaknesses, assess levels of public service, prioritize neighborhood needs, monitor neighborhood health and vitality, identify opportunities for investment and development, and visualize possibilities for the future.

Our ability to deliver this technology through TampaGov.net enables this type of neighborhood empowerment. Before the implementation of the

Neighborhood Information page, the Department of Strategic Planning and Technology responded to each request individually, generating a report, returning e-mail, or creating and mailing personalized maps. Providing the means to store and deliver huge amounts of data, maps, statistics, and measures to residents on demand has dramatically improved efficiencies. Between January 1 and September 1, 2004, the Neighborhood Information page had 9,599 visitors. Even budgeting five minutes of staff time to respond to a request, the Neighborhood Information page saved the city almost 800 hours of staff time in eight months.

EVOLUTION OF THE NEIGHBORHOOD INFORMATION PAGE

Like most things on the Internet, the Neighborhood Information page and its tools are works in progress. The Department of Strategic Planning and Technology continually tests and evaluates new indicators and ways to use the information.

The Web page was initially developed using geographical information systems (GIS) indicator software obtained from the Florida Department of Community Affairs through the 1998 statewide Sustainable Communities demonstration program. Under that program, the city of Tampa agreed to test and evaluate a new geographic indicator mapping software called INDEX. The project introduced new ways of managing and interpreting information at the neighborhood level, and the concept of measuring neighborhood quality of life emerged out of that experience. Detailed, in-depth profiles were produced, displaying indicators both graphically and numerically; so, not only was it possible to measure and assess quality of life in the neighborhood objectively, but it was also possible to see variations in conditions across the neighborhood. The INDEX software was capable of modeling 43 neighborhood indicators.

The INDEX Demonstration Project was a success, but its acceptance and application were limited because the information could not be easily disseminated. That limitation disappeared as the city's Internet capabilities increased. Beginning in 2000, Tampa embarked on a significant program to develop its TampaGov.net site, which pioneered the development and implementation of many specialized e-government services. The city's website grew from 2,500 pages of information in 2000 to more than 5,500 pages in 2004, with an increase in traffic from 250,000 monthly page requests to more than 1.5 million monthly page requests during this same period. Revenues collected through the portal also expanded, from $18,000 per month to more than $265,000 per month. The surge in the Tampa's Internet development and usage culminated in awards for first place in 2002's "Best of the Web" and in 2002's and 2003's Digital Cities Surveys. The lessons learned in developing the successful TampaGov.net website were applied to the community-indicator project, spurring the development of the current Web-based Neighborhood Information page.

CHALLENGES

Once the Neighborhood Information page was placed into production, the challenge of reaching Tampa's citizenry was solved. The page quickly emerged as one of the most visited sites attracting more than 1,400 visitors per month. At this point, the efficiencies of delivering information to so many people were realized.

The success of the Tampa's Neighborhood Information page to date also illustrates the challenges that arise in applying new technologies to traditional business practices. Its production and continued maintenance require knowledge of community planning, analytics, GIS, database and spreadsheet operations, photo-imaging techniques, Web-based design software, and Internet considerations. Implementation of technically driven resources requires employees to provide a higher level of service, as well as to understand a broader array of sophisticated software programs. They also need the ability to work in highly collaborative teams where knowledge sharing becomes a major focus.

But the biggest challenge has been, and continues to be, the acquisition and presentation of reliable and accurate data. At the program's inception, data for all city neighborhoods was not available in comparable forms or was missing altogether. Getting every neighborhood up to speed requires a substantial investment of resources and time. New databases, additional research, and geocoding databases need to be created.

Another ongoing challenge is to ensure that the sources of information remain very reliable, not only across the city but across time as well. In the production of indicators, where even slight changes in the values can produce measurable directional shifts, the quality of the data must always be considered. Otherwise, the page could produce indicators and comparisons that do not make sense or that are unrealistic. If the data are bad, then the potential exists for the information to mislead people, putting them at risk to make bad decisions.

To minimize the effect of these limitations, Tampa's system presently collapses the entire city into 16 neighborhood subsectors. The 16 subsectors also reduce the time and resources required to maintain the system. Where the information is readily available, key demographic and community indicators are produced for each subsector. This gives the city the ability to present information easily and, more importantly, to manage the entire Internet system from a single database. As information changes or new data become available, the neighborhood subsector pages are automatically updated. New indicators and calculations can be initiated without major design or site-maintenance implications.

FUTURE PLANS FOR THE NEIGHBORHOOD INFORMATION PAGE

As part of our Investing in Neighborhoods initiative, city departments will be evaluating the level of services they provide throughout the city. Based on what has been learned to date with the Neighborhood Information page, we are striving to make that information not only more intelligible but more dynamic as well.

We also hope to continue to make the site more user friendly. Additional maps and information and an interactive mapping tool will allow users to select and view statistical information layered on familiar city streets. Such features will increase the flow of information to our neighborhoods, helping to prepare our citizens better to make decisions and direct the activities of their city government.

The city of Tampa's ultimate objective is to publish information and indicators for each of our 85 registered neighborhoods. Not only is it our goal to match the commitment and resolve of our residents to improve the quality of life in their neighborhoods and provide them with easy access to information that they can use to effect change, it is also our aim to help others access this information to stimulate planned growth, appropriate development, and infrastructural investment.

SUMMARY

The city's goal in developing systems such as the Neighborhood Information page is to discover new ways to use technology, informing and empowering our citizens in the ongoing and important effort to create our city. By leveraging technology to promote citizen, and contextually, neighborhood empowerment, Tampa is achieving powerful objectives—greater effectiveness coupled with greater efficiency in the effort to improve our community. The Neighborhood Information page represents only one of the successful new initiatives the city of Tampa is developing to do business, harnessing today's technology to create a better tomorrow.

24

E-Government Innovation in Honolulu

Jeremy Harris, Mayor of Honolulu, Hawaii

In 1998, the city of Honolulu embarked on a long-range program to expand and improve public services through the application of digital technology. Our goal was to create a "paperless city," where barriers to interdepartmental communication were broken down, operational efficiencies were maximized, and citizen access to information and services was easier and more seamless than ever before.

The decision to modernize was driven by necessity. Between 1994 and 2002, city revenues plummeted as real property values suffered from the prolonged effects of the burst of the Japanese "bubble" economy. While the national economy grew at an annual average rate of about 4 percent between 1992 and 1999, Hawaii's economy shrank by an annual average of 0.3 percent. Honolulu's tourism-based economy was also hit hard by the Asian currency crisis of 1997–1998, which cut into international visitor arrivals.

By the end of the decade, the city faced three choices: cut services, raise taxes, or increase government efficiency. The latter option was the only one that made sense during tough economic times. So, we set out to reorganize government, increase operating efficiencies, and reduce our workforce by leveraging technology. Technology was one of the tools that allowed us to build a smarter, more responsive government with increased police, fire, refuse-collection, and transit service, all of which were enhanced without raising property taxes. We continued to hold the line on spending as the city's fiscal condition worsened. By 2002, real property tax revenues were down $62 million from what they were in 1994.

Though city revenues have declined over the past decade, Honolulu has significantly advanced its e-government capabilities. In 2001, a comprehensive review of e-government applications in 223 American cities led the Civic Resource Group to determine that Honolulu had one of the best websites among cities of comparable size. Last year, for the second consecutive year, the Center for Digital Government's Digital Cities Survey ranked Honolulu first among cities with populations greater than 250,000 for using digital technologies to improve the delivery of services.

While the attention we have received has been gratifying, there is more to the expansion of e-government than an award-winning website. Honolulu's quest for greater efficiency through technology is rooted in discussions I had with our chief information officer more than a half decade ago about the role we expected technology to play in the city's future. Out of those conversations came a plan to make Honolulu one of the most digitally advanced cities in the country.

The information technology (IT) vision developed for Honolulu featured three main components. First, we set about building a more responsive, customer-centered government to deliver public services more conveniently and cost-effectively. We sought to accomplish this not with the intention of meeting customer expectations but with the aim of surpassing them. In an increasingly interconnected world, where people shop, retrieve information, and access financial and other vital services online, the time had come to make city services easier to access as well.

Second, we wanted to wean the city of its longstanding dependence on paper. The ability to publish documents in digital form significantly reduces the cost of storing, retrieving, and transferring information. Moreover, the paper trail creates unnecessary barriers to communication by separating the data essential to city functions along departmental lines. For many cities, the result can be a bureaucratic and highly decentralized operational structure. Computer technology helps remove the barriers to information flow and encourages interconnectedness throughout the city system.

The third component of Honolulu's IT vision was the development of a user-friendly Internet portal to promote tourism and international business. Our city has responded to an increasingly competitive, global travel, and tourism environment by marketing Oahu as a strategically located island paradise that offers numerous advantages to international businesses beyond sun and surf. The Internet provides not only increased visibility but also tremendous flexibility in spreading the word to visitors and entrepreneurs throughout the world. Perhaps the most widely acclaimed of Honolulu's Web-based marketing initiatives is our sophisticated geographic information system (GIS) that provides visitors and investors with site-specific, detailed information about commercial real estate opportunities on the island of Oahu. The enhanced GIS is one of the reasons our website has become such an important part of the city's economic development plan.

CUSTOMER SERVICE

Not long ago, the people of Honolulu had no choice but to renew motor-vehicle registrations by mail, stand in line at city hall to pay property taxes and apply for permits, and get their information about city programs and services over the telephone.

While many citizens still rely on traditional modes of delivery, for a growing number of islanders, the Internet has become a more convenient way of doing business. As technology improves and more people are made aware of the range of services available to them online, we are confident that they will take advantage of the electronic alternative.

The trend is encouraging. Over the past two years, our city has processed approximately 11,000 motor-vehicle-registration renewals online at an estimated savings in mailing and processing costs of $10,000 per year. While that's still only 1.4 percent of the total number of renewals per year, online service is growing at a terrific rate. The total number of online registration renewals in 2002 was up more than 326 percent over the previous calendar year. Equally encouraging are surveys suggesting that up to 60 percent of Oahu's 876,000 people have access to the Internet. Such figures have led us to believe that we have only begun to realize the potential of technology in our quest to improve the quality of life on our island. The less time people spend in their cars on their way to city hall and standing in line once they get there, the more time they will have to spend with their families and enjoy the natural beauty of Hawaii.

Honolulu's "satellite" city hall system may be revolutionized in the years ahead as the acceptance of online service delivery grows. Currently, the city operates 11 permanent satellite offices in neighborhoods and communities on Oahu, in addition to two mobile satellites serving citizens in outlying areas. Our island is a lot bigger than many people realize. Altogether, the city and county of Honolulu encompass an area of about 600 square miles. Hence, the rationale for the satellite system has been to bring services closer to where people live, instead of making them drive to the downtown area where the majority of government offices are located.

The growth of Internet service delivery may eventually allow us to rethink this sprawling, brick-and-mortar customer-service operation and reassign the 92 full-time employees that staff the facilities. But we are not there yet. The total number of customer-service transactions executed by the city in 2002 was just over one million. A realistic near-term goal would be to increase the number of online transactions to 10 percent of the total.

Public education will help stimulate acceptance of the Internet as a primary means of service delivery. At the same time, we recognize that some people prefer face-to-face interaction with city government, and we intend to honor that preference. Accordingly, the city has recently modified its on-site payment system to keep lines to a minimum and expedite the flow of transactions at our satellites. Under the old system, customers had to wait in line at a separate cashier station after getting their licenses, permits, or registrations. Now, all customer-service representatives take care of business transactions and accept payment at the same time. By adapting a point-of-sale software system to existing workstations, the city was able to forego the purchase of more expensive registers. This single innovation has enhanced customer service and resulted in a one-time savings to taxpayers of more than $2.6 million.

PUBLIC SAFETY

Digital technology has revolutionized law enforcement and disaster management, dramatically reducing response times and making it easier to send and retrieve information critical to our city's first responders.

In recent years, Honolulu has moved aggressively to equip law-enforcement personnel with the technology they need to do their important work more effectively. In 1998, the city obtained $9 million in matching funds from the federal government to reengineer the Honolulu Police Department's (HPD) electronic workflow system and take advantage of new methods of acquiring, sharing, and storing information. Our goal was to minimize the time officers spend doing paperwork manually so that the bulk of their energies can be devoted to community policing.

With the introduction of a state-of-the-art computer-aided dispatch (CAD) system and the installation of mobile data computer terminals in the city's fleet of patrol vehicles, HPD communication systems here are as advanced as anywhere in the country. The primary link between dispatchers and our officers in the field, the CAD system, has streamlined the call process and significantly reduced response time. Voice communication remains an essential part of the dispatch process, as there is no substitute for human contact in the immediate aftermath of serious incidents. However, the CAD system augments voice communication and promotes speed and efficiency by enabling dispatchers to transmit volumes of information crucial to police investigations using voiceless data transmission.

Police investigation procedures have been refined through the use of mobile data terminals in squad cars. These on-board computers allow officers to transmit their reports electronically to the department's records-management system. Because of the integration of automated field reporting with HPD's records-management system, detectives are able to access information in a fraction of the time it used to take. The city is currently field-testing additional enhancements to mobile field reporting. By the end of this year, it will be possible for officers to call up mug shots and other graphic data from their patrol vehicles.

Such advances are part of the broader reengineering of systems in Honolulu's emergency-response complex. Along with police reports, data from fire and emergency services is stored in computers at our Emergency Operating Center at the heart of the city's Civil Defense Agency. There, city personnel are able to track the locations of emergency-response vehicles using Global Positioning System (GPS) technology. The result is coordinated response to emergencies of all kinds.

THE PAPERLESS CITY

Honolulu's digital revolution involves more than selling services over the Internet and upgrading emergency communication systems. Much of our modernization is aimed at creating a workplace where data are organized and shared across departmental lines. It is also about enabling and empowering city employees to adapt to the changing demands of the information age.

Last year, we launched a multiyear project to address the need for departments to store, retrieve, share, and manage their documents electronically. Although still in an early stage of development, the Integrated Imaging and Document Managing System has improved productivity, eliminated duplication, and uncovered "islands" of useful data embedded in the paper files of many departments and agencies. By creating a common repository for electronic documents, teamwork is encouraged and decision-making processes are enhanced.

Part of this same initiative is our Web-based workflow system, which allows city employees to complete more than 80 forms by computer and route them electronically through the approval process. The electronic workflow initiative has simplified and streamlined the routing process citywide at a projected one-year savings of $250,000. This is a particularly significant development for paper-intensive departments, such as human resources, where reduced processing times and integrity of data are vital to personnel management.

The process of tracking and approving city permits was among the most labor intensive of activities under the old manual system. Today, the city uses an automated program that allows users to track permits as they move through the review process. The Automated Permit Tracking and Managing System, commonly known as POSSE, is used by city agencies to monitor operations related to the review, approval, inspection, and enforcement of departmental permits. The system allows managers to monitor the progress of city construction projects, permit review times, inspectors' mileage, and personnel workloads.

The POSSE system has recently been expanded to allow private businesses and the general public access to permit records and information over the Internet. The Department of Planning and Permitting has deployed the Honolulu Internet Permit System (HIPS) website, which provides Internet access to parcel and permit data stored in the POSSE system. Customers can now research permits and land records and check on the status of application reviews in real time. The system also provides expanded access to agencies and individuals through the city's intranet system, allowing users to access detailed information related to city construction projects.

Honolulu has also developed one of the most comprehensive GIS databases of any city of its size. The Honolulu Land Information System (HoLIS) is an enterprisewide system serving over 15 city departments with land-use, permit, tax, infrastructure, and environmental data. A central repository for data pertinent to each of our city departments has eliminated duplication and cut the time required to access information related to zoning, property boundaries, tax assessment, ownership records, sewer hookups, demographics, flood zones, and much more.

TOURISM AND ECONOMIC DEVELOPMENT

The idea of devoting significant portions of Honolulu's website to the promotion of tourism and economic development on the island of Oahu has been several years in the making. We set out to build a versatile marketing tool that would allow us to convey a vivid image of our city to the rest of the world, promote awareness of our island's history and diverse cultures, and provide a wealth of information to perspective visitors.

We wanted to create an interactive, educational experience that would overturn the prevailing image of government sites as cold and impersonal. Honolulu's presence on the Web once consisted of a few simple pages listing city departments and telephone numbers. Today, our website features 18,000 pages that act as a virtual extension of the city itself, as a user-friendly cyberoasis reflecting the beauty of our land and the warmth of our "aloha spirit." Overall, the Web's ability to enhance our brand recognition in the international community has been dramatic. The site averages about nine million hits a month, about three times as many as a year ago. Surveys indicate that up to 60 percent of the people who visit our site live outside Hawaii, many of them in Canada and Japan.

The Internet's use as a business development tool is of potentially greater benefit than its application in tourism marketing. Within the last year, Honolulu has launched a site featuring the latest in GIS, Internet, and database technologies. This sophisticated application allows businesses to access information needed to make informed investment decisions. The new Economic

Development Property Locator allows users to view, create, and print maps, perform site-selection searches, develop custom demographic radius reports, and locate commercial or business properties.

More flexible and powerful than most government websites, the GIS-based application allows users to access data that might otherwise take weeks and thousands of dollars to assemble. In addition to providing site-specific map overlays, the application provides everything from rental rates, sales prices, and information on square footage and development incentives. Since its development, it has been an invaluable resource for landscape architects, land-use attorneys, real estate appraisers, and a host of other specialized users. Business owners find it useful for obtaining demographic information used in determining optimal retail site locations and doing target marketing. Even Hollywood movie studios have used the system to do background exploration on prospective shooting locations.

Sophisticated business- and economic-development resources like this can be cost prohibitive for the public sector acting alone. By developing public–private partnerships, cities can leverage their limited resources in ways that serve the greater community. The property locator was made possible through a partnership between the city, the Honolulu Board of Realtors, and Enterprise Honolulu, a nonprofit economic-development organization that attracts new business to the island of Oahu.

COMMUNITY ACCESS

No vision for e-government would be complete without considering the issue of digital democracy. As cities across the country explore new ways of improving the quality of citizens' lives through digital technology, decision makers are considering its potential to stimulate public awareness and greater involvement in community affairs. Improved efficiency and cost effectiveness are vital, especially at a time when city budgets are stretched to the limit, but we must be mindful as well of the Internet's capacity to open new doors to the democratic process.

Honolulu is among a growing number of American cities using IT to promote civic discourse. We provide live webcasts of city council meetings, encourage the submission of electronic testimony at hearings and committees, and make it easier for constituents to keep in touch with their elected officials via e-mail. We have also responded to the challenges of citizen disinterest and apathy by using the Internet to educate young people about how local government is structured, how a bill becomes an ordinance, and how anyone can have a voice in deciding the outcome of urban issues.

In 1998, our city took the concept of participatory government a step further with the establishment of what we call Community Visioning. This unique process enables thousands of people in communities throughout the island to work with planning and design professionals to set priorities for public works projects in their areas. Vision groups have been given the financial and material resources to bring dozens of ideas to fruition, everything from the construction of underground utility lines to traffic-management systems. The response to this experiment in democratization has been nothing short of spectacular.

IT plays an important part in facilitating the flow of information between citizens and design professionals. The city has made Smart Boards available at public meetings, with special software that allows citizens to review design options with project planners and architects without meeting face to face. This technology has revolutionized the process of citizen participation by making it possible for city officials and consultants to work with multiple vision groups across the island.

While Community Visioning has been an empowering experience for many of our citizens, there are many people in Honolulu whose personal circumstances prevent them from meaningful involvement in public affairs. The city is exploring ways to help them overcome obstacles to technology use that are often exacerbated by poverty, physical disability, geographic remoteness, or lack of computer training.

One initiative that has generated broad community support is our Neighborhood Online project, which is a collaborative effort between the city's IT and Parks departments. This program places computers in district parks throughout the island of Oahu, where Internet access and word-processing, spreadsheet, and printer services are offered to the public free of charge. With the establishment of Neighborhood Online, many of our park facilities have been transformed into community centers, where people of all ages gather to learn computer skills in a relaxed and informal setting.

SMART GOVERNMENT

The quest for smarter and more responsive government is the driving force behind IT advances in the city and county of Honolulu. While budget limitations have prevented our moving as quickly or aggressively as we have wanted to, every effort has been made to give investment in digital technology the emphasis it deserves. Anything less would be false economy.

In the coming years, cities of all sizes will be expected to adopt disciplined and creative approaches to the application of IT as they confront the ongoing challenge of doing more with less. In Honolulu, that means setting realistic priorities, writing more of our software programs in house, and forging public–private partnerships to achieve the goals we set for our community. Privatization is an option that may be expected to come under increased scrutiny.

The modernization of city government is not without uncertainty. But we can be sure that as new technologies are developed and the demand for government efficiency increases, cities will be expected to deliver services in increasingly convenient, customer-centered, and cost-effective ways. We must respond to these rising expectations with confidence and a commitment to improved public service. The future of our cities depends on it.

25

Using Technology to Reduce Cost and Improve Service

Lee Brown, Mayor of Houston, Texas

Houston relies on technology for everything from entertainment and information to business and critical services. The Internet is one of the tools that Houstonians use on a daily basis to get things done, so much so that Houston is one of the top cities in the country in both technological advancement and access to the Internet. At the onset of my term as mayor of Houston, I made a commitment to developing technology both as an industry and as a resource for everyday city activities. With the goals of using technology to reduce cost, limit the growth of the workforce, and improve services to both citizens and employees, our Internet technology (IT) vision statement is, "Using technology to reduce the cost of government and improve customer services."

In October 2000, I created the office of chief information officer (CIO). The CIO is responsible for providing strategic vision and implementing all citywide IT initiatives. On July 1, 2002, the IT Division of the Finance and Administration Department became its own department. The CIO serves as its director.

COLLABORATIVE IT MANAGEMENT CITYWIDE

Under my direction, the CIO reconstituted the Technology Steering Committee (TSC) to facilitate citywide collaboration in a highly decentralized IT environment and to ensure the fulfillment of the IT vision. The CIO chairs the TSC, which includes chief technology officers (CTOs) from each large department. The CTOs are, in most cases, assistant-director-level executives who report to the department director, as well as the CIO.

The CIO also works with each CTO to provide oversight regarding IT investments for department-specific systems. With a highly decentralized IT environment (i.e., between $80 and $100 million in annual spending, depending on how one counts data entry, automated meter reading, radio communications, etc.) in nine different organizations, the concept of having CTOs in each business unit with significant IT spending has proven very rewarding.

The IT department supports the TSC and provides a forum for collaboration with departmental CTOs to address citywide and departmental IT issues.

This management structure provides the citywide benefits of some centralization or, in this case, collaboration at the IT executive level, while retaining the effectiveness of IT support within each business unit. Departments that currently have CTOs include the Houston Airport System, the Houston Public Library, Planning and Development, the Houston Emergency Center, the municipal court, the Houston Police Department, and Health and Human Services. The only future CTO designation is planned for the Parks and Recreation Department.

CITY OF HOUSTON EGOVERNMENT CENTER LAUNCH

In our quest to provide citizens and visitors alike with quality service, the eGovernment Center was launched in March 2001. Through the tools and information offered here, we provide a vast number of options for interacting with the city 24 hours a day, 7 days a week.

The eGovernment Center is one of the key elements within one of my five guiding principles (i.e., neighborhood-oriented government). The center provides citizens access to city government from home, work, or school "online instead of in line." We strive to improve the services the city already offers, as well as to identify new ways to serve our citizens better. In an era where technology is the norm instead of the exception, providing these services online makes sense.

Since the launch, we have demonstrated our commitment to increasing citizencentric eGovernment opportunities. These opportunities are met with applications that provide direct services to citizens and constituents over the city's Internet portal. The services include applications that provide monetary transactions, as well as interactive sharing of information between city departments and citizens.

The city of Houston initiated its Web presence in 1997. At that time, the information was presented and managed according to the city's organizational structure. Because of the city's decentralized IT environment, there was no consistency in Web development or the availability and application of technology, and there were no uniform training initiatives. Information was difficult to find, and that found on various departmental Web pages was inconsistently presented. Also, not all departments had a Web presence. Finally, the city's webmaster did not have responsibility for citywide coordination of the city's Web presence.

As a precursor to the city's eGovernment Center, several departments took the lead and made significant contributions to improving the online delivery of city services and information. Houston's Planning and Development Department has provided Online Plan Submittal since 1991, and Online Commercial and Resident Permitting since 1997. The Houston Police Department has provided online crime statistics and other frequently requested information for some time. The Houston Public Library's consistent commitment to providing technology, e-services, and vast amounts of online information about the library has been evident for a number of years.

The launch of the eGovernment Center marked a new era in the presentation and management of the city's Web presence. Our award-winning website has received four-star reviews for its design, vast amount and variety of content, frequency of updates, appeal, links, interactivity, navigation, and search capability. The city's IT department now has responsibility for citywide coordination of the city's Web presence, promoting a consistent look and feel and developing and enforcing policies and procedures. To ensure a thorough online population of information and services, the IT department is also responsible for developing and maintaining the Web presence for city departments that do not have a dedicated Web-content administrator.

Our eGovernment Center provides citizens, businesses, and visitors with easy access to information based upon topics of interest, without regard to the city government's organizational boundaries. The eGovernment Center contains over 12,000 pages and 30,000 documents. It features continuously expanding online services, from Online Ticket Pay to Online Tee Times, as well as numerous downloadable forms and applications. We are very proud of the improvements to our site that were developed in-house, such as the Houston Neighborhood ZIP Code Reference and the Calendar of Events. Information on over 2,000 city facilities, parks, libraries, fire stations, and so forth in over 100 zip codes is one click away from our home page. More than 400 Houston events are listed with weekly updates and are accessible with one click. A robust in-house search engine is the third most-viewed page in our entire site, right behind the Employment and City Departments links. Our eGovernment Center averages 3,865 hits per day, a 72 percent increase since its launch, which is a testament that visitors to the eGovernment Center find our website helpful and useful.

Our Spanish-speaking visitors to the eGovernment Center also find our website helpful and useful. In December 2002, I announced the launch of our Centro Electrónico del Gobierno, or the city of Houston's Spanish-language eGovernment Center, which is one of the most comprehensive Spanish-language municipal websites in the country. This 90-page mirror site of information provides Spanish-speaking Houstonians with online access to information about city services and programs, covering everything from departmental services and city government to Houston tourism and economy. With the expansion of our online initiatives into Spanish, we are enabling access to city services and information for a larger segment of our community.

The next phase of development for the site will include increasing Spanish content. While some of this content will be translated from the eGovernment Center, there are also plans to create Spanish-specific content to meet the needs of that community. The continued development of and long-range plans for the Spanish site will include recommendations from our 311 Houston Service Helpline, the Citizens' Assistance Office, and the Mayor's Office for Immigrant and Refugee Affairs. This will allow us to make the site a more effective tool in reaching all Houstonians.

As mayor of this great city, I have made a commitment to developing technology, both as an industry and as a resource for everyday activities. In addition to initiating the eGovernment Center, where you can now pay traffic tickets and will soon be able to pay water bills, you can find out about Houston events and fun facts and learn about the city government that serves our citizens and visitors. I have also implemented technology initiatives as a part of our continuous management improvements to improve the city's technology infrastructure, as well as to standardize our e-mail systems and provide additional online transactions, to bring us up to date on ways to improve our services.

ONLINE TICKET PAY

When the city's Online Ticket Pay application launched in December 2001, Houston was the only city that allowed citizens to pay all allowable municipal fines and fees online. No one matched Houston's convenience and functionality. New York and Chicago, which both ranked above Houston on the "Digital Cities" list, only allowed online payment of parking fines. Where other systems only displayed the exact ticket requested for payment, the city of Houston's Online Ticket Pay system displayed all tickets linked to the requested ticket to maximize the collection of violation fees.

The Online Ticket Pay application provides another convenient payment method and was readily accepted, with adoption rates at 2 percent in the first year, representing $620,000 in violation collections in 6 months. Adoption increased to 4.2 percent in the second year, representing $2.7 million in violation collections in 12 months.

ASSESSMENT OF OPPORTUNITIES

After the formation of the IT department in 2002, an Online Opportunities Working Group was formed to increase the delivery of online transactional services, with a focus on sharing ideas and best practices that existed within city departments and consistently leveraging existing funding opportunities available to the city. The working group consists of decision makers from each department, who can readily determine the viability of a proposed project and activate the team to make it happen.

The initial approach to identifying online opportunities was a review of the 2003 fiscal year budget for each department, focusing specifically on licenses, permits, fees reservations, and so forth. Over 130 opportunities were identified, with approximately $1.3 billion in related revenue. Monthly meetings held to review and report progress on identified initiatives and to identify and resolve barriers to successful implementation were a motivating factor to ensuring a consistent focus.

Since the formation of the working group, the Online Auctions and Online Tee Times initiatives were launched. A new project underway will build upon the convenience of online payment and facilitate payment of a majority of municipal fees.

WORKING GROUP INITIAL PROGRESS

Early on, the working group reached a consensus on transactions fees (i.e., use them where it makes sense, but avoid them if they will discourage online use). It made sense to charge a transaction fee for business-to-government transactions and when it is cheaper for the business to go online rather than coming to city hall (e.g., building permits). However, when there is the potential for reducing operating expenses, then support cost should come down to fund the capital and ongoing support costs (e.g., water-bill mailing and payment processing cost Houston ratepayers $2.3 million). The following is a brief description of the city's current online transactional services:

- Online plat submittal
  —Launched: 1991
  —Funding source: General Revenue Fund
  —Average transactions per month: 625
  —Average Web visits per month: 533
- Online vital statistics (birth and death certificate) order processing
  —Launched: March 1992
  —Funding source: Free to the city of Houston.
  —Convenience fee: $6
  —Average transactions per month: 567
- Online permitting
  —Commercial and residential permits
  —Launched: February 1997
  —Funding source: Special Revenue Fund
  —Adoption rate: 19 percent

—Average monthly transactions: 2,500
—Average Web visits per month: 2,937

- Online ticket payment
  —Traffic, nontraffic, and parking fines
  —Launched: December 2001
  —Funding source: Free to the city of Houston
  —Convenience fee: $5
  —Adoption rate: 4 percent
  —Average Web visits per month: 6,472
- Online auctions
  —Launched: March 2003
  —Funding source: General Revenue Fund
  —Average Web visits per month: 2,091

Our Property Disposal Management Office offers surplus property, confiscated property, and unclaimed airport lost-and-found items through the online auction service esurplusauction.com. This service makes surplus available 24/7 and will potentially increase the revenue received by expanding the customer base to a national level and increasing the exposure to local buyers. The online auctions will supplement the live auctions that are currently being used to dispose of the surplus property. The service will also generate and maintain state-regulated reports and manage the collection of revenues from purchases.

- Online tee time reservation
  —Launched: April 2003
  —Funding source: Free (pilot project)
  --Adoption rate: 75 percent
  —Average Web visits per month: 1,658

An automated lottery process allocates tee times. This process starts when a Tee Time Lottery Request is initiated. The requestor enters a desired time to play and the range of times desired. This pilot will be continued through September 2003 at our Memorial Park Golf Course. Future rollout is being planned at two additional golf courses.

PLANS—PIPELINE AND FUTURE

As the city of Houston has recently completed our 2003 fiscal year budget and initiated the 2004 fiscal year budget, we will leverage past successes, work to complete projects currently underway, and identify new initiatives and funding opportunities. As such, the following are projects currently underway.

Online Water-Bill Presentment and Payment

The city's Utility Customer Service is responsible for reading and maintaining customer water meters, producing bills, receiving and processing payments, depositing cash receipts into city of Houston bank accounts, handling customer inquiries, and maintaining records of all related activities.

The emphasis on quality customer service has meant adding more payment options and making it easier for customers to access services each year. Customers appreciate the ease and convenience of making payments at nearby grocery stores and receiving same-day credit and handling payment problems with one quick telephone call.

In building upon our emphasis on quality customer service, we are in the process of selecting a vendor to assist the city in offering another convenient method of payment. Online Water-Bill Presentment and Payment will allow our citizens the option of paying through electronic checking. This payment method will be offered without additional cost to citizens, thus without convenience fees.

We also look forward to offering the online payment option by the first quarter of 2004.

Municipal Courts Integrated Case Management System

The city of Houston is in the process of replacing a 15-year-old, paper-intensive, mainframe system that has been used to mange the court's processing of parking tickets, traffic tickets, and other municipal violations. This new system will not only allow our city to convert its courts processes to a near-paperless environment but will also provide a component that will allow our citizens to perform online inquiries into their case information. An eCourts system will allow citizens, attorneys, and bond companies to post bond and send and receive relevant information. While we are currently providing citizens with the opportunity to pay their violations online, online case inquiry will be a new service offering.

Our municipal court has 24 courtrooms at 6 locations, is operated by more than 500 full- and part-time staff, and processes over 100,000 violations per month at a value of over $3 million; more than 10,000 citizens visit or call the court daily. As one of the largest organizations of its kind in the United States, the city of Houston will again take the lead in providing services to its residents at a magnitude that is currently unprecedented.

Handheld E-Ticket Program

The city formed a partnership for the development of a solution to streamline the ticketing process for the Houston Police Department, whose officers currently write approximately 800,000 tickets a year, with many procedures involved in the processing of each ticket. A solution was created to facilitate these procedures, as well as to give police officers portable access to reliable information. Features include the ability to

- Scan a driver's license with a magnetic stripe reader
- Wirelessly query a database for real-time information
- Gather required citation data and manipulate it within the handheld device
- Capture an electronic signature
- Print a ticket(s) for the offender
- Assemble all of these items on a single-piece, small, rugged handheld device
- Quickly upload the electronic ticket information to a host system, providing the ability to print a ticket for data entry and municipal courts and deliver an electronic record of the ticket to the municipal courts' host computer

Youth Opportunities Website

This site is designed to help kids, parents, teens, and youth leaders find out about the activities and programs offered in Houston and Harris County. Our list of planned initiatives include the following opportunities:

- Online payment for various commercial licenses
- Online request and payment for police accident reports for use by businesses
- Online payment for alarm permits
- Online food dealer's permit renewal
- Online charitable donations
- Leveraging funding opportunities

Houston, like other governmental entities, has been challenged to develop new and enhanced customer services, while managing with reduced funding. During this bleak economic season, the city has successfully created and leveraged funding opportunities to provide a continuum of electronic services and information.

A public–private partnership established between the city and BearingPoint (formerly KPMG Consulting) in 2000 allowed the city to participate in the Texas Electronic Government Framework to develop a portal, or Internet gateway, which would become the city of Houston's home page, and launch new online transactions. Through this framework, which entailed no initial investment by the city, the eGovernment Center and Online Ticket Pay applications were developed. The funding model used for the technology development and hosting services is based on the payment of convenience fees by users of the Online Ticket Pay application.

The city's municipal courts administer a Technology Fee Fund at the direction of our city council. The Municipal Courts Technology Fund charges a $4 fee for convictions on all traffic and nontraffic offenses occurring on or after June 26, 2000. The purpose of the fund is solely to finance technology enhancements for the municipal court, including computer systems, networks, hardware, software, imaging systems, electronic ticket writers, and document-management systems. It is through this fund that the city is able to finance the Integrated Case Management System and the Handheld E-Ticket project with no additional cost to the taxpayer.

SimHouston: Providing "eTools" to Citizens

In addition to eGovernment, Houston is bringing viaGovernment to its citizens with SimDesk technology. This is a service provided via government instead of by government. SimDesk Technologies offers SimHouston, in which the city of Houston is the first city in the country to give its citizens access to the global information highway, thus being the first city on the planet to "bridge the digital divide." SimHouston—a Web-enabled, virtual software application—allows all Houstonians with a Houston Public Library card (whether or not they own a computer) to access software programs over the Internet, including word processing, e-mail accounts, spreadsheets, address books, calendars, and a file explorer. The city of Houston purchased three million licenses, which are being made available absolutely free to any resident. Files created via SimHouston are available on a virtual drive from any computer anywhere in the world. Because of the launch of SimHouston, the city of Houston has received national recognition for its efforts to ensure that no one is left behind due to a lack of access to new technology.

Since concluding the successful pilot program at all of our library locations, an extensive marketing and community outreach strategy is underway to ensure that as many residents, community and faith-based organizations, schools, churches, and businesses know that this valuable resource is available at no charge. Almost 80,000 had signed on as users by July 2003. My dream has been to make sure that technology is available to every citizen, no matter what his or her socioeconomic situation. We are on our way.

There is also an enterprise deployment underway to reduce the cost to city government of its 14,000 desktops through the conversion of PCs to cheaper internal devices, acquisition of fewer software licenses, and use of fewer support personnel. The enterprise deployment is in its early stages and expected to continue through 2003.

AWARDS AND RECOGNITION

The city of Houston has been honored with numerous awards for the eGovernment Center's content, frequency of updates, links to related and helpful information (e.g., county and state information), interactivity, appeal, design, and search capability, as well as for its technology initiatives. These awards include the following:

- "2003 City Livability Award Winner: Houston Awarded Top Honors for Improving Quality of Life for SimDesk," sponsored by the U.S. Conference of Mayors and Waste Management, June 7, 2003.
- "City of Houston eGovernment Center Selected Best Municipal Government Website in Texas," presented by Texas Association of Municipal Information Officers at their spring conference in Corpus Christi, Texas, June 6, 2003.
- "Best Is Yet to Come for Houston E-Gov," presented by *Government Computer News*, April 7, 2003.
- "Mayor Lee P. Brown Named 2002 Public Technologist of the Year," presented by Public Technology Inc. (PTI). PTI formally announced Mayor Brown's award in Miami at the PTI Technology Leaders of the Year Ceremony, April 11, 2003.
- "City of Houston eGovernment Center Selected among Top Ten E-Government Cities in Nation," presented by Brown University, which ranked Houston ninth (up from thirty-sixth in 2001), October 2002.
- "City of Houston Recognized as One of the 2001 Top 25 Cities for Bridging the Digital Divide," presented by PTI, June 11, 2002.
- "City of Houston Website Receives 4 Star Review," presented by *Muninetguide*, December 12, 2001.
- "Houston Ranks 5th in 2001 Digital Cities Survey," presented by the Center for Digital Government.
- "City of Houston a Finalist in 2001 Best of the Web Contest," presented by the Center for Digital Government.

The advent of the mainframe computer in the 1950s, and more recently the Internet in the mid-1980s, has changed the way the world does business. As mayor of the fourth largest city in our great nation, I recognized early on that technology would be a critical element in controlling cost and the size of the workforce, as well as improving citizen service. I hope this chapter will inspire other government leaders to adopt Houston's technology vision (i.e., using technology to reduce cost and improve service).

26

Leveraging City Assets in a Public–Private Partnership to Build a Fiber-Optic Infrastructure

Dave Bronconnier, Mayor of Calgary, Canada

The city of Calgary's programs and services touch the daily lives of every man, woman, and child in our city. City staff operates buses and CTrains, designs and maintains our roads, picks up the garbage, keeps the parks green and blooming, teaches children to swim, ensures that out water is safe, lights the streets, and protects our families.

Calgary is a Canadian city of just under one million citizens in the footsteps of the Rockies. The city of Calgary, more than other city in Canada, is confronting ongoing financial constraints compounded by an exponential growth in the number of people migrating to the city and the downloading of responsibilities from other levels of government without an appropriate transfer of the corresponding funds.

Calgary uses information technology (IT) extensively, but the sustenance of an appropriate level of investment in technology remains an ongoing challenge. The investment in technology competes with other critical citizen-facing services and life-cycle upgrades. The city is challenged with finding innovative ways of applying and funding technology, while ensuring that the focus is kept on the primary concerns of Calgarians.

One of these concerns has historically been transportation and the challenges of maintaining a viable transportation framework to serve a growing "uni-city," growing towns outside city limits whose residents commute into Calgary, and regional traffic flowing through the city. The city of Calgary operates a Light Rail Transit (LRT) system and is responsible for all roads within the city limits, with the exception of provincial highway portions that extend through Calgary. A traffic-management system manages the flow of our complex road network.

THE LRT STORY

Calgary's LRT System comprises the downtown section and three legs to the south, northeast, and northwest. The construction of the first leg, the south, began in 1978, and the 10.9-km section was officially opened on May 25, 2001. The northeast 9.8-km line commenced service in 1985, and the 6.6-km northwest section was completed by 1990. Calgary Transit carried 76.1 million passengers in 2002.

A number of technologies are used to provide safe, accessible, and courteous service to satisfy the needs of our citizens. These can be categorized into station-focused technologies and systemwide integrated elements, both of which ensure that the operational and safety needs of the services are achieved within a sustainable framework.

The station systems include cameras for video surveillance and an audio/public address system, an emergency alarm system, a ticket-vending control system, and telemetry systems. The individual station systems are integrated across the network and monitored from a central location. This central location is also the hub for managing the train-signaling system. The signals from each station and signaling device are transmitted back to the central control point. At the time these lines were built, the media used to transmit these signals were multipair copper cable and heavy-duty coaxial cable in four-inch ducts laid parallel to the LRT tracks. In the south leg, one duct was allocated for telecommunications, while two were allocated for this purpose in the northeast and northwest legs.

In 1999, further extensions to the south leg were in the planning stages. Also at that time, some of the existing copper and coaxial cable were reaching the end of their planned life. The city of Calgary had been exploring fiber-optic communications for some time, but the total cost of ownership was prohibitive based on leased costs. Also, providers were reluctant to lease dark fibers and offered a managed fiber service, which was even more expensive.

The city of Calgary conducted a review of its requirements, and the cost to replace existing copper and coaxial cable was estimated at $1 million. This figure did not include the replacement of terminal equipment and transmission devices, which were also due for replacement as part of normal life cycle programs. A Fibre, Cable, and Duct Systems Team (FCD) was formed in January 2001 to provide stewardship for Calgary's immediate and long-term telecommunications needs in a coordinated way. The team was formulated to plan, operate, optimize, and look for business opportunities for the use of these facilities. The team evaluated the existing facilities, the condition of the existing plant, alternatives for optimizing the existing ducts, and the use of fiber optics. Thereafter, a request for proposal was issued to the marketplace looking for innovative alternatives to optimize the duct space available, install fiber-optic cable for the city, and reduce the financial impact to a manageable level. The vendors were requested to look at subducting options and their own requirements to arrive at a solution that could be beneficial to both parties, while ensuring that the city retained ownership of all of its existing assets.

A vendor was selected who offered to subdivide the four-inch duct into three sections and to install fiber for the city in one of the subducts, or sections, in return for access to one of the three sections for a set period of time; the third section was available for the city to use as appropriate. The vendor would use its leased section to further its business offerings in the northeast part of the city by installing fiber optics for its own use to serve its customers. The city would provide appropriate personnel to ensure the safety of all contractors working in the LRT corridor. The financial outlay for the city would be minimal.

At the same time, the team started exploring a systemwide replacement of the transmission medium based on fiber-optic cable. A key criterion was that the transition from the existing systems to the new fiber-optic-based system was to be done with minimum disruption. An existing four-inch duct was subducted in the northeast leg, and a 48-pair fiber was installed for the city over a 12-week period by the selected vendor. This put in place the first leg of a proposed fiber-optic backbone for the Municipal Corporation.

A second request for proposal for the provision of transmission equipment based on fiber-optic cable was issued. From among some interesting offerings, the one selected optimized the transmission of all signals over a four-fiber ring circuit based on a redundant ring configuration. Also, the total cost was less than the amount budgeted for the replacement of equipment based on copper cable and coaxial cable. This Optical Transmission Network was the first of its kind in North America at that time. The vendor was interested in expanding into the Americas, and the city agreed to a "show-case" arrangement. This enabled the vendor to show the installation to other prospective clients, while ensuring that the city received the appropriate benefit.

The FCD team then focused on the northwest and south legs to extend the fiber network in a star configuration. The arrangement was similar to the variant of public–private partnership used for the northeast leg. The main principles for the partnership were that the city would have clear and complete ownership of dark fiber, all ducts and subducts would remain under the ownership of the corporation, access to city facilities would be on a lease basis after the initial term, and all partnerships would be of mutual benefit and not encumber the city with any additional operating costs.

The Optical Telecommunication Network for Calgary Transit is now complete and resulted in cost avoidance of over $1 million. It also achieved the key goal of establishing a core fiber network within a very prudent financial framework.

INTELLIGENT TRANSPORTATIONS SYSTEMS

The city of Calgary manages the traffic-light systems within the boundaries of the city. This provides centralized control over 50 percent of the installed base of traffic lights. As the city approaches one million residents, it is apparent that, apart from building new roads and upgrading intersections, there is a need to manage the flow in a more integrated fashion. The city of Calgary is guided by a document entitled "Intelligent Transportation System Strategies, 2003–2013," which defines a vision for the implementation of such technologies in Calgary. The strategic plan is a roadmap that sets the direction, pace, and priorities of intelligent transportation systems investments in a coordinated and focused manner over the next ten years. It also accomplishes the following:

- Provides a vision for the deployment of intelligent transportation systems throughout the Calgary region
- Identifies a range of strategies to pursue over ten years
- Provides a framework to help facilitate the coordination and integration of various systems

The city of Calgary went through an extensive consultation process with stakeholders to determine what intelligent transportation systems would be right for Calgary. This process involved identifying the challenges that are facing our transportation system and determining if technology can help address the problem.

Intelligent transportation systems use new and emerging technology to reduce congestion, save money, improve safety, and reduce the environmental impacts in all areas of transportation. These systems are made up of several components, such as sensors, electronic signs, cameras, controls, and communication technologies. The components of an intelligent transportation system work together to provide information and allow greater control of the operation of the transportation system.

The present system uses copper cable for the control of traffic lights via controllers at the intersections connected back to a central traffic-control console. As part of the IT initiative, the city has installed video cameras at a few intersections. Signals are transmitted back to the central hub via wireless technology and backbone fiber optics owned by the Municipal Corporation. This ability to use various wireless technologies for the "last mile" and to use the fiber-optic network as a backbone for this application provides a very cost-effective way of meeting our requirements. As the implementation of this multiyear plan unfolds, the communication system is key to the delivery of signals from sensors and other field devices to the central consoles. The fiber-optic network is at the heart of this framework.

THE FUTURE OF FIBER COMMUNICATION—CALGARY COMMUNICATION NETWORK

Short-Term Goals

The present three legs of the fiber network were built to address a specific need for Calgary Transit. These legs have been further extended as the LRT System has been expanded over the last two years. This has also established a base of core fiber-optic network available for use by other city departments.

The first priority was to replace the presently leased fiber-optic cable with city owned facilities and leverage the savings to further extend the core network. This is underway, and most of the leased fiber is serving diverse departments like the Calgary Fire, Waterworks, Waste Water, and Solid Waste departments. Other departments, like the Calgary Police Service and Calgary Parking Authority, which needed more bandwidth for critical operations, are also connecting to the fiber backbone network. These have replaced leased copper circuits.

Based on the experience of other Canadian municipalities, the fiber team is now exploring the concept of a community broadband network. A community network is a locally based enterprise that specializes in meeting the needs of local government, associated entities, and community groups and can be extended to other tax-supported groups. This network can leverage the base fiber framework but can also use a number of emergent wireless technologies to extend the reach of the network, such as the following:

- Point-to-point laser links
- Microwave radio links
- Hot spots (based on 802.11)
- 802.16 or Wi Max technology

The key to success is the formation of a multidepartment core team with the mandate to establish an integrated transmission framework for serving all business units.

The city of Calgary has had to be prudent in its plans and is extending the network on an opportunity basis. This includes partnering with the road-building companies to install ducts for telecommunicating as part of road-widening projects, installing ducts in bridges, approaching entities building a ring road around Calgary, and partnering, as appropriate, with the city-owned electricity-distribution company. Once the duct is in place, fiber is installed based on the requirements of city departments or business users.

The city of Calgary employs more than 11,000 people and operates from more than 400 locations. These locations range from small office areas to large, campus-type service areas. These locations all require telecommunications facilities, and many of these services are leased today. As the need for higher data speeds increases, the city of Calgary would be well served by establishing a telecommunications transmission framework based on city-owned fiber-optic facilities.

The optical fiber has tremendous bandwidth, and only using dark fiber is a less than optimal way to exploit the properties of this medium. Although this approach is easily sustainable by the city of Calgary, it is very conservative. A better way would be to establish a so-called managed network, which allows the same fiber to be used by many more users at a lower sustainable cost. This technology, which uses dynamic bandwidth allocation to serve the users, is available today. The concept is to use four of the fibers in a ring framework to serve the majority of the city sites. This can be achieved by using multiplexing techniques that allow the available bandwidth to be used very efficiently and provide effective, secure separation to serve the unique needs of different entities. This can be thought of as "logical separation" with "physical sharing." For example, Calgary Transit can monitor its stations, Roads can monitor closed-circuit television cameras for traffic flows, and Emergency Services can channel its critical information to appropriate areas, all on the same fiber.

It is expected that the telecommunications framework will be implemented over five to ten years. The pace of expansion will depend directly on the ability to attract private-sector partners to expand the network, generation of revenue by leasing ducts, fiber, or both, reinvesting into the framework, and exploring prudent alternatives as the existing copper cable reaches the end of its life.

Long-Term Goals

The city of Calgary is growing by leaps and bounds, and the influx of new Calgarians shows no signs of abating. The traditional source of funding is primarily based on property taxes. This cannot be relied on to meet the needs of the Municipal Corporation. It is necessary to explore other alternatives to ensure effective use of emergent technologies to meet the growing needs of Calgarians.

This chapter illustrates but one example of an innovative approach to leveraging the technology to meet the needs of citizens. In the future, the city could set itself up as a nondominant carrier, which is allowed under Canadian federal communication rules. Some smaller Canadian cities have already registered as such and extended their service to other tax-supported entities. In some cases, the smaller municipalities are extending this service to citizens and offering Internet services for a small fee.

CONCLUSION

An effective, secure, and robust communication framework is critical for efficient operation of traffic systems in a growing city. The people of Calgary have indicated year after year that transportation is a key concern. At the same time, the city of Calgary is struggling to meet the demands of a growing city with limited sources of income. It is therefore necessary to leverage all available city initiatives to ensure that critical emergent technologies are leveraged with a prudent financial framework. The base or core fiber network is an example of one such initiative.

27

Applying Innovations in Midsized Cities: 311 and Chattanooga's Results

Bob Corker, Mayor of Chattanooga, Tennessee, and David Eichenthal, Chief Financial Officer and Director of the Office of Performance Review

New technology has provided an important tool for improving municipal service delivery. At the same time, it has also made it possible for cities to engage its citizenry and provide more democratic access to government in new ways.

The advent of a one-call system for local government through 311 and the concomitant development of performance-measurement systems around data from that system have launched a revolution in municipal government. The 311 system, like 911 before it, provides citizens with one easy-to-remember phone number to access local government. Citizens no longer have to test their knowledge of government by guessing which of the dozens or hundreds of different telephone numbers often listed in so-called blue pages is the right one to call to address a particular question or concern. The 311 number shifts the burden of determining the right place for a call to go from the citizen to the government, for which they pay.

At the same time, 311 creates a single portal for the public and enables government to collect information about how government responds to citizen service requests much more easily. It is not an accident that the most robust data about local government performance has often come from law-enforcement and fire-protection agencies, whose work output is often driven by calls to 911. Now, performance by other government services can be measured by 311 calls, just as crime has been measured by complaints to 911.

The power of 311—and related technology that can be used to track government response to citizen requests—is evidenced by its rapid growth. It took 30 years for 911 to make it across the Atlantic from England to the United States in the late 1960s. By comparison, the federal government called for the creation of a national community policing number for nonemergency response in 1996. Later that year, the city of Baltimore became the first U.S. city to designate a three-digit number for nonemergency police services in the form of 311. A year later, the city of Chicago moved to develop a 311 system that incorporated nonpolice nonemergency services as well. Today, seven of the ten largest U.S. cities now have 311 systems.

While 311 can provide benefits and eventually cost savings, significant upfront investments in technology and human capital are required. For 311 to be effective, an intensive commitment of both city staff time and, in most cases, consultant time is needed. However, these are investments that larger cities have been willing to make.

But what about the vast majority of American cities that are smaller in size and have limited resources? While there are 29 U.S. cities with a population of more than a half million, there are 121 cities with a population between 150,000 and 500,000. Can 311 and strong performance measurement work in those cities as well?

Chattanooga is an in-progress case study of how it is working. Just a year after a public launch of 311, the service is widely regarded as a success by city officials and the public. And Chattanooga is now in its sixth month of using 311 and other data to regularly measure the performance of city departments through a process known as chattanoogaRESULTS. In many ways, 311 has already redefined city government in Chattanooga. As a result, it is emerging as a model for implementation in other similar-size jurisdictions.

HOW 311 WORKS

In most U.S. cities, multiple government departments are responsible for pothole repair, sanitation services, traffic-signal and sign repair, animal control, drainage and erosion problems, the delivery of social services, and a host of other local government functions. For citizens to access each of these service types, they need first to determine whom to call—usually by going through a long list of phone numbers in the local telephone directory.

Sometimes, citizens actually need the assistance of more than one department. For example, after a rainstorm, a citizen might have an erosion problem, downed trees, and the need for brush collection: this single problem would, in some cities, require separate calls to three different departments.

Other times, citizens are not calling to request a specific service or register a complaint. Instead, they may be trying to gain information, such as what the hours are of a recreation center, when the next scheduled trash pickup will be, what roads will be closed due to repairs, and when will they reopen. They also frequently have to make multiple phone calls before they reach a city employee who might happen to know the answer. And, frequently, the answer they get depends on the employee they reach.

Initially, 311 was launched to provide a mechanism for citizens to reach their local police to report nonemergency conditions. Thus, it was conceived primarily to relieve 911 call volume. It was not long before some realized that the potential for 311 reached beyond policing and extended to all government services.

The number 311 is not a switchboard. While, in theory, a city could create a 311 Call Center that screened calls and routed them to the appropriate government department, that would result in an additional layer of bureaucracy. Instead, a 311 Call Center takes a series of functions already performed by city workers and, through consolidation and with the aid of technology, allows those functions to be performed better and at a lower cost. Rather than routing a phone call, 311 customer-service representatives actually have the ability to provide information from and accept service requests for various city departments. Calls are almost never transferred to operating departments.

The 311 system eliminates the silolike division of responsibility for government service. When a citizen calls 311, he or she does not need to know what department will solve the problem, just what the problem is. Moreover, government response is divided by task rather than jurisdiction. The 311 Call Center is a customer-service gateway for all nonemergency services, allowing departmental personnel to focus on the actual performance of service. Rather than having to teach phone-answering and customer-service skills to employees throughout city government, that expertise and skill is concentrated in one place.

Technology is used both to assist customer-service representatives answering questions via an information database and to ensure that they ask the right questions to process service requests. Client-relationship management technology, now commonplace in the private sector, has become revolutionary in the public sector. Through system configuration, customer-service representatives are prompted to ask the same questions that departmental personnel would ask in response to citizen calls. We have essentially transferred the knowledge and expertise of operating departments to customer service through use of technology. The software manages the intake, routing, and resolution of requests and provides a complete work-order management system.

THE DECISION TO BRING 311 TO CHATTANOOGA

Chattanooga is Tennessee's fourth largest city with 155,000 residents. It is located in the southeast corner of Tennessee, less than a two-hour drive from Nashville and Atlanta. Surrounded by mountains and on the banks of the Tennessee River, Chattanooga is truly a beautiful city in the midst of a decade-long renaissance. After years of decline, Chattanooga's citizens decided that their city had a future. Beginning with a visioning process in the mid-1980s, Chattanooga has revitalized its downtown and waterfront through a series of public–private partnerships. The current phase calls for implementation of the $120 million, twenty-first century Waterfront Plan, including expansion of cultural institutions and parks, new housing and retail, and transportation-access improvements.

Chattanooga is governed by a popularly elected mayor and a nine-member city council. While the county has responsibility for schools and jails, the city is responsible for the delivery of most essential services. In fiscal year 2004, the city had a $145 million General Fund budget and employed approximately 2,500 employees.

In 2001, Bob Corker was elected mayor with 54 percent of the vote. Prior to becoming mayor, Corker had served as commissioner of finance and administration for the state of Tennessee and was a successful commercial real estate developer in the city. During Corker's campaign, he went door to door and visited more than 9,800 households.

Shortly after taking office, Corker started a series of regular "cabinet" meetings with department administrators. While Corker sought to use these meetings to help manage city government, he soon realized he had a problem. In many cases, there was neither accurate nor timely data to track what departments were actually doing. As a result, meetings produced few results and were quickly terminated. Corker's experience on the campaign trail also convinced him that citizen access to government was a real problem in Chattanooga. Voters expressed frustration at their inability to reach certain city departments and their lack of information as to which departments provided which services.

Corker turned to lessons from another city, namely Baltimore, as a model for solving two of Chattanooga's problems: lack of performance data and lack of easy citizen access. Baltimore mayor Martin O'Malley's innovation of 311 and CitiStat appeared to be a solution to the problems.

There were, however, obstacles to implementing this model. First, unlike Baltimore, Chattanooga did not already have a 311 number in place for nonemergency police calls. Second, it was unclear who would oversee 311 and CitiStat and how the two functions would be staffed. Third, early research by the city's Information Services Division suggested that there would be costs associated with startup for hardware, software, telecommunications technology, and consulting services, in addition to potential ongoing costs. Note that cost was especially significant given that Corker had just won council approval of a combination of workforce reductions and a tax increase to begin to close a structural deficit. Finally, it was unclear how city employees would react to change. After all, for years, different departments had been responsible for their own customer calls from citizens. Moreover, collecting performance data suggested that managers and employees would be held accountable for results.

IMPLEMENTATION OF 311 IN CHATTANOOGA

By late 2001, the city's Information Services Division began the process of surveying other one-call systems around the nation. Early on, several important operational decisions were made. First, because of the desire to limit cost and expedite implementation, 311 would initially be limited to nonpolice and fire nonemergency calls. Nonemergency police calls would continue to go to a dedicated seven-digit number. Second, there was a strong desire to maintain the human touch. As a result, there would be no use of interactive voice response technology: citizens calling the city would reach real, live human beings. Finally, Information Services determined that for a city of Chattanooga's size, the most cost-effective way to implement 311 would be to contract out for the software and configuration of the system, as opposed to developing it in house. So, in early February 2002, the city issued a request for proposals for technology solutions to operate a one-call center.

At about the same time, Mayor Corker decided that while technology would play a major role in the development and operation of 311, it should not become part of the Information Services Division, as was the case in other cities. Instead, the mayor sought close coordination between the call-center function and the performance-review function that it would hopefully generate. During the mayor's transition, he moved to improve the city's process for seeking and administering grants and the internal-audit function. All of these functions—audit, grants, and 311—were placed under a single new position, the performance audit manager, and recruitment began.

In Corker's May 2002 State of the City address, he made public his plan to create a 311 system and, in July 2002, he named David Eichenthal, a former New York City government official, as the first director of the Office of Performance Review (OPR). One month later, based on the earlier work of the Information Services Division, the city tapped Motorola as its lead consultant on the implementation of the 311 system. In his presentation to the city council on the proposed $268,000 contract, Eichenthal committed to having a functioning 311 system within six months.

Between September and December 2002, OPR and Information Services staff and Motorola consultants conducted literally dozens of meetings with key staff in each city department. This configuration process helped develop a comprehensive information database, established the questions that customer-service representatives would ask in response to approximately 200 different possible requests for service, and set out the work process for each of those requests.

At the same time, Eichenthal began the process of hiring 311 Call Center staff. Initially, the goal was to transfer individuals currently taking calls in individual departments to the call center. Not surprisingly, city departments were unwilling to give up staff that they valued and only too happy to transfer underperforming staff. Instead, OPR worked with department heads to transfer vacant positions to the call center. Thus, over time, the city hired a staff of seven, which consisted of a customer-service coordinator and six customer-service representatives. All had experience in customer service, but only two had ever worked for city government before.

Like any change, 311 was greeted with skepticism and concern by city workers. Regular communication between 311 Call Center staff during the planning stage was essential and remains so now during implementation. In addition to the work meetings with consultants, there was a series of town hall meetings, sometimes with the participation of as many as 100 city employees, on concerns and questions about 311.

By January 2003, an initial staff of five was in place, and staff members proceeded to go through a one-month period of intense training and visits to various city departments. It was incredibly important for customer-service representatives not just to hear about the services for which they would be taking requests but to go out and see what they would be talking about.

In February 2003, the 311 Call Center went through a test period, where calls to existing city phone numbers were gradually transferred to the call center. Chattanooga 311 was launched to the public on February 27, 2002. In addition to media coverage, the city expended approximately $50,000 on paid advertising, including billboards, busboards, and radio ads. Perhaps the most effective means of advertisement, however, has been the placement of 311 ads on most nonpolice and nonfire city vehicles and on city-funded public buses.

THE CUSTOMER SERVICE IMPACT OF 311

A large number of Chattanoogans now believe that 311 is city government. When 311 customer-service representatives answer calls, they greet callers by thanking them for calling the city of Chattanooga, not 311. And, because of the presence of 311 signs on city vehicles, some members of the public assume that 311 is responsible not just for processing their service request but for actual service delivery. The 311 customer-service coordinator regularly receives letters of commendation for her staff, which are then passed on to Public Works or other departments where the employees actually work.

In its first full year of operation, 311 received just over 125,000 calls. Approximately half of the calls were service requests, and half were requests for information. By comparison, there are approximately 10,000 emergency and nonemergency calls to the police and fire departments on a monthly basis.

The top ten service requests account for 60 percent of all service requests to the city. Different cities, which deliver different services, have different types of service requests. In Chattanooga, fully 25 percent of all service requests are for a special collection of bulky trash items. Other requests among the top ten include complaints about missed garbage pickups, litter, abandoned vehicles, housing-code violations, and erosion problems.

Information requests are varied. 311 has received requests for information about noncity services as well as city services. Customer-service representatives do not have the ability to take service requests for county or state government but can provide basic information and transfer calls to the right point of contact.

In Chattanooga, while 311 is answered 24 hours a day, 7 days a week, customer-service representatives are available from 8 a.m. to 6 p.m. on weekdays. At other times, citizens reach an answering service that can refer some calls to on-duty city personnel, but in most cases, the operators urge callers to call back during normal business hours. The city experimented with having 311 fully operational on Saturdays, but call volume was so limited that it was not cost effective.

Based on surveys of citizens who call 311, the call center provides a high level of customer service: 80 percent of telephone respondents rated 311 customer-service representatives as good or excellent on courtesy and 69 percent rated them as good or excellent at handling the customer's problem.

Tracking and survey data also provided interesting information on who uses 311 and when. Call volume is significantly higher on Mondays, accounting for 24 percent of all calls during a week. The 311 callers are disproportionately women (two-thirds) and older (42 percent are 56 or older).

THE LIMITED IMPACT OF 311 ONLINE . . . SO FAR

Chattanooga is one of several cities with a 311 program that provides online access. In other words, citizens can request virtually the same services available by calling 311 by logging on to www.chattanooga.gov. Early surveys of 311 callers gave city officials hope that a significant number of service requests would be generated through the Web: one early survey found that 49 percent of callers would use a Web-based option if one were available. The more service requests processed via the Web, the fewer the calls to the 311 Call Center and the shorter the hold time for those who do call. Once the online version of 311 was available, the city conducted an advertising campaign directed at shifting calls to www.chattanooga.gov.

In one respect, the effort has succeeded. Based on informal surveys, Chattanooga apparently has one of the highest rates of Web use of all 311 programs. Unfortunately, though, just 4 percent of all service requests are coming in via the Web. There are several reasons for this disappointing result to date, at least in a city the size of Chattanooga.

First, because of the ease of the telephone alternative, there is relatively limited incentive to use the Web. Only callers seeking to request service during times when the call center is closed have a real incentive for using the Web.

Second, unlike places like New York City, Baltimore, and Chicago, it is relatively easy for citizens to access government in Chattanooga. National data indicates that while the majority of people believe that Internet access has improved citizen relationships with state and federal government, only 30 percent believe the same is true with local government. Contrary to the speculation of scholars, this may not necessarily be due to the superior quality of federal and state websites. Instead, it may be due to the ease of non-Internet access to local government.

Third, the real advantage of 311 online will be in the processing of information, rather than service, requests. Approximately 50 percent of 311 callers are seeking information not an opportunity to request service. National data shows that most people use government websites to get information not solve problems. They prefer personal contact to deal with complex issues, and even e-mail provides greater flexibility than online 311 forms.

Finally, there are digital-divide issues. The demographic profile of 311 callers (older and female) is virtually the opposite of the demographic profile of people most likely to use Internet (slight male predominance and younger/middle age).

CHATTANOOGARESULTS

By creating a single gateway to nonemergency government services, it is possible to track information about complaints and nonemergency service requests in a way that many cities—including Chattanooga—had not done prior to 311. Prior to the implementation of 311, many departments did not have call-tracking systems. Moreover, city officials had no idea how long it took to respond to service requests. Much of this data did exist for emergency-service delivery, largely because of 911. With 311 and 911 data, the city was now able for the first time to begin to track demand for city service and how city departments and employees responded.

Performance review was an important part of OPR's mission from the start. Two internal auditors who had been in the city's Finance and Administration Department were reassigned to OPR and initiated a series of performance audits. They also worked on the first effort to begin tracking performance on a regular basis using existing data, which was the departmental use of overtime.

The city's reporting of overtime is actually remarkably transparent. At every weekly city council meeting, a report details city overtime expenditures for the prior week. Managers receive a regular report of overtime use and cost within their departments. But, despite this transparency, managers have lacked a tool for regularly comparing overtime use and costs to the prior period or fiscal year. A preliminary citywide review by OPR found that after one quarter of fiscal year 2003, overtime costs were up 25 percent over the prior period last year. OPR, working with Information Services, developed a standardized program that would report on overtime trends by department, division, and employee every two weeks.

OPR's director began sending the results with a cover e-mail that highlighted findings. The results were impressive. By the end of the fiscal year, instead of rising at a rate of 25 percent, overtime cost actually had declined by 7 percent: through the first half of the current fiscal year, overtime has declined an additional 5 percent.

The overtime-effort results bode well for a larger undertaking—the planned use of 311, 911, and other available data to measure financial and operational efficiency and effectiveness on an ongoing basis. The effort was bolstered by the appointment of Eichenthal in February 2003 as the city's finance officer. In addition to monitoring departmental performance, Eichenthal now had considerable oversight over the spending process as well. Also, for the first time, Eichenthal had access to a professional staff that could focus on regular performance review, rather than the internal audit's focus on long-term audit projects. For years, the budget staff had looked almost exclusively at revenue and expenditure issues with little attention to actual performance. Under Eichenthal, this changed: the city's budget officer became the director of a Management and Budget Analysis (MBA) staff, and the budget staff was charged with responsibility for overseeing the performance measurement and review process as well.

Beginning in July 2003, the MBA staff worked with departmental administrators and other senior city personnel to develop a list of the 100 most important indicators of efficiency and effectiveness. In October 2003, the city inaugurated the chattanoogaRESULTS program. Every month, MBA staff work with Public Works, Parks, Police, Finance and Administration, Fire, and Neighborhood Services staff to develop monthly results reports based on selected indicators. The reports are reviewed at meetings with the mayor, the chief financial officer, Information Services, MBA staff, and other senior aides to the mayor. Four other departments and agencies funded by the city—the Personnel and Human Services departments, Chattanooga Neighborhood Enterprise, the Chattanooga Area Regional Transportation Authority, and the chamber of commerce—report to and meet with the mayor on a quarterly basis.

Less than four months after its start, chattanoogaRESULTS is still in its infancy. MBA and departmental staff are still honing their approach to determining the best indicators (i.e., "what counts") and assuring the accuracy of the data (i.e., "counting it"). But chattanoogaRESULTS meetings have already contributed to improvements in performance, as department administrators review and improve timely response to citizen requests and function as a forum for collaborative problem solving. The most important RESULTS meetings are actually those that take place in preparation for meetings with the mayor. There, department officials can now use data on performance to drive management.

NEXT STEPS

In the next year, 311 will begin to take phone calls for two nonemergency services, the treasurer's office and our city court clerk, which were excluded from phase. The city is also developing a process whereby city departments will provide regular updates to citizens on service requests that are taking weeks or months to complete rather than just hours or days. Concerns regarding the online version of 311 have prompted the city to fund a total revamp of its website, which should be underway by this summer.

The effectiveness of 311 has also led the city to increase the number of services available by subscription. In addition to "trash flash" bulk collection, the city is also looking at the possibility of making brush collection and recycling available by subscription: together, these initiatives could generate savings on the order of $1 million annually. The city is also using the same software that supports 311 to support internal service requests, including requests for building maintenance and fleet services.

As part of the constant effort to improve the chattanoogaRESULTS process, OPR is now beginning to audit service-request data to ensure that departments are accurately reporting the timeliness of their response to citizen requests. Eventually, the city also hopes to engage citizens in the process of determining what the indicators should be for the some departments and collecting independent data on performance.

28

Transforming E-Government into E-Service

Loyd Neal, Mayor of Corpus Christi, Texas,
and Susan Cable, Director of E-Government Services

Since the late 1990s, cities across the country have been establishing a strong presence in the world of e-commerce. The application of new electronic tools to customer communications and business transactions has opened doors of challenge and opportunity for building a citizencentric government.

DEFINITION OF E-GOVERNMENT

A good working definition of "e-government," similar to e-commerce, is "streamlining government by providing efficient and effective services and information to citizens and businesses through advanced technology." Key words here are "streamlining" and "efficient," which imply improved use of resources and maybe even some cost savings, and "effective," which means citizens (customers of government) are satisfied with the services delivered. Following the definition, this positive position of government is accomplished through the use of state-of-the-art technology. Primarily, e-government, like e-commerce, is associated with transactions and interactions on the Web, although "electronic" has broader reference, including Interactive Voice Response (IVR) technology, through which customers obtain information, pay bills, and conduct business on the telephone without speaking to a person.

EVOLUTION FROM THE PRETENDING STAGE TO "CITIZENCENTRIC" GOVERNMENT

E-government has evolved over the years, moving from basic information posted on the Web to online payment and interactive applications, and from service through the Web to service through multimedia, including the Web, telephone, e-mail, kiosks, and call centers. A good example of this evolution is the online job application, which is probably the number-one destination Web page for most city governments, with thousands of transactions each month. Like most cities, Corpus Christi started out with PDF forms, which visitors printed off the Web, then filled out and mailed or faxed to the Human Resources Department, whose staff manually entered the information into other forms. This was the "pretending" stage as the PDF forms were convenient but not too "automated." Later, the city updated the PDF forms so that the job applications could be completed online before they were printed, then to forms that could be completed online and submitted, although the form was just e-mailed to the Human Resources Department, whose staff continued to enter the information manually. Today, visitors complete forms online and submit their application for a job or several jobs. The information populates the back-end applicant database and remains in the system for this and future, similar job openings. People have access from their personal or work computers, from over 100 computers with Internet service at public libraries throughout the city, and from kiosks located in the lobby of the Human Resources offices at city hall, complete with staff assistance to coach users through the process.

An example of the use of multimedia channels is our utility-bill-payment and account-information process. City utility customers can pay their bills and access account information, including historical billing and usage data, through the city's website, or they can pay their bill and have copies of bills and information faxed to them through a phone IVR. For the first year and a half, the number of online utility payment transactions increased from 40 to 100 each month. When expanded access services were added, transactions more than doubled in two months, and growth is continuing on a steady basis.

TECHNOLOGIES IMPROVE SERVICE AND REDUCE COSTS

Web applications have significant appeal to city government. With the remarkable growth of interest in and use of the Web, and with the evolution of TQM principles of quality customer service, by the late 1990s, many organizations identified the use of Web-based business processes as a new, critical approach to improved service and operational efficiencies. In 1997, Ernst and Young conducted a study for the Telecommunication International Benchmarking Consortium on the costs of providing service to customers using various communication channels. The results indicated significant improvement opportunities through the Internet (see table 28.1).

Table 28.1. Cost of Providing Service Using Various Communications Means

Channel	*Cost/Channel*	*Functionality*
Call center (Human)	$1.56/minute*	Two-way communication channel used for complex, value-added functions
Kiosk (bank machine)	$1.05/transaction*	Distribution outlet for automated transactions, money, tickets, certificates, cards, bill payments, and so forth.
IVR (self-serve)	$0.35–$0.56/ transaction*	Automating transactions: More effective call routing Information advertising (while on hold)
Internet/Web	$0.01/transaction*	Convenience of self-service and flexibility: Information vehicle Advertising vehicle Education Tools Sales and services

**Sources: Financial Post* (January 25, 1997) end-to-end costs; TIBC Ernst & Young.

CUSTOMER PREFERENCES

In addition to lower costs, the Internet offers improved access to and for citizens. In an environment in which having ten people attend a city-hosted public-outreach meeting is a great success, getting 150,000 hits a day on the city's website provides an amazing outreach volume for communication. However, even with all of the technological advances related to the Internet and the large increases in businesses and homes with computers, some people still prefer other communication media. This reality is an important consideration, as e-service is built on being responsive to the needs and preferences of citizens. According to the Pew Internet and American Life Project, which produces reports that explore the impact of the Internet on families, communities, work and home, daily life, education, health care, and civic and political life, "Internet users benefit from the efficiency of e-government, but multiple channels are still needed for citizens to reach agencies and solve problems."

The Pew Internet and American Life Project aims to be an authoritative source on the evolution of the Internet through collection of data and analysis of real-world developments as they affect the virtual world. The project releases 15 to 20 pieces of research a year, varying in size, scope, and ambition. Internet users are increasingly turning to e-government sites to carry out their business with government. But Internet users and nonusers alike value having more than one way to get in touch with government. The July

2003 survey by the Pew Internet and American Life Project shows that 97 million adult Americans, or 77 percent of Internet users, took advantage of e-government in 2003, whether that meant going to government websites or e-mailing government officials. This represented a growth of 50 percent from 2002. At the same time, citizens who contact government said they are more likely to turn to traditional means—either the telephone or in-person visits—rather than the Web or e-mail to deal with government. Of the 54 percent of Americans who contacted government in the past year, the telephone or in-person visits were preferred to the Web or e-mail by a 53 percent to 37 percent margin.[1] Preferences for Web use increased if Internet users had high-speed connections. So, it is beneficial to city government to encourage making broadband or high-speed Internet service accessible in all areas of the city, such as through cable franchise agreements, WiFi initiatives, and other efforts.

BLOCKS OR OPPORTUNITIES

Even with the appropriate balance of communication channels of choice, several components of e-government can function as either blocks or opportunities to success in e-service. The first key component is effective communications, which means that what you say must be current, accurate, and relevant. It is imperative that communications be coordinated among individual departments, such as e-government, including the call center, public information, service departments, and the city manager's Office. The same message, dates, hours of operation, contact numbers, rules, processes, and so forth, should be available from all sources.

Centralized databases with Web-based forms and reports become the standard of choice, and interfaces between the two become the critical link. An example is the city of Corpus Christi departmental FAQs. Individual departments developed frequently asked questions and answers that are posted online and have helped to offload customer calls. Through the use of Macromedia RoboHelp, the same database is used in setting up a desktop-computer "Help" feature for call takers in the Customer Call Center, which ensures that regardless of how a customer calls in or accesses information, the response is consistent and current.

One side benefit of Web-based applications is that they create, for some reason, increased accountability. It seems that people have an easier time handing off incomplete or out-of-date information to an individual one-on-one because they can verbally communicate caveats and qualifiers to the individual receiving the information. People are much more uncomfortable putting incomplete or outdated information on a website for millions to access. So, the end result is that staff will usually work hard to ensure that information is current, accurate, and complete before they post it online. The challenge is ensuring that the same good information is distributed through other communication channels.

Another key component in transforming e-government into e-service is being flexible and seamless. Years ago, a story was told about a company that was losing market share due to problems in research and development. The company was spending a lot of resources on ideas that seemed promising but turned out not to be feasible; the end result was that the company was always late entering the market with new ideas. The chief executive officer finally established a best worst-idea award, even shooting a canon off in front of headquarters to celebrate the best worst idea. Unfortunately, the research-and-development staff would continue with a bad idea because of the resource investment; now, the improved concept was to recognize and let go of an idea as soon as it was determined not to be worth continuing. This has much relevance to today's technology evolution. What may have been the very best choice three years ago may be the worst choice today because of changes in vendors, products, technologies, partnerships, and the like. Knowing when to maintain and build on an existing system versus when to let go of an investment and move on with new technology and opportunities for future cost savings is important. The city of Corpus Christi implemented online utility-bill payments, job applications, and youth sports registrations with a state subsidiary of a national firm. It was a great application, which had consistent growth. Three years after applications with this vendor were implemented, other vendors entered the market and demonstrated very successful online modules and interfaces with back-end systems. By letting go of the "good" system, making an additional one-time investment, and doing the extra work to "stand up" a new system, services and options for users were greatly improved and significant long-term cost-savings were achieved. Not only did the city accomplish savings of $80,000 annually with the new system, but, without advertising, online transactions more than doubled within two months.

Other important issues that can be either blocks or opportunities to success are security, in-house hardware and technical expertise, and competent external providers. As a city progresses in e-government services, a major focus is building interactive online customer forms, applications, and reports that interface with the back-end databases used by staff in daily operations. With these interfaces and functionality, security becomes a crucial issue. The forms must be located outside a firewall, or in a DMZ, and the databases must remain in a secure, internal-access-only area. Establishing the connectivity between the form and the database, while maintaining security, often becomes an enormous challenge. In implementing a Web-based presentation of the airline flight arrivals and departures that are shown on monitors at the airport, city staff ran into numerous obstacles with PIXs, connectivity, proprietary programming, scripting, and working within the framework of established security of the airport server and the Web server. With tenacity and determination, the goal was accomplished after three months of trial and error. The same challenge occurred in putting vendor-supplier information and purchasing-bid information online, interfaced with the purchasing database that city staff uses on a daily basis. Eventually, an old Access database was transferred to Structured Query Language on a server in the DMZ, training was provided to staff on the new system, and the interactive format was a big success, providing not only improved customer service but significant efficiencies through a new, consolidated, streamlined, and robust database. Many people have the perception that you decide to put something on the Web, so you just plug it in. Dealing with security, databases, customers, and back-end employee processes are key result areas of the implementation process, and, typically, there are no straightforward solutions.

ROLE OF ELECTED OFFICIALS

The role of elected officials in this process has been vital. First, elected officials are often the source of new ideas. We learn of innovative approaches from our visits to other cities, counties, countries, and conferences and from conversations with constituents. Then, city staff does the research and feasibility study, and if it is a great idea, the implementation process begins. That is how the city of Corpus Christi Internet website was initiated, as well as a number of the electronic service applications.

Elected officials have also played a key role in focusing the Web as "the new media." At weekly meetings, when discussing an upcoming bond project for street repair, a concept for bayfront development, CDBG funding, or getting citizen input on the budget, city council members continuously ask, Are we putting the information on the city website? and How are we getting citizen input? The answer to the latter question now has to include multimedia opportunities. Through annual goal-setting processes or less formal direction, elected officials set and fund priorities. Our city council considered putting building permits and inspections online as a priority goal. City staff then conducted a series of focus groups to develop the implementation details and moved forward with a new online business application, both through the Web and IVR. Our elected officials continuously champion a customer focus for government business, decisions, and activities. The council consistently directs staff to put a survey on the website, get input from citizens on a draft plan, and use technology tools to find out what the community thinks. City staff has a short survey on the front page of the city website that is used to gather comments about priorities for the website and for city services. So far, 23 different surveys have been posted with thousands of responses. Citizens also can provide weekly input on cost savings and service improvements through the Budget Builder online form. Complaints and comments are submitted on a regular basis through the Citizen Comment form, and responses are coordinated through our Customer Call Center. Input on special projects is obtained through special city hall briefings, which are televised live on cable government access, with viewers submitting comments and questions in real time via phone, e-mail, and a Web forum. Ad hoc committees, such as the Blue Ribbon Committee examining the city's unified development code, are using both a new online discussion forum and a group listserv e-mail application to communicate with each other on a regular basis. Elected officials in Corpus Christi have set citizen interaction as a benchmark for conducting business, and the city staff has responded with multimedia channels for citizens to obtain information, communicate feedback, and conduct business.

HISTORY

Around 1995, a city council member came back from a trip to Austin, Texas, and said there is this cool thing called the Internet that Austin is using to communicate information. The city staff's response at that time was, Austin is a technology center; we are South Texas, and it will be years before some of our population even has computers. The next year, the city had a "skunkworks" going, with several individual departments developing websites because they partnered on another project with the university or because a staff person had a nephew who was a computer whiz. By 1999, all of these initiatives were centralized in the Communications and Quality Management Department, a front page was designed, development tools were centralized through a cheap ($60) software program called PageMill, and the city was receiving 3,000 hits a day, amazed to be able to offload this amount of potential phone calls or visits. In 2002, recognizing the importance of electronic opportunities, the city established a separate, new E-Government Services Department, redesigned the website, implemented a new, customized content-management system, and launched a number of e-commerce applications; immediately, hits increased to 18,000 per day. By 2003, e-government was transitioning into e-service, with integrated systems for multimedia customer contact. Citizen interaction has grown to 150,000 hits per day on the city website, with over 2,000 calls per day in the Customer Call Center, and eight online citizen comments submitted per day. Hundreds of other phone calls or in-person visits to city offices are offloaded by the city's IVR phone applications.

PLAN AND STRATEGY

Transforming e-government into e-service means making multiple channels available for citizens to access information and conduct business. With emphasis on citizencentric government, the city of Corpus Christi is now providing seamless contact with and service for the customer by integrating computer hardware and software, telephone systems, work processes, and information in the back-end systems that support delivery of information and services to customers through the communication media of their choice.

In 2003, the newly established Customer Call Center was moved into the E-Government Services Department, which is responsible for the city's Internet and intranet sites and telephone IVR systems. This functional consolidation occurred in conjunction with the citywide deployment of MAXIMO for work management, MAXGIS for work orders, Voice over IP telephony, and RoboHelp for departmental FAQs. Instead of the traditional Customer Response Management system, the city of Corpus Christi Customer Call Center uses a centralized work-management system. Call-center representatives take calls and enter work requests into a database system that records complaints and service requests and notifies designated contacts in city departments with a physical mapped location. With the work order in a centralized database, the customer can call back, and various staff can access the system and provide responses regarding the actions being taken and the current status of those actions. As the work-management system is deployed throughout the organization, call takers from individual departments are moved into the centralized call center; thus, expansion is accomplished with no additional staffing costs. Customer-call takers are cross-trained in the field by various department staff in both call-center policies and procedures and in such relevant skill areas as customer service. Tracking of call data provides direction for addressing and resolving departmental problems, in developing communications with customers, in establishing more effective business processes, and in improving the customer-service attitudes of city staff.

CURRENT STATUS

Currently, the city offers multiple services through diverse channels to citizens. Through the Internet, the E-Government Service Department provides the opportunity for payments and job applications, forms and applications, and citizen comment and survey forms and applications, as well as to access airline flight information, bids and supplier packets, live and archived video streaming of city council meetings, city facility rental information, a community calendar, live Web cams and virtual tours, tourist and business information, interactive maps, departmental FAQs, municipal codes, city plans, and agendas of the city council and boards and commissions. The city currently has installed the infrastructure for a 20-square-mile WiFi area, initiated a pilot project for automated meter reading, is completing a WiFi business model, and is working on other wireless projects in the downtown district.

Through the intranet, an internal Web service for city employees, e-government provides access to city policies, employee forms, departmental weekly reports, IT forms, fleet-maintenance forms, budget information, employee newsletters, special-event information and updates, and an internal fire department communication site.

Through IVRs, e-government provides utility-bill payment and account information (with fax capabilities), building permits and inspections, departmental-services information, and a document library.

The Customer Call Center provides knowledgeable and well-trained call representatives who process thousands of calls each day, answering questions, providing information and direction, and issuing work orders and special requests for citizen calls on animal care, utility services, streets, solid-waste services, and other city services. The call center also functions as the phone bank in such emergency situations as hurricanes (see figure 28.1).

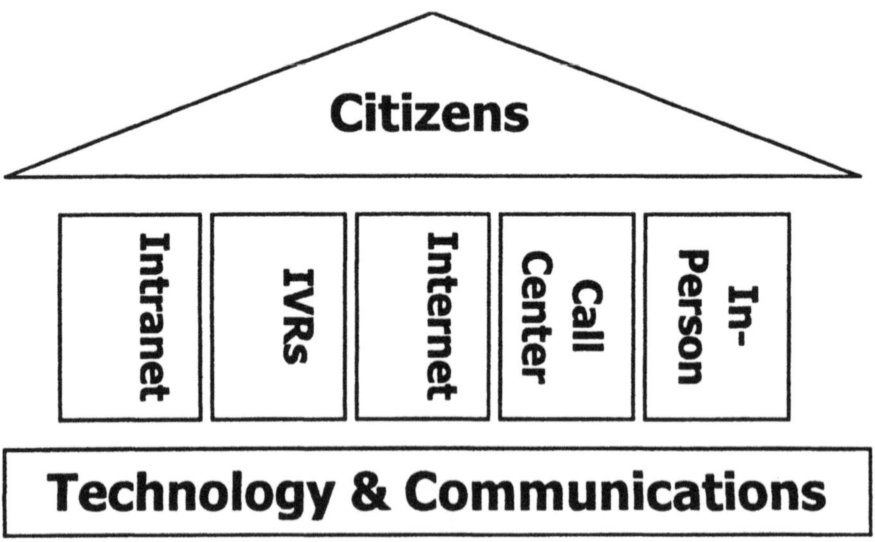

Figure 28.1. City Services Provided by Various Channels.

CONCLUSION

Huge increases in customer contact, significant decreases in specific complaints, and continuous growth in electronically offloading communications and business transactions have allowed city staff to perform other functions, thus increasing operational efficiencies.

E-government and the more advanced e-service model of the city of Corpus Christi address many of the traditional problems citizens have with city government. The benefits of this approach are a single point of contact, choice of preferred user media, fewer hand offs, easier navigation of government, 24/7 access, a more efficient flow of service, better tracking and accountability, and satisfied citizens.

Success in e-government requires leadership and vision of elected officials and executive management, along with a plan and strategy based on a commitment to responsive customer service. To transform e-government into e-service, multimedia channels must be available to address customer preferences, and these communication channels must be built on a solid foundation of integrated technology and communications.

The city of Corpus Christi has been awarded designation as a Top 10 Digital City in 2003 and 2004 and has been recognized as a City Portal Finalist in the Center for Digital Government's 2004 "Best of the Web." We are convinced that Corpus Christi will continue to be an e-service leader because of our multimedia approach and focus on citizencentric government.

ENDNOTES

1. See www.pewinternet.org/pdfs/PIP_E-Gov_Report_0504.pdf and http://207.21.232.103/index.asp.

Index

PROPER NAMES

SUBJECT

WEB-SITES

About the Contributors

Erwin A. Blackstone is professor of economics at Temple University and a senior researcher in its Center for Competitive Government. His special areas are privatization, industry studies, economics of crime and security, and health economics. He has published extensively in these areas. His Ph.D. in economics is from the University of Michigan.

Michael L. Bognanno is associate professor of economics at Temple University and IZA Research Fellow. His primary research interests are in the area of personnel economics, particularly pay, promotion, and incentives in organizations. He has published in *The Journal of Labor Economics, The Industrial and Labor Relations Review, The Journal of Political Economy,* and *The Labor Law Journal.* His Ph.D. in economics is from Cornell University with labor economics as his major field.

Simon Hakim is professor of economics and the director of the Center for Competitive Government at Temple University. His special areas are privatization, public policy, and security and economics of crime. He has a Ph.D. in regional science from the University of Pennsylvania. He has published numerous articles in academic and professional journals and fifteen books.

Kay Barnes was elected as Kansas City's first woman mayor in March 1999 and was reelected in 2003. In 1979, she was elected to a four-year term on the city council, serving the Fourth District At-Large. She has taught college-level classes at the University of Missouri at Kansas City and Central Michigan University. For 23 years, she was president of Kay Waldo, Inc., and she currently serves as cochair of the U.S. Conference of Mayors Small Business/Partner America™.

David Bronconnier was elected Calgary's 35th mayor on October 15, 2001. During his first year in office he coordinated and hosted the 2002 G8 Summit. Through his leadership, the city of Calgary's responsible planning and effective management helped ensure the Kananaskis Summit was a successful and, more importantly, a safe event for Calgarians and its international visitors.

Lee Brown was elected as the 50th mayor of Houston in 1997 and was reelected in both 1999 and in 2001. He served from 1993 to 1996 in the Clinton administration as director of the Office of National Drug Control Policy. He also served as the commissioner of police for New York City, Houston, and Atlanta. He was elected to the Conference of Mayor's Advisory Board in 1999 where he was an active member of various standing committees and task forces.

Willie Brown was mayor of San Francisco from 1996 to 2004. He was the longest-serving speaker of the California State Assembly, serving from 1980 to 1995. He was part of the California State Assembly from 1964 to 1995 and served as the chair of Committee on Ways and Means. He is an attorney, admitted to practice law in the state of California and all federal courts including the Supreme Court.

Jeb Bush was elected governor of Florida in November 1998. Before that, he helped launch, and served as president and chief operating officer of, the Codina Group, now the largest full-service commercial real estate firm in south Florida. He served as Florida's secretary of commerce from 1987 to 1988 and is the coauthor of *Profiles in Character*, a book profiling fourteen of Florida's civic heroes.

Susan Cable was appointed director of e-government services to the city of Corpus Christi in 2002 after serving for ten years as director of communications and quality management. Previously, she established and directed the Management Development Center in the College of Business at Texas A&M–Corpus Christi and received recognition from the Society for Training and Development for Organization of the Year and Outstanding Professional Services. She has had articles published in *Government West* and *Texas Town and City* magazines, and the *Society for Advancement of Management* international journal.

Bob Corker was elected mayor of Chattanooga in March 2001. Through his leadership, Enterprise South, a 1,200-acre industrial park, was developed.

He has worked with the Bush administration to secure a Renewal Community designation for the downtown and other areas, which has resulted in significant tax credits for eligible businesses that are expanding and adding jobs in Chattanooga.

Otto Doll was appointed South Dakota's first chief information officer (CIO) in July 1996. He has advised Fortune 1000 companies and federal, state, and local governments on information technology assessment and alignment to business needs. He received his computer science degree from Virginia Tech and is a Senior Executive Fellow of the Kennedy School of Government, Harvard University. He is a past president of NASCIO, a national organization of state CIOs. Mr. Doll has helped wire more than 660 public schools for telecommunications and power.

David Eichenthal began working for the city of Chattanooga in 2002 as director of the new Office of Performance Review and then in February 2003 as city finance officer. He was previously the chief of staff to New York City's public advocate, the city's second highest elected official. Mr. Eichenthal received a degree in public policy from the University of Chicago and a law degree from New York University. Currently he is the new president and chief executive officer of the Community Research Council Inc.

Mark Forman was appointed on April 2003 by President Bush to be the administrator for the Office of E-Government and Information Technology. He has served as an associate director for IT and e-government at OMB. Before joining the OMB, he was a vice president of e-business in Unisys Global Industries and led IBM's Americas Public Sector e-business Consulting Services. He was the senior professional staff member on the majority staff of the Senate Governmental Affairs Committee. He has written numerous papers and reports on government management, e-business, e-government, and defense economics issues.

Mike Foster was elected Louisiana's 49th governor in 1996 and ran for a second term and won in the first primary. This was the first time in many years that anyone has won the governorship outright without a runoff election. His second term expired in 2004. Before becoming a governor, he was a member of the U.S. Senate for two terms. He has also been a board member of several local banks, a junior warden of St. Mary's Episcopal Church, the president of the St. Mary Parish Farm Bureau, and a member of the American Legion.

Rudolph W. Giuliani was elected mayor of New York City in 1993 and was reelected in 1997. Before serving as mayor, he attended law school at New York University, was associate attorney general of the Department of Justice, the third highest position in that department, and served as U.S. attorney for the southern district of New York.

Neal Giuliano was elected the 26th mayor of Tempe in May 1994 and was reelected in 1996, 1998, 2000 and 2002. He received his master's degree in higher education administration in 1983 from Arizona State University. Prior to being elected mayor, he served on the Tempe City Council from 1990 to 1994, and was vice mayor from 1992 to 1994. His leadership experiences include serving on numerous boards of directors for nonprofit agencies, including the Tempe Community Council, Valley Big Brothers-Big Sisters, and Home Base Youth Services. He was the 2001 recipient of the Superior Service Award from the American Society of Public Administration.

Stephen Goldsmith was elected mayor of Indianapolis in November 1991. He was the recipient of *Governing Magazine*'s Public Official of the Year Award and the prestigious Innovations in American Government Award from the Ford Foundation. He is also the author of *The Twenty-First Century City: Resurrecting Urban America*. Mr. Goldsmith served as an advisor to former governor of Texas George W. Bush and is currently a chairman of the U.S. Board of Directors of the Corporation for National and Community Service.

Jeremy Harris was elected mayor of the city and county of Honolulu in September 1994 and was reelected in 1996 and 2000. Term limits made him ineligible for reelection in 2004. He previously served as a delegate to the 1978 Hawaii Constitutional Convention and in 1979 was elected to a seat on the Kauai County Council as a council chairman. In 1984, he joined the city and county of Honolulu government, and was soon promoted to deputy managing director and then managing director. He also holds the distinction of being the city's longest serving managing director, having held that post from 1986 until 1994.

Mike Huckabee was elected Arkansas's 44th governor in 1996 when his predecesor resigned. He was then elected to a full four-year term as governor in 1998, attracting the largest percentage of the vote ever received by a Republican gubernatorial nominee and was reelected to another four-year term in November 2002. He previously served as president of Cambridge Communications from 1992 to 1996. He also served as president of the Arkansas Baptist State Convention from 1989 to 1991 and received an honorary doctor of humanities degree from John Brown University in 1991.

Pam Iorio was elected mayor of the city of Tampa in April 2003 for a four-year term. She serves on the Aviation Authority, the Port Authority, Tampa

Bay Water, and the Board of Trustees of the University of Tampa. Previously, she served on the Hillsborough County Commission from 1985 to 1992. In 2000, she was elected president of the Florida State Association of Supervisors of Elections. She also earned a master's degree in history from the University of South Florida in Tampa in 2001 and has published several articles on Tampa's civil rights and political history.

Sharpe James was elected as the 35th mayor of the city of Newark in May 1986 and was reelected in 1990, 1994, 1998, and 2002. In 1988, he was awarded an honorary doctor of laws degree from Montclair State University and in 1991 an honorary doctorate from Drew University. In June 1999, he was appointed to the state senate and in November 2001 was reelected for a full term. He was voted "The Most Valuable Public Official" in municipal government by *City and State Magazine* and currently serves on the Board of Trustees of the U.S. Conference of Mayors.

Vera Katz was elected mayor of Portland in 1992 and later became the only one in state history to hold the post for three consecutive terms. She was elected to the Oregon House of Representatives in 1972 and was chosen in 1985 as the first woman Speaker of the Oregon House. She holds honorary doctorate degrees from Lewis & Clark College and Portland State University.

Tony Knowles was elected governor of Alaska in 1994 and reelected in 1998. He previously served two terms as mayor of Anchorage from 1981 to 1987. Mr. Knowles served as chair of the Western Governor's Association in 1997, a two-term chair of the Interstate Oil & Gas Compact Commission, and a member of the Pew Oceans Commission. He earned a degree in economics from Yale University in 1968.

Patrick McCrory was elected mayor of the city of Charlotte in 1995 and in December 2003 became the first to serve a fifth term as mayor. He founded the Mayor's Mentoring Alliance in 1995 and was presented the *2001 Governor's Outstanding Local Official Award* for his mentoring work. He also received an honorary doctorate degree from Catawba College in 2001. Mr. McCrory has also held several management positions with Duke Energy Corporation.

Joan McGee is the information technology database analyst for the Office of Electronic Services in the Louisiana Division of Administration. She has a master's degree in English Literature and taught at the University of California at Santa Cruz, University of Oklahoma, and Louisiana State University. She also has a master's degree in library and information science. Currently she manages ASK Louise, an online knowledgebase of the most frequently asked questions about state services and information resources.

Loyd Neal was elected mayor of the city of Corpus Christi in April 1997, and was reelected for his fourth and final term in April 2003. He has served as chairman of Corpus Christi Economic Development Corporation, the Corpus Christi Chamber of Commerce, the South Texas Homeport Committee, and the Leadership Corpus Christi Alumni. He is currently serving as a director on several agency boards and was recently appointed as a Driscoll Foundation trustee and to the Driscoll Children's Hospital Board. Since 1973, he has been an adjunct professor of insurance at Texas A&M–Corpus Christi.

Richard O'Donnell serves as executive director of the Colorado Commission on Higher Education. Previously, he was executive director of the Colorado Department of Regulatory Agencies where his leading accomplishments included the establishment of the Office of Economic Competitiveness and Regulatory Reform that helps the private sector keep track of regulations via the Internet and get involved in the regulatory process; this system is the first of its kind in the nation. Mr. O'Donnell also is a senior fellow at the UCLA School of Public Policy and Social Research.

Martin O'Malley was elected mayor of the city of Baltimore in December 1999. Previously he served as an assistant state's attorney for the City of Baltimore from 1988 to 1990. In 1991 he was elected to the city council representing the 3rd District and served as chair of both the Legislative Investigations and the Taxation and Finance Committees. He is an attorney and received his law degree from the University of Maryland.

Bill Owens was elected as Colorado's 40th governor in January 1999 and was reelected in 2002 with the greatest majority in Colorado history. He has been called "the best governor in America" by *National Review* magazine and touted as one of the major emerging leaders in American politics by *The Economist* magazine. He has served in the state house and senate and as Colorado treasurer. He holds a master's degree in public administration from the Lyndon B. Johnson School of Public Affairs at the University of Texas.

Sonny Perdue was elected Georgia's 81st governor in January 2003. He has been a businessman, community leader, Sunday school teacher, state senator, majority leader, and president pro tempore of the Georgia State senate, as well as an officer in the United States Air Force. He earned a doctorate in veterinary medicine in 1971 from the University of Georgia.

Ed Rendell was inaugurated as Pennsylvania's 45th governor in January 2003. He previously served two terms as mayor of Philadelphia from 1992 to 1999. Mr. Rendell graduated from Villanova Law School, served as chief of homicide in the Philadelphia District Attorney's Office and in 1977 was elected district attorney, becoming the youngest district attorney in the city's history. In September 1999, he was elected general chairman of the Democratic National Committee.

Gail Roper is the first female director of information technology for Kansas City. She was recruited from Austin, Texas, to develop an infrastructure strategy for network computing for the city in August of 1996. In 2001, she was one of three local government officials to receive the 2001 Technology Leadership Award. She is currently studying for a master's in business administration with an emphasis in management information systems and finance at the University of Missouri in Kansas City.

M. Michael Rounds was sworn in as South Dakota's 31st governor in January 2003 He served as state senator from 1990 to 2000 and represented District 24, including Pierre and the surrounding areas. In 1994, he was chosen by his peers to serve as senate majority leader, a post he held for six years. He earned a bachelors of science degree in political science from South Dakota State University in Brookings.

Bill Smith was elected mayor of Edmonton in 1995, Canada's fifth largest city. Previously, he founded Alberta Supernet, the first private company in Alberta to receive a license to market Internet service. He was also the founder of Tire Town, a retail force in Western Canada. Mr. Smith has served as chair of the Northern Alberta Mayor's Conference and as a board member to the Economic Development Edmonton and Alberta Capital Region Alliance.

Fran Ulmer was elected lieutenant governor of Alaska in 1994. She previously served as state representative from 1987 to 1994, as mayor of the city of Juneau from 1983 to 1985, and as policy director and legislative advisor to former governor Hammond from 1975 to 1981. She earned a J.D. cum laude from the University of Wisconsin Law School. She is currently a distinguished visiting professor at the University of Alaska in Anchorage.

Mark Warner was inaugurated Virginia's 69th governor in January 2002. He has helped found the Virginia Health Care Foundation, which has provided health care to more than 476,000 underserved Virginians in rural and urban areas. In 1997, he developed the Virginia High-Tech Partnership, which helps students from Virginia's five historically Black Colleges and Universities pursue technology careers through a summer internship and job placement program.

Anthony A. Williams was inaugurated as the 4th mayor of the District of Columbia in January 1999 and was reelected in January 2003. In December

2004, he was elected president of the Washington, D.C.-based National League of Cities, the oldest and largest national organization representing municipal governments throughout the United States. He was elected vice chair of the Metropolitan Washington Council of Governments in January 2005.

www.ingramcontent.com/pod-product-compliance
Ingram Content Group UK Ltd.
Pitfield, Milton Keynes, MK11 3LW, UK
UKHW041103150926
475561UK00001BA/22

9 780742 549128